The Life of an Oak

AN INTIMATE

PORTRAIT

The Life of an Oak

AN INTIMATE PORTRAIT

GLENN KEATOR

SUSAN BAZELL

Heyday Books

California Oak
Foundation

Photo Credits:
All photographs taken by Glenn Keator or Susan Bazell, with
the exception of the following; Cover-Tamia Marg, title page
spread-David Cavagñaro, pages 12–13-Stichting Arboretum
Trompenburg, page 139-Mark Moffett, page 148-special thanks
go to Dr. Stephen Edwards who contributed the beautiful
image of the oak fossil, page 231 top-Diane Burk, page 233-
Zhou Zhekun, page 236-Oren Pollak, Nature Conservancy.

Library of Congress Cataloging–in–Publication Data
Keator, Glenn.
          The life of an oak : an intimate portrait / Glenn
Keator ; artwork
          by Susan Bazell.
          p.   cm.
          ISBN: 0-930588-98-3
          1. Oak   I. Title
QK495.F14K435 1997   97-29094
583' .46—dc21
CIP

Cover & interior design: Diane Burk
Cover photo: TK
Printing and binding: Imago Publishing Ltd., Singapore

Please address orders and inquiries to:
Heyday Books   or   California Oak Foundation
P.O. Box 9145   1212 Broadway, Suite 810
Berkeley, CA 94709   Oakland, CA 94612
Tel: (510) 549-3564   Tel: (510) 763-0282
Fax: (510) 549-1889   Fax: (510) 208-4435
heyday@heydaybooks.com   oakfdn@igc.apc.org

Printed in Singapore

10 9 8 7 6 5 4 3 2 1

Contents

Introduction   8

OAK ARCHITECTURE

Oak Design   11
From the Basement up: Oak Roots   21
Oak Framework: Trunk, Limbs, and Branches   37
Epiphytes   47
A Tour Around a Leaf   60
The Oak as an Ecosystem   96

THE OAK LIFE CYCLE

Flower Basics   99
Life Cycle of the Oak   106
Acorns   124
Seedlings   142
An Overview of the Life Cycle   147

OAK DIVERSITY, RELATIONSHIPS, & EVOLUTION

What is an Oak?   149
Diversity Among Oaks   153
Relationships Among Oaks   161
What's in a Name?   170
Oak Relatives   171
Origins and Evolution   182
Where is Oak Evolution Headed?   196

OAK HABITATS

Snapshot Visits to Oak Habitats   199
Oaks: The Final Overview   235

Fagaceae Family   238
Glossary   241
Index   250

Acknowledgments

The California Oak Foundation joins Heyday Books in acknowledging the generous contributions of the following sponsors of *The Life of An Oak:*

International Oak Society
Melvin B. Lane
Mennen Environmental Foundation
The Strong Foundation for Environmental Values
The Sam and Mary Mills Fund of the Vanguard Public Foundation
Janet Cobb Oak Education Fund of the California Oak Foundation
Anonymous Contributor

California Oak Foundation

The California Oak Foundation is a nonprofit organization dedicated to the conservation and perpetuation of California's native oak woodlands. The California Oak Foundation educates the general public and decision-makers about the importance of oak woodlands to California's wildlife habitat, watersheds, and quality of life through its newsletters, bulletins, books, symposia, and workshops. To join or obtain additional information, contact:

California Oak Foundation
1212 Broadway, Suite 810
Oakland, CA 94612
Telephone: (510) 763-0282
Fax: (510) 208-4435
E-mail: oakfdn@igc.apc.org

International Oak Society

The International Oak Society is a nonprofit organization dedicated to the study, sustainable management, preservation, appreciation, and dissemination of knowledge to the public about oaks (genus *Quercus*) and their ecosystems. The Society produces journals each year and is sponsored by members representing more than thirty nations. For more information, contact:

International Oak Society
Department of Biology
Saint Mary's College
Notre Dame, IN 46556

Thanks also to the Santa Cruz Island Reserve, which hosted the author during his study of the unique vegetation there, portrayed in Part 4.

Introduction

Surely the world has a surfeit of books on oak trees, and for good reason. A familiar part of the world in which we live, oaks are widespread symbols of strength and endurance. Humans have marched down the millenia in close companionship with oaks. Myths and rituals have memorialized and honored them: Ovid spoke of acorns as the first gift of food bestowed by the gods, and many Native Americans would agree. Instead of rice, Romans threw acorns at weddings to bless the newlyweds with fertility. The Celtic priests who defied the Roman invaders were called "druids" for their knowledge of oaks.

Besides spiritual association, oaks have provided humans with material wealth as well. Masts crafted from the trunks of immense oaks were the mainstay of British sailing vessels. Barrels made from oak staves have served as the traditional receptacles for aging fine wines. Implements and furniture fashioned from fine-grained oak wood are cherished more than ever today, as good-quality hardwood is rapidly disappearing. Given oaks' importance, it really is no surprise that so many books have been written about oaks, from children's books that chronicle the miracle of an oak tree's growth from an acorn to the learned treatises of scientists investigating oak minutiae.

My reasons for writing this book are both personal and professional. I grew up in the San Francisco Bay Area—a region especially well endowed with oak species—and have spent a lifetime probing the mysteries of these trees and their environments. Although I have spent much of this time learning about California's oaks, I also wanted to understand oaks in a worldwide context. But no such overview existed. Bits and pieces of this worldview lie embedded in various books, floras, technical journals, and articles for the layman, so when I set out to write this book, I wanted to assemble these pieces to illuminate the nature of oaks. I began with straightforward goals: I would address the common aspects of oak architecture, reproduction, evolution, and relationships and simplify them for everyone to understand. But nature is whimsical, and in the pursuit of knowledge, it is easy to be led in new directions or to be taken on circuitous detours. Such detours are often unexpectedly revealing, and I have permitted a few to find their way into this book. In my research, I found some aspects of oaks surprisingly difficult and controversial; many facets of oaks have suffered neglect in the pages of this book for lack of space or because of their technical complexity.

One example of this complexity is the mysteries surrounding oak origins and evolution. Although my perspective reflects the training of a professional botanist, I remain a mere beginner in the intrigues of oak taxonomy, a study that could easily consume several dedicated lifetimes. The interpretation I offer on these matters is strictly my own, based on my best rendition of work done by a number of oak specialists.

Through my expanded knowledge of oaks, my admiration for them has grown deeper. Now that the book is written, I feel I have only scratched the surface. There's so much more to ponder and explain. Wherever I go, I will look at oaks with new wonder and curiosity. As with so many aspects of life, so it is with oaks: the more you learn, the more questions you want to raise. I hope that this all-too-brief overview of oaks will showcase the beauty of oaks, open the door to the wonder of evolution, and ignite in others a desire to probe into oaks' deepest mysteries.

Glenn Keator
Berkeley, 1997

Oak Architecture

Few trees elicit such immediate imagery or call up as many legends as oaks. Because oaks are so widespread and so familiar to those who dwell in the Northern Hemisphere, the names for the oak tree are diverse, extending far back into antiquity. Our English word comes from the Old English *ac,* related to the Dutch *eik* and German *Eiche.* Other European languages trace their words from completely different origins: oak is *chêne* in French; *roble* (deciduous oak) or *encino* (live oak) in Spanish; *quercus* in Latin. Scholars tell us that when different languages have distinctly different words for plants, it indicates the importance of those plants to the cultures that have named them, and so it is with oaks.

The English oak (*Quercus robur*) is renowned as the prototype of oak design. In overall shape, the English oak resembles an immense, unfurled umbrella of equal spread and height. Spring and summer leaves cloak the canopy so thickly that finer details of branches and twigs are obscured, but in winter, all is dramatically revealed as the pattern of branches is laid bare.

The English oak trunk is thick and steadfast, covered with pale brownish gray bark consisting of short, coarse furrows and ridges arrayed in offset vertical files. By the time the trunk grows to fifteen to twenty feet in height, it diverges into two or three

major boles. The boles continue to grow upward, sometimes
staying straight and true, sometimes gracefully curving. Boles
ultimately lose their identity as they taper and split into several
upper limbs. Along the boles, a series of limbs fork off, spaced at
definite intervals of several feet. Lower limbs jut straight out horizontally while higher limbs swoop upward at rakish angles; the
uppermost limbs finish by pushing stiffly up. Each limb forks
and reforks into a network of branches, especially toward its

The umbrella-like crown of English Oak (Quercus robur) *is an example of typical oak architecture.*

outer limits. The branches, in turn, richly ramify into a dense tangle of crooked twigs and even finer twiglets. Those final twigs and twiglets are lumpy from the many closely arrayed buds and twig scars. The overall shape is a canopy of surpassingly complex design on a tree that stands one hundred feet tall, with a spread of a hundred feet.

The basic shape of a broad, rounded umbrella applies to many oaks. Their general form has changed little from the first days, millions of years ago, when oaks radiated out into a wide variety of woodland and forest habitats, carried forward ever so slowly by foraging squirrels or dependent jays. Yet not all oaks are built this way. Some have trunks that carry the limbs and crown higher overall, a pattern designed to help oaks overshadow shorter trees in tight competition for light. Oaks that live in competition with taller trees, such as evergreen conifers, are frequently taller, with many upward-trending branches. Other oaks are smaller trees, hunkered down, twisted by environmental extremes: they grow in the form of dense shrubs or low mounds in hot, dry chaparral, in granite crevices on high mountains, in wind-blown coastal barrens, and in hammocks in limestone-encrusted swamps.

It is no accident that oak design tends to be successful. The broad canopy allows oaks to shade large areas, preventing the growth of competitors that depend on plentiful sunlight, thereby giving oaks more of what they need: minerals and water from the soil. Oak shade also cools the soil beneath, keeping feeder roots fresh and cutting down on evaporation from the upper layers of soil. The shade is deepest when it is most needed, in summer when air temperatures soar.

Oaks are also spared the plumbing problems that plague taller trees. Tall trees often place excessive stress on the continuous water columns that carry water from their root tips to the leaves of their highest twigs. Water columns are unbroken chains of water molecules that extend from near the root tip to the place where water is lost to evaporation from the leaves' surfaces. Remarkably, the driving force to move the entire column is capillarity coupled with evaporation through

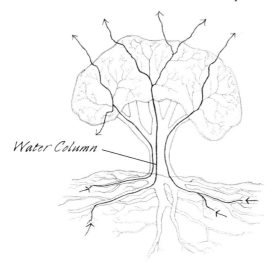

Water Column

innumerable microscopic pores in the leaves' skin. The column is held together entirely by the tenacity of attraction between water molecules. The higher a column has to reach into the sky, the more vulnerable it becomes to the unrelenting pull of gravity, and when the column is subjected to stress from too little water entering the soil, it breaks. Then the top of the tree dies, blasted by drying out. Oaks circumvent this problem by growing wide rather than high.

Another advantage of a stocky tree with multiple branches is that it has greater stability. Compare this shape to that of a slender, conical tree that soars into the sky. Taller trees often fall simply because their height exposes them to stronger, more persistent winds. It is this very feature of California's coast redwoods, together with their particularly shallow roots, that often brings about their death. When strong winds blast and rip through branches of an oak, the stocky tree will bear the brunt of their force. Although it may lose some limbs, it will seldom topple over. The heavy, broad-reaching limbs distribute the oak's center of gravity over a larger area, stabilizing the tree.

The oak's contorted branches, twigs, and twiglets present leaves to the sun in a close, dense canopy, thus catching as many of the sun's rays as possible and making vast stores of food available through photosynthesis. These food reserves serve oaks well for a variety of purposes. They may be drawn upon during long winters for maintenance of basic cellular processes. When spring comes, food reserves make bursts of rapid growth possible. If leaves are stripped by voracious caterpillars, food supplies spur the manufacture of a new set of leaves and also provide the means for manufacturing an arsenal of chemicals to defend leaves against further predation. Food fuels the lavish production of the pollen that will be carried to neighboring trees on the whims of wind. And food is stocked in large amounts in acorns to make them attractive to foraging rodents and birds. Food-rich acorns also give the seedlings a head start when they germinate.

Just as designs have their merits, they also have their weaknesses. The oak's downfall is that its rounded crown cannot bear up under great loads of snow in winter blizzards. Oaks prevail throughout temperate forests where cold winters occur, but they don't wander into subarctic, northerly climes or into the fastnesses of mountains. It may be this vulnerability to heavy loads of snow that limits their distribution. In snowy climes, conifers have a competitive edge with their slim, conical shape. Their downward swooping branches are perfect for shedding heavy loads of wet snow.

Oaks are lovers of light, and since they don't have the ability to grow tall and slender, they are at competitive odds with trees that do. When oaks compete with many tall trees, inevitably they lose the battle and slowly decline and die. The world's great conifer forests, which stretch in almost uninterrupted bands across the north's taiga, the high mountains' pine belts, California's redwood region, and the temperate rainforests of the Pacific Northwest, come close to totally excluding oaks. In such places, oaks are relegated to the role of opportunist, dwelling along the margins of forests and awaiting the spaces that the felling of conifers and conflagrations open up, where they'll have enough sunlight to feed their light-hungry leaves.

In California in particular, many forests that were once dominated by oaks are now hurrying toward an overstory of conifers. In the past, lightning-induced fires periodically consumed conifer saplings, allowing oaks to thrive. But with today's policy of fire prevention, the pines and Douglas firs are gaining ascendancy. The fast, tall-growing conifers tower over oaks, shading and weakening them, until finally the oaks succumb to disease and pestilence.

An example of changing dominance that favors oak trees is in peninsular Malaysia, where an alliance of tall trees of the laurel and dipterocarp families once thrust skyward, shading all lesser trees. But widespread logging of these giants has eliminated them from broad sweeps of forest, and the ubiquitous oaks and oak relatives have assumed dominance in their place. The oaks' shorter, broader crowns now enjoy the full potency of the tropical sun.

Some oak trees are remarkably malleable, changing form according to need. You might see the goldcup oak (*Quercus chrysolepis*) with its branches extended fully to the sun on the semidesert slopes of Southern California's interior mountains, where it preserves its basic umbrella crown. But when you find it competing for a place in the sun among the northern Sierra Nevada's coniferous forests, it sends its limbs into a steep climb, with a narrowly rounded crown. The Rocky Mountain Gambel's oak (*Q. gambelii*) is equally changeable. On well-watered plateaus, it sends up a few stout trunks and a dense, rounded canopy; on a rock-strewn slope or where it is subjected to frequent browsing, it quickly forms groves of miniature trees with slender trunks. When it takes root on steep rock shelves, it changes once again, forming sprawling woody mats only a few feet high.

This ability to assume shrub form has given oaks yet another architectural advantage. Shrub design is easily accommodated by a tree; simply reduce the overall dimensions and convert a single trunk into several smaller trunks. This changeover is especially easy, as many tree oaks already show a tendency toward multiple trunks. Dormant buds at the base of the trunk have the ability to spring to life when stimulated by pruning, cutting, or fire. Buds provide many lines of defense for oaks by preserving the germ of potential growth, sometimes over vast periods of time. Buds are an oak's means to rejuvenate after many of nature's harshest injuries.

Environments that favor a shrub design over that of a tree include coastal dunes and bluffs, and mountaintops relentlessly swept by drying winds or covered by heavy snows. Places with nutrient-poor soils, which slow growth to a snail's pace, also favor the shrub form. Look for these soils along the edges of acid bogs covered in spongy sphagnum mosses, in the barrens derived from slick bluish green serpentinite rocks, and in terrain made from crumbled, gray granite and tan sandstone rocks. Oak shrubs also thrive in the understory of dense forests. In these places, shading and vigorous competition for water leave little extra for plants that have high demands for these commodities. Finally, places that receive little rainfall and experience broiling hot summers, such as areas with Mediterranean or desert climates, favor shrubs.

The contrast between the understory of a Garry oak forest (above) and a dwarf Brewer's oak (below).

The common denominator in all these situations is the low nutrient value and poor water-retaining capacities of the soils.

Soils derived from California's bluish green serpentinite rocks offer a vivid illustration of the impact of these conditions on oak trees. Serpentinite soils are low in calcium, a nutrient needed for building strong cells. They're also low in potassium and nitrogen, which plants use in relatively large quantities. In addition, serpentinite soils are unusually high in magnesium and heavy metals such as copper and iron, all of which are toxic in large quantities. The toxicity of excessive magnesium seems particularly incongruous, for an atom of magnesium lies at the heart of every chlorophyll molecule. But, as with many of the vitamins living bodies require, a little magnesium is essential; a lot can be injurious for plants.

Plants that have managed to adapt to serpentinite soils have an edge over "ordinary" plants, and as a result, they have an environment nearly free of competition. But they pay a price for their success; their growth is painfully slow, and they seldom grow beyond the stature of low shrubs. The leather oak (*Quercus durata*) is a strong indicator of serpentinite soil and exemplifies the cost of living in such soil. It has the stunted look of a plant starved for food, and its curled leaves bear the stamp of a droughty environment: they're tough, leathery, and covered with a dense powdering of white, starlike hairs.

We use the short-hand term *adaptation* to describe the special characteristics of the leather oak, but actually it is *preadapted* to these harsh conditions. Its ancestors may have lived in ordinary soils, with ample minerals and water. Random changes in its leaf design—tough, hairy leaves, for example—may have appeared at a time when they didn't confer any special survival skills. But when other plants began to outcompete leather oak, it was able to move into new habitats with severe conditions because of these preadapted leaf characteristics.

Huckleberry oak (*Q. vaccinifolia*) hunkers down under heavy snowbanks for much of the year in the high mountains of California and adjacent areas. It has splendid isolation in crevices

Nature's miniature hedge, created by a thick growth of huckleberry oak on granite.

between chinks of granite, where it finds a cool, moist root run. Its dense, compact growth of glossy leaves is a testament to the effects of snow, wind, and cold, short growing seasons. Huckleberry oak's new leaves are bronzy red, a warning color to dissuade potential browsers, and they grow obliquely, to avoid the full impact of the harsh ultraviolet rays that pass through the thin subalpine air.

Silver-leaf oak (*Q. hypoleucoides*) forms dense shrubberies on the steep, rocky soils of southeastern Arizona's high desert mountains. Silver-leaf oak is especially effective at filling vacancies left when raging fires have reduced tall trees to charred stumps. Adaptations include long, tapered leathery leaves with curled edges and a dense, feltlike matting of closely intertwined white hairs underneath to reduce water loss from the hot summer air.

20

oots are the foundations on which a tree is built, yet because roots are seldom seen, they are poorly understood by most and rarely given their full importance. The oak root system is vast and richly branched to provide an anchor for the tree and a highway for absorbing water and nutriment. Except for carbon dioxide, which is absorbed from the air by leaves, all other nutrients enter through the roots.

Oak roots diverge from the trunk like the radiating spokes of a wheel, many burrowing outward just beneath the soil's surface. Although a taproot at first plunges straight down into the soil, plumbing its depths, it often withers and dies as lateral roots develop. Where they join the trunk, oak roots look like woody limbs and are covered with the same bark pattern that aerial branches wear. Gradually, the major roots split and fork, and those forks split in turn, until toward their tips, there is a rich welter of delicate, pencil-thin roots and even thinner rootlets.

While the details of oak roots vary among species, universal elements of design prevail. An oak seedling starts life by investing considerable time and energy in establishing a substantial taproot. The taproot begins as a thin root that quickly swells and thickens as it constantly pushes downward, guided by internal microscopic particles that are sensitive to gravity. When the taproot reaches four or five feet, its growth slows, then grinds to a halt. Its job may last for the first few years, but it usually atrophies as lateral roots grow and flourish.

The taproot's downward growth gives the oak a way to probe for hidden moisture. When all the surface moisture has evaporated or been sopped up by surface roots, taproots can draw on reserves far below. Taproots also provide ample room to store food for emergencies. When extra sugars have been sequestered for later use, capacious taproots provide a safe place to store them. Stored food is used for winter parsimony and for quick regrowth when tree tops are sawed or chewed off. Food reserves speed growth in spring by allowing leaves to unfurl and photosynthesize as soon as possible. Later in an oak's development, the

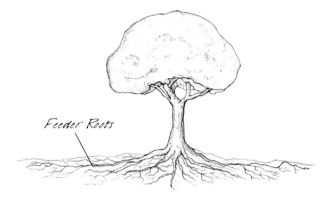

Feeder Roots

bases of the major lateral roots take over this all-important food storage function.

In addition to the initial taproot, oaks soon produce lateral and feeder roots. The feeders diverge again and again in a rich tapestry, always growing horizontally just below the soil's surface at the ends of the laterals. As trees increase their crowns, they also cast ever-larger networks of these feeders, acting like the seines a fisherman casts for his catch. The feeders develop richly toward the tips of the lateral roots, and as they age, these lateral roots develop wood and bark in the manner of the branches above ground.

Contrary to the popular myth that tree roots approximate the circumference of the crown or "drip line," recent studies show that feeder roots extend far beyond the limits of that imaginary line superimposed on the soil from the crown above. Expert tacticians, feeder roots enter complex configurations with competing feeder roots of sibling oaks, other trees, and a wide variety of smaller flowers and shrubs. Successful plantings of oaks must take feeder roots into consideration because confined spaces and soil compaction spell slow but certain death. Some oaks also develop sinker roots that hang vertically from near the ends of feeders. Sinkers make the most of any surface moisture missed by feeders, reaching deep into the soil. Oaks with prominent sinkers are especially adept at extracting the soil's moisture.

Feeder roots grow rapidly and extensively because they consume the essential ingredients that promote rapid root growth: oxygen from the air for efficient respiration and minerals that have been recently recycled into the topsoil by the millions of microscopic bacteria and fungi that mine the humus. Feeder roots also take quick advantage of any surface moisture from superficial rains or melting snows, absorbing the moisture before it penetrates deeply into the soil and drains away.

Each root is a marvel of design, from its tiny tip to its woody base. Under the lens of a strong microscope, the root tip is revealed as a minute center of active cell division, the *root meristem,* where the future root cells are produced during active growth. The root meristem is delicate, fraying easily as it pushes against sharply abrasive soil fragments. So the root tip, for the fractional measure at the extreme end, wears a root cap, like the thimble worn on a seamstress's finger. The root cap consists of a loosely knit, multilayered wrapping of cells. The root meristem is constantly adding new cells to repair the root cap as it is relentlessly stripped away.

Just above this flurry of activity lies the millimeter-long *zone of elongation,* where cells grow bigger and longer as they adopt their mature form. It is solely through the activity of these cells that roots manage their downward travels; in the *zone of maturation* above, root cells remain the same size and length. The zone of maturation occupies the bulk of the root—in it, cells have matured into tissues, each with its own special role to play. The outer layer is the *epidermis,* a thin skin that covers all parts of the plant and keeps them from drying out. Cells in the center of the root become *xylem* and *phloem,* the vascular plumbing system that moves water and minerals upward and distributes food throughout the plant. Encircling the vascular tissues is a sheath of cells—the *endodermis*—whose function is to regulate water flow into the vascular tissue. Just inside the endodermis lies the *pericycle,* a narrow sheath of unspecialized cells that produce branch roots. The pericycle is the fount from which all branch roots push out of the parent root, just as tree limbs diverge into branches. Cells between the epidermis and endodermis comprise the *cortex,* a tissue that serves many purposes and is intimately involved with food storage in winter.

Despite this precise arrangement of primary root tissue, roots do change with age; as they enter their second year of growth, they put on girth by adding an outer layer of bark and an inner

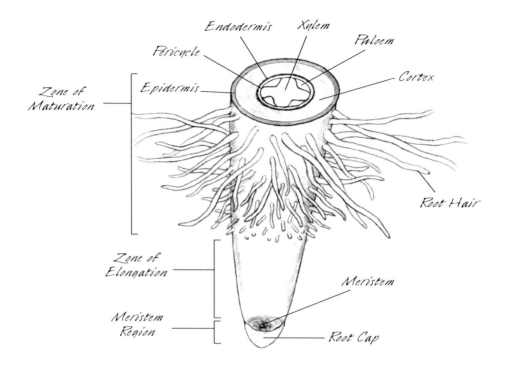

Endodermis   *Xylem*
Pericycle   *Phloem*
Epidermis   *Cortex*

Zone of Maturation

Root Hair

Zone of Elongation

Meristem

Meristem Region

Root Cap

core of wood. Every year thereafter, more girth accrues, following the same fundamental patterns as trunks and limbs above ground. Indeed, when one examines the exposed base of an oak trunk, it's difficult to distinguish the bark-covered roots from the trunk; they look identical.

Water and mineral absorption occurs in the region between the zone of elongation and the place where roots become woody. This area is covered by a furry coat of fragile tubular projections from the epidermis called *root hairs*. The sheer number of hairs on a single root is staggering: there are thousands of hairs per cubic inch, with a total surface area for a single tree that spans many square miles. Root hairs assure the best possible contact between a root and the surrounding soil particles.

The membranes of root hairs, which allow passage of water and minerals, are equally amazing, for they're able to select what substances they take in. Such *semipermeable membranes* surround all living cells, taking some materials in passively, while actively drawing in others. Small molecules like water pass in both

24

directions unimpeded, but the direction of flow is determined by a gradient. If there is more water outside the root hair than inside, there is an overall movement of water into the root. This gradient concept also applies to the movement of many mineral ions—charged particles that are plucked from soil fragments. As in a beehive, this coming and going is in a constant state of flux, but for healthy roots, more nutrients need to enter than leave.

While helpful, this passive *diffusion* of molecules cannot supply root cells with all the minerals they need. Often, mineral ions are also carried across the root hair's membrane by *active transport*, a process in which the tree expends energy to carry the ion into its roots. Using photosynthesis, the oak produces sugars in its leaves, transports them to the roots, and then burns them, thus spending stored energy (sugar) to obtain other nutrients in a dramatic illustration of the interdependence between parts of the tree.

In addition to using root hairs, oak roots gather water through a fuzzy white covering known as *mycorrhizae*—a symbiotic partnership between fungi and roots. The fungi obtain sugars from roots and, in turn, they give minerals and water to the roots. The name mycorrhizae comes from two simple Greek words: *mykos* for fungus, and *rhiz* for root. Oak root mycorrhizae actually go by the name *ectomycorrhizae*, which are specialized mycorrhizae associated with specific plant groups, including oaks and pines. The fungi which engage in ectomycorrhizal relationships are characterized by their specificity to their host and the short distance they penetrate into roots, and it's probably no accident that tree groups with this hidden relationship have achieved widespread success.

The mycorrhizal relationship evolved some time in the distant past, when land plants first became trees. It is likely that a group of fungi, acting as aggressive parasites, invaded roots for the food they contained. Sometimes these fungi were thwarted by the chemistry of the host roots. The roots released enzymes that reduced the invaders' cells to mush, killing them off. Initially defeated, these unwanted villains evolved forms that could grow into the roots for a short time before they were destroyed. The invasion became a sort of standoff until advantages to this specialized parasitism were acquired and became finely tuned, so that a true symbiosis between both parties evolved. To understand how such a relationship could be mutually beneficial, we need to sketch a portrait of fungal life.

Fungi obtain food using hundreds of minute, branched, tubular threads—*hyphae*—that thrust their way through soil duff, living leaves, dead bark, or acorn hulls. Usually fragile and hidden, these hyphae nonetheless occur in great abundance in the humus. So vast is this network of fungal hyphae that ancient fungi that have lived for hundreds—possibly thousands—of years may comprise the largest of all living organisms, in some cases spanning more than a mile underground. Hyphae absorb water from the soil and release enzymes that break down leaf litter and animal debris, allowing the hyphae to obtain mineral nutrients. Because hyphae create a huge network of threads to absorb nutrients, they stabilize and hold the soil together in a complex and ever-changing configuration.

Now imagine the advantages to tree roots of being hooked up to such a network. Each hyphal tip is walled off, detached from the rest of the hypha, and eventually engulfed by the root's living protoplasm. As the root releases its enzymes to break down the penetrating hyphae, it absorbs water and nutrients, and the fungus gains sugars that are stored in the roots, so both partners benefit.

Most mycorrhizal fungi have evolved from the club fungi (Basidiomycetes), a group that includes the common mushroom and various so-called toadstools. The world has hundreds of species of mycorrhizae, and these vary from place to place and from one kind of oak to another. Two fungi, the cêpe (*Boletus edulis*) and truffles (*Tuber* spp.), are not only illustrative of ectomycorrhizal fungi, but make a delicious contribution to our diet.

The cêpe signals its identity by its handsome fruiting body, a substantial tan mushroom with a classically sloping cap, a massive stalk that bulges at its base, and a white underside. The fruiting body, or mushroom, is the seat of reproduction, where

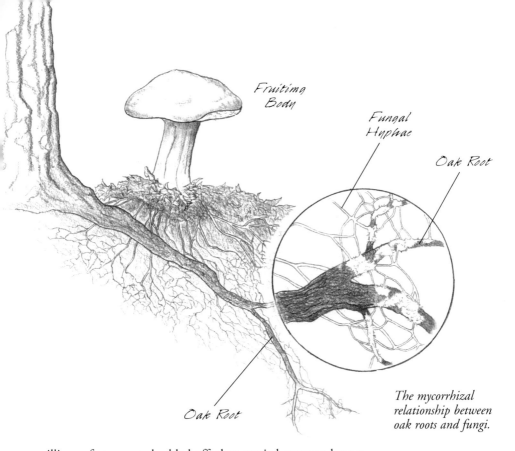

Fruiting Body

Fungal Hyphae

Oak Root

Oak Root

The mycorrhizal relationship between oak roots and fungi.

millions of spores are budded off, then carried away on breezy convection currents. Instead of a lining of gills beneath the tan cap, cêpes carry hundreds of tubes that end in a spongelike pattern of pores. The cêpe is something of a generalist, benefiting from an underground partnership with more than one kind of tree: the cêpe also finds itself intertwined with that other far-flung tree group, the pines. Perhaps cêpes have accommodated to more than one host in order to attain broad distribution. If so, their strategy has succeeded handsomely, for cêpes thrive across the temperate zone of the Northern Hemisphere from Great Britain to Russia and Japan, from China through Southeast Asia, and across the breadth of North America.

Whatever the habitat, cêpes seasonally produce those delicious fruiting bodies. So choice is their flavor that they are a delicacy in many nations, known as *king bolete* in English-speaking countries, *Steinpilz* in German-speaking lands, and *porcini* in Italy. David Arora, in his book *Demystifying Mushrooms,* describes

The fruiting body of the cêpe, (Boletus edulis).

the cêpe this way: "It is a consummate creation, the peerless epitome of earthbound substance, a bald bulbous pillar of thick white flesh—the one aristocrat the peasantry can eat!" The main fungal body—all those hyphae—remains permanently in the soil, interlaced with tree roots. The emergence of the fruiting body depends on the year, condition of the host tree, and the current climatic conditions. (Of course, not all members of *Boletus* are delicacies—some are quite poisonous.)

The various species of truffle (*Tuber* spp.) paint an entirely different picture, for they are not ubiquitous and perhaps would not have even been discovered were it not for the animals that often root through oak leaf duff. Truffles are not physically large, nor do they have a handsome appearance. Truffle fruiting bodies are small spheres—often smaller than a pea—with a wrinkled skin. The interior of truffles is marbled from numerous interconnecting "veins" that are lined with microscopic spore-producing sacs.

Truffles thrive in the Mediterranean climate of California's foothills and southern Europe, where they associate mostly with evergreen oaks. When truffles fruit, they remain invisible to humans because their tiny fruiting bodies are subterranean.

Italian white truffle, (Tuber magnatum).

The spores are doubly buried—concealed inside the fruiting body which itself is buried beneath the leaf duff—so they can't use the wind the way cêpes do. Instead, truffle spores depend on rooting animals such as pigs, with their fine sense of smell. Lured by the intense truffle fragrance, pigs unearth the fruiting bodies, break them open, and liberate the spores. Their fragrance is what makes truffles so valuable in human feasts, but so unique and strong is that odor that some are repelled rather than attracted by it. The two most valuable truffles are *Tuber magnatum* and *T. melongatum,* both from Europe; California's truffles are seldom used for food. Since California did not originally have indigenous wild pigs, rooting animals such as ground squirrels and pocket gophers oblige truffles by distributing their spores.

Soil is one the most miraculous components of the environment. It is here that roots grow, browse, feed, anchor, and drink. If roots were unable to carry on their duties, all trunks, branches, twigs, leaves, buds, flowers, and fruits could not survive. Oaks have to absorb all their water and a wide array of mineral nutrients from the soil in order to satisfy the needs of photosynthesis and counter water loss in the leaves. All green plants have these needs, so they compete intensely to obtain water and nutrients from a finite resource. The minerals sought by roots include nitrates, potassium, phosphorous, iron, magnesium, calcium, and sulfur—and these are only the components needed in the greatest quantity. Some of these—nitrogen, phosphorous, and potassium—you will recognize from the bag of fertilizer you use in your garden. Others—zinc, copper, manganese—are seldom talked about because most healthy soils have them in plenty. (An easy way to remember these components is by the jingle C HOPKN'S CaFe, Mg [mighty good]. The components are: C for carbon, H for hydrogen, O for oxygen, P for phosphorous, K for potassium, N for nitrogen, S for sulfur, Ca for calcium, Fe for iron, and Mg for magnesium.)

Of these nutrients, roots need nitrogen in the greatest quantity. In a strange twist of nature, plant roots are unable to use atmospheric nitrogen, which comprises some 78 percent of the air we breathe. Instead they take nitrogen from such compounds as ammonia (NH_3) and nitrate (NO_3). Among the teeming legions of soil bacteria, there are certain kinds that convert atmospheric nitrogen to ammonia or nitrate. Each step of this chemical conversion requires a different kind of bacterium. All the necessary bacteria thrive in healthy soils with a near-neutral *pH*. (pH is the scale used to indicate whether a soil is acid, neutral, or alkaline; most oaks live in neutral to slightly acid soils where these important bacteria thrive.)

Certain kinds of bacteria convert pure nitrogen from the air into ammonia. Then, other bacteria remove hydrogen from the ammonia and replace it with oxygen in a process known as oxidation. During this process, ammonia is converted first into nitrites (NO_2) and then into nitrates (NO_3). In the course of these conversions, energy is liberated. Bacteria rely on this energy to fuel other metabolic processes and eventually release the nitrates into the soil where they can be absorbed by oak roots. At the other end of the cycle, when oak leaves, bark, and wood are decomposed by other kinds of bacteria, the complex nitrogen-containing substances of the oak are broken down once again into the starting components: ammonia, nitrite, or nitrate. Once an oak woodland is established, the cycle tends to balance itself and constantly recharges itself by going around again and again.

The basic building blocks of soil are billions of near-microscopic rock fragments. Nutrients in the form of charged particles cling to each tiny fragment. Most nutrients come from weathering

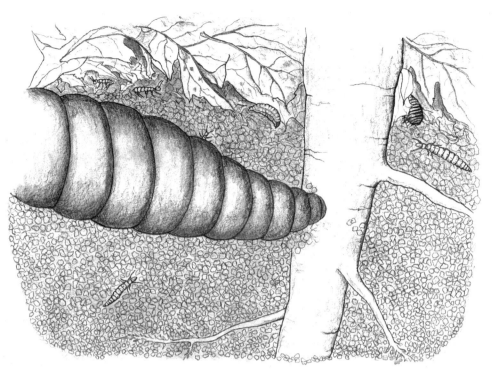

A subsurface view of
the taproot and branch
roots of an oak
seedling: soil particles,
the tail of an earth-
worm, springtails,
proturan, centipedes,
and a topdressing of
oak leaf litter.

processes like rain, which carries dust particles to the earth, or
from the decay of animal, fungus, and plant remains that accumulate on the soil's surface. Many of the oak tree's nutrients
come from the decomposition of other organisms, and the
machinery that recycles those nutrients is as complex and fascinating as any above-ground forest ecosystem. Every animal pelt,
every bone, every leaf, bit of bark, piece of wood, or fungal fruiting body is ultimately recycled to the soil's top layer. A bit of sulfur from a squirrel, a fragment of phosphorous from a fern, or a
sliver of calcium from a bird feather may ultimately end up in an
oak leaf. The functioning parts of this recycling machinery are
often microscopic and hidden. Within the matrix of the soil,
nonphotosynthetic bacteria, blue-green bacteria (formerly known
as blue-green algae), fungi, slime molds, actinomycetes, and pro-
tozoans swarm and multiply, feeding on the various bits of debris
that come their way and recycling them. Alongside these nearly
invisible life forms, there are millions of very small creatures,

including flatworms, segmented worms, round worms, crustaceans, millipedes, springtails, centipedes, spiders, and insects, also doing the work of salvaging and recycling.

There is an abundance of organisms, known as *saprophytes*, that feast on dry oak leaves, rotten acorns, fragments of bark, insect skeletons, and animal carcasses. There is an equal number of *parasitic* creatures that thrive on the living, eating each other or consuming plant and tree roots. Parasites make struggles for water and minerals even more difficult, for oak roots face a hoard of browsers, chewers, and borers. If roots are not eaten wholesale by some large burrowing creature—ground squirrels, pocket gophers, or prairie dogs, for example—then they're likely to suffer the smaller but significant predations of parasitic bacteria, voracious worms, and pathogenic fungi. And when roots grow under less than healthy conditions—densely compacted soil particles, soggy soils with low oxygen content, or soil laced with harmful chemicals—the roots are weakened and even more vulnerable to predation.

While oak roots depend on the ectomycorrhizae, a fuzzy white covering of helpful fungi, they are sometimes heavily preyed on by many opportunistic members of the fungal world. Notable among these is the honey mushroom (*Armillariella mellea*). An oak root fungus of many guises and cosmopolitan in distribution, it grows in large, conspicuous patches of tan or honey-colored mushrooms on stumps and pieces of old wood. Prodigious quantities of spores line the white gills underneath each mushroom cap, powdering the caps and wood that may lie beneath them. These microscopic spores are capable of traveling great distances on the wind, and they move easily from forest to forest and woodland to woodland.

Once a spore alights in new soil, it may infect living roots or thrive on old pieces of buried wood—both ubiquitous commodities. Healthy oak roots are seldom distressed by the fungus's presence, but when conditions are shifted drastically—by summer flooding or irrigation, for example—then roots slowly succumb to the fungal invasion and are turned into a white mush. The oak tree dies branch by branch. Evidently, oak root fungus

A massive fruiting of the honey mushroom, (Armillariella mellea).

thrives only when the combination of abundant moisture and warm temperatures coincide. During winter, when temperatures remain cold, plentiful water does not promote fungal growth. And regardless of the season, oak taproots are able to strike water and flourish because they access water that lies deep in the soil, where the fungus cannot get the oxygen it needs to survive.

Honey mushrooms use a strange means of local propagation, forming black, ropy *rhizomorphs* that extend from root to root, infiltrating otherwise healthy roots from one originally infected source. These rhizomorphs also penetrate pieces of dead wood and produce a glowing biological "fire" known as *foxfire*. This term probably originated from the old French *fau feux,* or false fire, which was transformed into foxfire.

An oddity among oak parasites is *Mitrastemon yamamotoi,* a little-known plant without a common name. Mitrastemon's tiny brownish flowers sprout from the ground to encircle Japanese

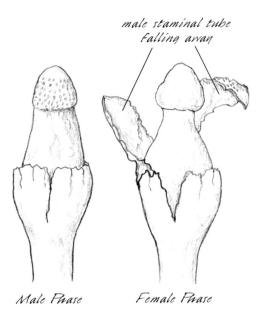

male staminal tube
falling away

Male Phase   *Female Phase*

Two stages of Mitrastemon yamamotoi *flowers: (left) the male phase; (right) male structure ruptured to reveal the female stage.*

oaks in circles similar to the "fairy rings" created by the fruiting bodies of many fungi.

In fact, mitrastemon belongs to the world's strangest parasitic flowering plant family, Rafflesiaceae, which takes advantage of a wide range of hosts. In this family, the parasites have created an ultimate match with their host: the entire plant grows inside the host as a series of branched threads that resemble the hyphal threads of a fungus.

Not until the parasite's flower emerges is there any evidence that there is a parasite within. The flower buds of mitrastemon develop inside the host oak, near the tips of its feeder roots. There, each flower bud develops in synchrony with the new roots, and by the time the flower pushes through the root tissue, it emerges near the growing edge of the roots. A single mitrastemon can invade the entire network of feeder roots, so that the leading edge of the roots is wreathed by mitrastemon flowers. To the casual observer, such flowers look like so many fanciful mushrooms emerging from the soil.

Oak roots are marvelously efficient at pulling water out of the soil, either via the extended web of mycorrhizal fungi or across the fuzzy network of root hairs. Once inside the root, most water moves toward the root's center, into the vast pipeline of the vascular system's xylem. Water moves from cell to cell on its journey toward the vascular system, diffusing across the membranes of living cells or moving freely in the spaces between cells. The cells of the endodermis engirdle the vascular core and channel the flow of water inward to the xylem. Each endodermal cell wears a beltlike strip of wax along all surfaces except for those facing outward, toward the root hairs, and inward, toward the xylem. Since water can't penetrate wax, the only route for the water is through the endodermal cells and toward the vascular tissue's xylem. On its route inward, water is sometimes moved by *root pressure,* which is caused in part by the active movement of salts across cell membranes into the xylem. The accumulation of these salts within the xylem causes a decrease in the number of water molecules, and more water rushes in to dilute the salts and compensate.

Vascular tissue consists of phloem (usually on the outer margins), which moves sugars and other foods within the plant, and xylem (usually on the inside or center), which transports water and dissolved minerals from the soil. Because these tissues form a complex, interconnected system that extends from near the tip of the roots all the way to the surface of leaves, water that enters the system flows uninterrupted from the bottom of the roots to the uppermost leaves. In the root, the vascular tissues form a solid central core; in the trunk and branches, they diverge into concentric rings; and in the leaves, they fan out into an extensive system of pipelike *veins* that travel to all corners of the leaf.

Water moves through the xylem in cells called *vessels,* which are arranged in ringlike vertical chains. Vessels begin as squat, barrel-shaped cells full of living protoplasm, but the protoplasm soon builds a multilayered wall around itself—a wall which starts with cellulose on the outside and is followed by layers of woody *lignin* on the inside. Then the vessel self-destructs, leaving a tiny empty tube that is a perfect vehicle for moving water without impediment. The vessel's protoplasm contains special enzymes that dissolve its living fabric, including the membranes at the

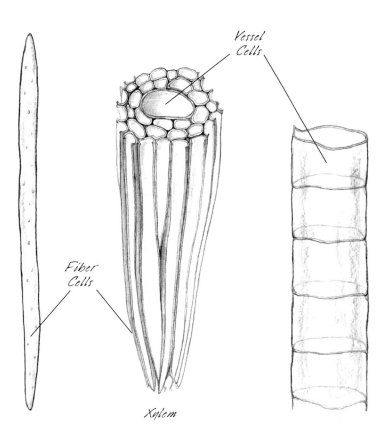

Vessel
Cells

Fiber
Cells

Xylem

Details of xylem:
(left) a single, long
fiber cell; (middle)
lengthwise view of
a vessel surrounded
by fibers; (right)
lengthwise view of
a stack of vessels.

upper and lower ends of each vessel, so that neighboring vessels
form a continuous vertical pipeline. They line up row upon row
and layer over layer to form an unbroken channel from near the
root tip all the way to the leaf margin. The vessels' side walls (the
sides of the barrel) are reinforced with cellulose and lignin to
keep them from collapsing—after all, water is dense and heavy.
Oak vessels are among the most specialized of all trees, for their
design of squat, drumlike cylinders, fully open at each end, is
about as effective as you can get.

Although root pressure is partly responsible for getting the
water into the xylem and forcing it up a short distance, the transport of water into the upper reaches of oak branches depends on
other physical forces. Water molecules are shaped so that they
have a strong attraction for one another, and they also tend to

stick to the smooth walls of the vessels. The combination of attraction and stickiness allows the chain of water— consisting of millions of individual water molecules—to move upward in a continuous stream. This phenomenon is referred to as the *cohesion-tension* of water molecules, although it also involves the adhesion of water molecules to one another.

While the cohesion-tension of water molecules holds the water column together inside the vessels, evaporation from the leaves is what moves the water upward. Over 95 percent of the water taken in through the roots is lost through simple evaporation (*transpiration*) from leaf surfaces. This nearly relentless water loss from the tree's leaves lifts the vessels' water columns and sucks more water out of the ground. Whenever a water molecule evaporates from a veinlet, it places tension on the entire column, moving it one molecule higher. Every time the column moves higher, more water must enter the root at the bottom to maintain the continuity of the column.

OAK FRAMEWORK :

TRUNK, LIMBS,

AND BRANCHES

Т he complex and elegant design of oak trunks, limbs, and branches provides the "frame" of the tree, which supports and deploys thousands of leaves. Besides holding up tremendous weight and carrying leaves to the sunlight, this frame also provides the conduit by which water, minerals, hormones, and food travel throughout the tree. Food moves from leaves to places of active growth or travels to the cortex of the roots to be stored. Hormones diffuse downward from the shoots' growing tips.

The pattern of the oak's framework depends on the interaction of the environment with the genetic blueprint that resides in every cell. Wind, availability of water, potency of light, and richness of soil dramatically affect the oak's genetic program, determining the rate of growth, ultimate height, and overall shape of the tree. Even under the best conditions, the size of the oak is still limited by its genes. However, the determination of whether stems become branches, limbs, or trunks is a complex dance involving not only the genes, but also the age of the tree and the production of key hormones that influence the development of buds, the initiation of secondary growth, and the direction of growth from the terminal bud. The precise choreography of these events remains a mystery that we are barely beginning to unravel.

As oaks grow to maturity and then old age, their shape changes. What was once a slender slip of a tree, with numerous ladderlike limbs ending in drooping or widely splayed twigs, gradually becomes a sturdy tree with a cauliflower-like crown and a clean, unfettered bole. The mature tree may endure for several hundred years if fate is kind. Record oaks in Europe are up to 900 years old, but this is extremely uncommon. Sooner or later, stress, disease, or wild and violent weather will weaken and kill the tree. But in the interim, it has had many springs and summers in which to bear its flowers and acorns, in a process that is repeated over and over again. Even in an ancient tree showing symptoms of its age—abundant growth of mistletoe, large aggregations of ornamented galls, jagged breaches in the bark where limbs have fallen away, shelf fungi protruding from the dying bark—the cycle of life goes on. Even in the throes of death, the oak will furnish sustenance to hordes of bark beetles, legions of fungal spores, armies of ants, and swarms of microscopic bacteria. Every bit and scrap of leaf, bark, and wood are recycled to help make life possible for brand-new oaks.

The bulk of an oak's massive framework consists of wood and bark. Like all trees, oaks have a thin cylinder of cells between the bark and wood that extends from the base of the trunk out to the tiniest woody twigs. The cells of this *vascular cambium* multiply rapidly in spring, slow their pace in summer, and quit in fall (except, of course, for subtropical and tropical oaks, where growth occurs throughout the year). These cells add new girth and bulk to the trunk each year. Each new cell—as in the root tip—enlarges and assumes its mature form. New cells produced toward the inside of the cambium's cylinder add to the wood, so that each year a new ring of wood is laid down just outside last year's. New cells produced to the outside mature into *sieve tube members* that add to the phloem layer. In addition to the phloem of the inner bark, the outer bark consists of multiple layers of cork and *cork parenchyma.*

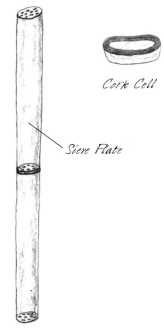

Cork Cell

Sieve Plate

Sieve Tube Cells

Wood is what botanists call secondary xylem. It gives trunks and limbs their bulk, carries their water, and provides their support. Wood is not a simple tissue, but a complex congregation of cells, each with its own role. Included in this aggregation of cells are fibers, single and multirowed vascular rays, vessels, and wood parenchyma. Parenchyma cells are generalists with little specialization. In wood, they fill in the gaps between the more specialized cells, like putty between layers of a rock wall. Oak wood carries hundreds of vertically oriented reinforcing rods called *fibers* that help hold up the tree's weight and give it sturdiness. Fibers—which are among the longest of all cells, measuring up to an inch long—are very slender tubes with tapered tips. Fiber cells die when they reach maximum size. Before dying, fiber cells systematically lay down intricate layers of cell walls impregnated with lignin.

The basic framework of these (and other) cell walls consists of long chains of cellulose molecules. Cellulose is the stuff of paper, rayon, and cardboard. The cellulose molecule itself is a chain made up of unit upon unit of glucose molecules.

In the fiber cells, strands of cellulose called fibrils are laid down first in one direction, then in another, each complementing the other. Spaces between fibrils are potential weak spots in the cell wall that can be compressed unless they are filled. This is where lignin comes in handy, for it permeates these spaces. Cellulose and lignin together give fiber cell walls their structural rigidity.

In addition to vertical fibers, both narrow and broad *vascular rays* cut directly across the wood in a horizontal direction, going from the inner heart wood all the way out to the vascular cambium, where they cross into the bark's phloem. These rays consist of a variety of thin-walled cells that continue to live and metabolize when fibers and vessels no longer do. Water is carried sideways in these rays, flowing from cell to cell, from the xylem's wood out to the living cambium and phloem, while food passes inwards from the phloem to nourish the cells in the vascular rays.

Vessels, which continue their vertical, linked pipeline from roots into leaves, constitute a major portion of the trunk's wood. The vessels of white oaks are often so large in cross-section that they give oak wood a characteristic porous look; the term *ring porous* is used to describe this pattern of vessels in the wood. By contrast, the vessels of black oaks are often partially blocked by intrusions of adjacent cells called tyloses. The largest vessels, those that form early in spring as the vascular cambium resumes its growth, are arranged in distinctive rings that can be seen with the aid of a simple magnifying glass.

Vessels grow smaller in diameter as spring cedes to summer and fall. This patterning—from large spring vessels to tiny fall vessels—results in the phenomenon we call *annual rings*. When we count rings in a cross-section of wood, we get an accurate idea of a tree's age, for each ring usually counts for one year's growth.

The science of *dendrochronology* studies the annual rings and their relationship to the tree and its environment. Annual rings not only reveal a tree's age, but they also say something about its growing conditions from year to year. The annual rings of an ancient 300- to 400-year-old oak tell a story about what the climate was like in the past. Drought, plentiful rains, early rains, and summer flooding are all revealed by a careful microscopic examination of rings in conjunction with comparisons of

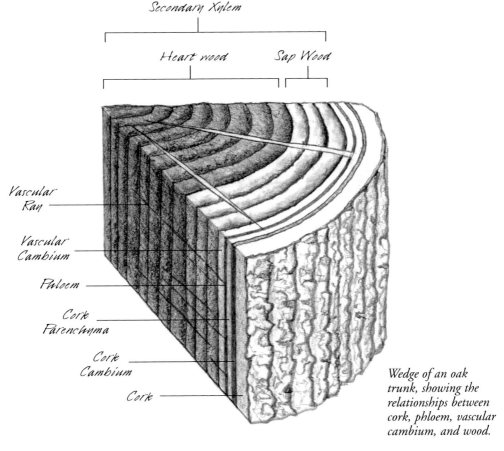

Secondary Xylem

Heart wood   Sap Wood

Vascular Ray

Vascular Cambium

Phloem

Cork Parenchyma

Cork Cambium

Cork

Wedge of an oak trunk, showing the relationships between cork, phloem, vascular cambium, and wood.

rings from known climate patterns.

Ring patterns also depend upon the seasonal rhythms of climate. In the tropics, where day length, temperature, and precipitation—all the environmental cues that rule seasonal growth patterns—are nearly constant, oaks often fail to produce rings. And if they should make rings, the rings don't coincide with the yearly cycles we're accustomed to. Subtle environmental cues (minidroughts or warming trends, for example) may start or finish a round of ring building. So determining the age of tropical oaks is much less certain. Tropical trees may become voluminous and hefty relatively quickly, with a pattern of year-round growth. In such circumstances, the only satisfactory way to estimate a tree's age is to carefully correlate growth rate with girth.

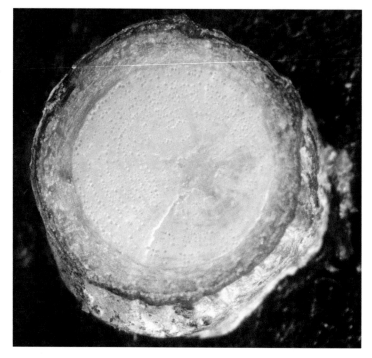

A thin slice through an oak twig reveals bark, sap wood, and heart wood. Annual rings form concentric circles in the wood, while vascular rays radiate out from the center.

Another pattern in the wood that is visible to the naked eye is the difference between the outer, lighter sap wood and the central, darker heart wood. The striking difference in color merely reflects what is going on at a functional level, for sap wood (the newest few rings of wood) is where the sap or water flows from root to leaf. Heart wood looks dark because its vessels have become clogged with various waste products, chemicals that accumulate and block the passage of water. Why heart wood loses its ability to carry water is counterintuitive, for one would think that if all the oak's wood carried on this function, the tree's ability to move water would increase. But the heart wood is where bitter tannins gather, and their presence guards the interior of the oak, inhibiting the growth of fungi. Heart wood vessels can also become clogged by *tyloses,* contorted or bulging outgrowths of wood parenchyma cells that protrude into vessels, partially blocking their openings.

Despite the oak's development of defense mechanisms such as tannins, organisms have evolved ways to get around this defense. Various fungi have overcome the effects of tannins and are responsible for a major cause of the oak tree's demise: heart rot. As the heart is literally eaten away by thousands of fungal hyphae, the tree collapses. Any point of entry is the beginning of the end, allowing other fungal spores, bacterial propagules, and beetles to enter and consume the tree.

One of the most spectacular creators of heart rot are the giant woody mushrooms known as *conchs*. Their massive fructifications often appear only after the fungal strands inside have labored long to break down the wood and turn it into fungal food. By this time the tree is already in the process of collapse and decay. Conchs demonstrate how quickly materials are recycled, for their

Young conch (Fomes sp.) fruiting bodies on trunk.

texture resembles the woody substances they have consumed.

Each conch juts like a shelf from the oak trunk, looking somewhat like a fat, puffy lip. Fruiting bodies are zoned in half-circles, adding a new ring annually along their outer periphery.

Large conchs' tremendous output of spores can be gauged by looking at their undersides, where the surface is riddled with thousands of tiny pores that are merely the tips of vertical tubes. Within each tube, thousands of specialized cells bud off microscopic spores. When the spores fall out the ends of these tubes, winds easily blow them to distant places and a new population of host oaks.

Dramatic examples of conchs on oaks include the artist's conch (*Gandoderma applanatum*), which has a rich mahogany brown fruiting cap and a white underside that would-be artists have long scribed fanciful patterns upon, and the maze gill (*Daedalia quercina*), which produces a mazelike network of elongated spore-bearing pores underneath a dull grayish cap. There are also legions of lesser wood rotters of the shelf fungus persuasion, whose fructifications last only a season but add colorful trimmings to bark during the wet season. Among these are the turkey tail (*Trametes versicolor*), whose common and scientific names give testimony to its artful and colorful design, and chicken of the woods (*Laetiporus sulphureus*), whose massive sulfur yellow caps are fleshy and dubiously edible.

The qualities of oak wood have been heralded since time immemorial. Oak wood has served as a fine-grained hardwood for building all manner of furniture and implements. The English oak was once famed as a source of timber for ship masts. The wine industry has also long depended on oaks: cork oak for the stoppers in wine bottles and oak barrels in which to age the wine. The very tannins that inhibit fungi also lend fine wines a nuance that would otherwise be missing. Today, oak furniture and other crafts have become more expensive and less available because of the difficulty of obtaining first-rate boards from old-growth forests.

In France and other European countries, the *coppicing* of

oaks was long practiced to accomplish several objectives. Coppicing is the severe cutting back of a tree to promote new growth. The new shoots thus encouraged often grew straight and true, providing slender poles for a variety of uses. Periodic cutting back also prevented the development of several competing trunks, so that the tree could focus all its energy on growing one main trunk.

Yet not all oaks are equally valuable for their wood; many species of oak, in fact, have decidedly inferior wood. California's valley oak, for example, was often given the derogatory name mush oak because its wood easily rotted. Other oaks have wood that easily cracks despite its dense, tough grain. The variation in wood from species to species depends first on how straight or crooked the oak grows; some oaks were actually prized for their curved trunks because this made for boards that were already bent and could be shaped accordingly. Other factors affecting the quality of the wood include the quantities of fungus-inhibiting tannins, the overall pattern and kinds of wood fibers, and the presence or absence of tyloses in the vessels. Tyloses seem to lend extra strength to oak heart wood and make wood watertight for wine barrels.

Wood accumulates, thickening the trunk with every passing year, but a tree's bark always has the same thickness because the main constituents of bark, cork and phloem, are sloughed off year after year. The cells that compose bark lack the tough durability of woody xylem. Phloem is a fragile tissue; it is the living layer that carries the foodstuffs manufactured by the leaves. The phloem consists of sieve tube members, narrow tubes joined end to end. Unlike the vessels that transport water, sieve tubes are alive while they function, and food passes from tube to tube across a sievelike partition between cells. How the food is dispatched with such efficiency and speed is still a mystery, because the living protoplasm inside each sieve tube impedes rather than aids speedy transportation. Foodstuffs dissolved in the protoplasm must move by rather inefficient diffusion from sieve tube to sieve tube instead of gushing through an open pipeline, as water does in vessels.

Sieve tubes are easily crushed and mangled, and when cork parenchyma cells die, they deteriorate, compromising the integrity of the bark's structure. Each spring, old phloem is squashed and eventually peels off, along with accompanying layers of cork. Thus, phloem does not accrue from year to year, and there are no rings of phloem as there are of wood. A sapling of ten years age or an elder 300 years old have about the same thickness of phloem in their trunks.

The cork that composes the bulk of bark is created by its own special *cork cambium*. The cork cambium consists of a series of long, semicircular arcs that form just outside the current year's functional phloem. Sometimes these arcs join up to form a continuous cylinder; sometimes not. And just as the vascular cambium produces new cells to the outside and inside, so, too, does the cork cambium. Cells produced to the outside become the substantial and protective *cork cells*. Cells produced inwardly develop into *cork parenchyma,* rather undistinguished, small cells that have insubstantial cell walls. Cork cells are dead, wax-impregnated cells that prevent the phloem from drying out and insulate it from temperature swings. Cork parenchyma are living cells that act as a cushion between the stiff, tough layers of cork, like the filling of a sandwich between layers of bread. The springiness of cork parenchyma lends bark its particular resilience.

Cork cambium is sloughed off annually with the old bark. In its place, a new cork cambium is formed just outside the living layer of phloem. The pattern of the cork cambium is responsible for the distinctive appearance of bark that characterizes each oak species. When trees lie leafless in winter, bark still speaks eloquently of each tree's identity.

The common name for major oak groups is based on bark color: the subgenus of white oaks usually has pale gray to near-white bark, while the subgenus of black oaks is characterized by dark gray to near-black bark. Whether these differences in bark color or other attributes of bark design strongly affect adaptability or reproductive success is doubtful, for throughout much of North

America, black and white oaks grow side by side. Bark is also described by the depth and patterns of ridges and furrows, which is often shallow in white oaks and deeply fissured in black and red oaks.

Young saplings seldom display the characteristic bark of their older parents, making them more difficult to identify. The bark of a young twig undergoes a remarkable metamorphosis on its way to becoming a branch. Young twigs are often smooth-skinned, with a thin epidermis full of microscopic holes or *stomates*. They are soft and flexible to the touch. In the process of becoming branches, they stiffen perceptibly and take on the first wrappings of the cork that forms the outer boundary of bark. Young bark also exhibits a liberal sprinkling of fissures—called *lenticels*—that allow oxygen exchange with the inner tissues. These lenticels function until bark assumes its characteristic mature pattern of furrows, cross-hatchings, and cracks, which provide oxygen to older branches, limbs, and trunks. (A crazy network of lenticels, going blindly in many directions, character-ize pieces of cork from cork oak bark.) The subtle changes from smooth new bark riddled with lenticels to the rough-textured bark of a mature oak trunk can be followed by tracing the progress in patterning from twigs to branches, branches to limbs, and limbs to trunks.

Epiphytes (from the Greek words *epi,* meaning on and *phyte,* meaning plant) are plants that grow on the limbs and trunks of bigger plants and thrive on the hospitable environment of oak bark. Scores of different plants live on oak trunks and branches, including ferns, lichens, liverworts, lycopods, and mosses. Although most of these epiphytes are spore-bearers in temperate climates, many tropical oaks host flowering epiphytes. Epiphytes favor tree bark because there is less competition, better light, and improved oxygen circulation for their roots. Fortunately for oaks, epiphytes have a neutral impact on their host; they don't penetrate into living tissues or harm the tree.

When you walk through a mixed hardwood forest, notice the

number of plants clinging to tree trunks. Some kinds of trees house very few mosses or lichens, while others seem almost overburdened with them. Epiphytes avoid certain trees, particularly conifers such as redwoods, but most have no such strictures about oaks.

The density of epiphytes on trees depends on their bark texture and chemistry. Many trees, such as madrones (*Arbutus menziesii, A. arizonica, and A. jalapensis*), manzanitas (*Arctostaphylos* spp.), sycamores (*Platanus occidentalis* and *P. wrightii*), and gumbo-limbo (*Bursera simarouba*) have smooth, even slippery bark, while most oaks, particularly of the white oak group, have hundreds of crevices, furrows, and troughs separated by ridges in their bark. Craggy bark affords ample sites for an epiphyte's water-absorbing hairs, called *rhizoids,* and aerial roots to obtain purchase, and it provides abundant opportunity for spores blown about by wind to lodge and start growing. Epiphytes benefit from the wrinkled texture of oak bark, but no one has proposed what advantage or disadvantage this wrinkled pattern might have for oaks.

The chemistry of various other trees bothers epiphytes. Conifers such as incense cedar (*Calocedrus decurrens*), red cedar (*Thuja plicata*), and redwoods (*Sequoia sempervirens* and *Sequoiadendron giganteum*) have plenty of cracks and crevices for epiphytes, but these trees get few takers because of the high levels of fungus-inhibiting tannins that infuse their bark. Tannins are celebrated for their ability to kill the harmful parasitic fungi that attack bark and wood, and wood from tannin-rich trees is valuable where fungal rot is a problem. Oaks also contain tannins, but the amount of tannin that serves oaks to discourage browsers and munchers is probably far less than the concentration required to kill epiphytes.

To learn why oak-dwelling epiphytic plants and fungi don't simply grow on the ground like other plants, consider the vigorous competition between plants in an ecosystem. All plants, we know, need light, water, minerals, and space. Small plants, growing low to the ground, don't require much space, but they're

A thick growth of mosses and leafy lichens adorn California black oak bark. Just right of center, a small cluster of Mycena *mushrooms peeks out.*

unlikely to find enough light—they're shaded by the taller plants that pre-empt most of that light for themselves. Plants without vascular systems, such as lichens and mosses, are also at a disadvantage, because water moves slowly from cell to cell in their bodies, and instead of roots, they have only slender, delicate hairs. Other plants are sure to get almost all the water first.

In order to avoid competition for light, space, and water, epiphytes have taken to the trees. There, they have room to spread and grow slowly, they can grow at a high enough level to receive ample light, and although they don't get much water unless it rains, they can soak up plenty during a downpour. Indeed, epiphytes have adopted a strategy to deal with dry times: they go into suspended animation, a condition in which they nearly stop

Epiphytes

Oak bark is home to a wide variety of *spore-bearing epiphytes.* These fall into several major groups, including fungi, lichens, mosses, leafy liverworts, ferns, and lycopods.

Fungi send colorless or white filaments into the bark, then reproduce by mushroom-shaped fruiting bodies. Each mushroom cap is lined beneath with spore-bearing gills.

Lichens consist of two organisms living as one: a fungus, which provides structure and anchors the plant; and algae, minute green cells or filaments which live within the fungus, where they're protected from drying out. Lichens come in diverse forms and colors but are never spongy and deep green, as are mosses. Lichens reproduce by fragmenting or by creating tiny powdery balls that cover their upper surface. Lichens may also bear discs or cups that make the spores of the fungus partner, but these don't reproduce the entire lichen.

Mosses grow as tufted bunches of leafy branches, with spongy texture. Their fragile leaves are tissue thin, with only one layer of cells. When the leafy branches reproduce, their fertilized egg, located near branch tips, grows into a separate plantlet. This plantlet has a slender stalk, with a bulbous capsule at the end. Inside this capsule, spores are produced.

Leafy liverworts look like flattened mosses that splay against bark, almost as though they had been spray painted on. Close inspection reveals precisely aligned overlapping leaves that resemble tiny shells or rounded shingles. Reproductive structures are usually not obvious.

Ferns grow from rhizomes embedded in bark or moss. Fern leaves—called *fronds*—develop from a coiled fiddlehead. Brown spots, stripes, or lines on the backside of fronds represent sori, collections of spore sacs that explode to release spores (use a strong hand lens).

Lycopods (genus *Lycopodium*) look like coarse mosses, with thick, mosslike leaves attached to substantial branches. Lycopods bear slender white to greenish cones that produce spore sacs.

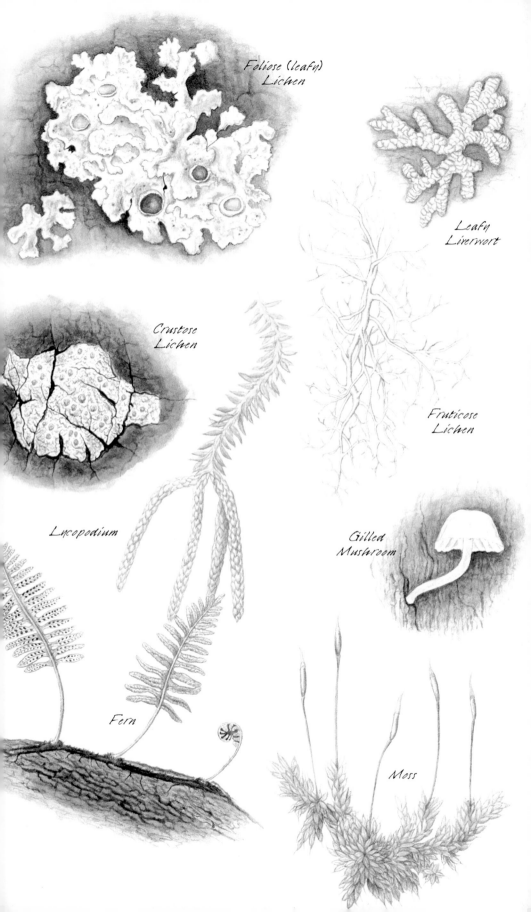

Foliose (leafy)
Lichen

Leafy
Liverwort

Crustose
Lichen

Fruticose
Lichen

Lycopodium

Gilled
Mushroom

Fern

Moss

metabolizing. They can remain in this state for months or even years. When rains return, they immediately come alive and start growing once again.

Take a walk through the woods on a cloudy day, after it has rained. The world is transformed. Where there were once dingy clumps of greenish brown or blackish mosses and curled strips of gray lichens, now sit plump cushions of mosses, redolent with green leaves, and the kaleidoscopic ribbons, miniature shrub-beries, patches, and ruffled leaves of multifarious lichens. On bare patches of bark, if you're lucky, you'll find green filagree designs that look as though they've been spray-painted onto the bark; these are the leafy liverworts.

And then there are the ferns. Many epiphytic ferns, especially the polypodies (*Polypodium* spp.), appear dead during the dry season but magically "resurrect" after rain. Of course, their slen-der creeping stems, called rhizomes, live on the bark year-round, cached out of sight under tufts of moss. But after rain, new sets of leafy fronds begin uncoiling. The resurrection fern (*Polypodium polypodioides*), from the southeastern United States and tropical America, has old brown fronds that can quickly spring to life and turn green.

If you visit a tropical rainforest in Malaysia or a pine-oak for-est in the mountains of Mexico, you'll find an even richer com-munity of epiphytes living on oak bark. In these places, the diversity of mosses and lichens is almost beyond imagination, and the number of ferns leaps from a select few to dozens of kinds. Of course, you'll be disappointed if you're wandering through the cathedral depths of a mature rainforest, for all the epiphytes there are perched high up, closer to the sun, and far from the gloom of the forest floor. But even so, you may chance upon a twig that has been shed, or an entire tree that has toppled as a result of a monsoon. Then you can really get a true sense of epiphyte diversity. You'll also be rewarded with a plethora of flowering plants. If you're in Southeast Asia, there will be exotic orchids, curious Malaysian pitcher plants, even colorful rhodo-dendrons. If you're in Mexico or Central America, you'll find an

*Bare oak branches
are home to colonies
of epiphytic
bromeliads in
Mexico's Sierra
Madre Occidental.*

*Massive fronds of the
bird's nest fern often
sit on oak limbs in
the cloud forests of
Southeast Asia.*

Long chains of the gray bromeliad (Tillandsia usneoides) *hang from the tips of live oak branches in the south-eastern United States.*

array of different orchids, succulent-leaved peperomias, and brilliantly flowered tank bromeliads.

It's difficult to imagine that epiphytes don't have some effect on oaks, even though they are not parasitic. The epiphytes that cover a large branch can weigh several pounds when wet. Such great weight spread over a giant tropical oak adds to its burden and may cause it to keel over during an intense wind storm. But it is a misconception in the temperate zone that epiphytic lichens, hanging in delicate tapestries or thick draperies from oak branches, can kill the tree. The error springs from the proliferation of lace lichen (*Ramalina usneoides*) and old man's beards (*Usnea* spp.) on trees about to die. Similarly, in the bayou country of Louisiana and Mississippi, Spanish moss (*Tillandsia usneoides*), which is really a flowering plant of the bromeliad alliance, abounds on dying oaks. But this is simply a matter of opportunity, for as oak branches lose most of their leaves to disease and stress, they provide well-lit homes for large numbers of lichens or bromeliads.

Lichens are another kind of epiphyte, and they have the uncanny ability to live in some truly hostile places, including on oak bark, where they endure long periods of drought, obtain meager amounts of minerals, and—when their host tree goes leafless in winter—are subjected to the full brunt of sun, wind, and snow. Lichens occur in bewildering and wondrous variety, with thousands of species conveniently arranged according to their overall shape: flattened and bladelike (*foliose*), branched and twiggy (*fruticose*), or crust-forming and inseparable from the bark they cover (*crustose*).

Lichens represent a long and highly successful relationship between two different organisms. Although lichens may still occasionally form anew today, it is likely that most were formed in the distant past. Just as certain parasitic fungi entered into the mutualistic mycorrhizal relationship with oak roots, other fungi (mostly from a group that produces its spores in microscopic sacs called *asci*) had completely lost the ability to live on their own. Unlike other fungi, they could scarcely sustain themselves as saprophytes or parasites. By chance, though, some of these ineffective fungi had the good fortune to trap among their strands the minute, single-celled plants referred to by the blanket term algae. Algae have the green pigment chlorophyll and manufacture their own food, just as land plants do. So when certain fungi and algae met, a magical new relationship evolved in which the fungus enfolded and protected its algal partner, channeling water and minerals to it, while the algal benefactor passed on extra food to its fungal jailer. The result was the first lichen. Sometimes, of course, things must have gone awry; either the fungus was too aggressive and soon killed the alga, or the alga couldn't produce food enough for both, and the lichen perished.

But this relationship frequently succeeded, and in many instances fungi and algae were better off than if they had continued struggling on their own.

Despite the unsavory image they may project, lichens don't harm their host oak tree in any way. On the contrary, some lichens may have actually rewarded their hosts' hospitality, courtesy of the algal partner. The algae in lichens belong to two fundamentally different groups: true green algae (Chlorophyta) and blue-green bacteria (Cyanobacteria). Most types of green algae still live tied to the watery environments of ponds, slow streams, lakes, and tide pools. When they do live freely on their own, green algae live chiefly on twigs, where humidity is high year-round. The blue-green bacteria, by contrast, live in a wide variety of habitats, including some of the most hostile environments on the planet: snow fields, sulfur vents, and edges of hot springs.

Blue-green bacteria are more adaptable overall than green algae and are able to convert simple nitrogen-containing compounds into more complex ones. Blue-green bacteria, together with the more conventional soil bacteria that live in most healthy soils, are called nitrogen-fixers because they convert nitrogen to a form that plant roots use. Some of the blue-green bacteria that live inside lichens carry on in the same manner, which means that nitrogen fixation occurs in lichens attached to oak bark. Whether the oak can easily absorb nitrogen produced this way is still a question, but recent evidence from research on tall tree crowns suggests that some lichens do "leak" extra nitrogen onto tree bark. Since this research mainly involves cone-bearing trees such as firs and spruces, it remains to be seen whether it holds true for oaks.

As befits a large and ancient group of trees, oaks also offer room and board to parasitic flowering plants. Sacred to the ancient druids and familiar today because of the sweet, foolish custom of kissing beneath its pale berries, no other group of parasitic plants is as conspicuous as the mistletoes. Mistletoes are semi-parasitic; they still photosynthesize, yet for some reason,

Bare in winter, a Garry oak in the mountains north of San Francisco Bay reveals its large, dense clumps of mistletoe.

they have lost the ability to absorb water and minerals from the soil. This large family, the Loranthaceae—which includes more than 1,200 species worldwide—has evolved from ancestors that once lived with their roots planted in the earth. Some mistletoes still do, but even then their roots suck the juices from other plant roots in order to get by. Most mistletoes have taken to the air, perched high in the crowns and branches of trees, and their roots have been converted into massive sucking organs—haustoria— that pierce and penetrate the bark. Inside the tree, the haustoria fan out into the tree's plumbing system to drink substantial amounts of water and minerals. So large are these haustoria that they often cause a conspicuous swelling of the branch.

Their aerial habitat affords mistletoes several advantages, for there they receive abundant light and elicit the services of wind for pollination and birds for pollination and seed dispersal. Some mistletoes, especially those that infest oaks in temperate North America and Europe (*Phoradendron* spp. and *Viscum album*) do not have obvious flowers, and many people mistakenly think they reproduce without them. But look closely, and you'll find greenish spikes of minute male and female flowers, whose pollination, like that of oaks, depends on wind. In the tropics, though, no such scrutiny is necessary: oaks wear mistletoes that make them look as though they have burst into flamboyant flower with vivid splashes of red, orange, or scarlet. Such mistletoes (many are in the genus *Loranthus*) lure a variety of birds to their tubular flowers and reward them with abundant nectar. Each group of birds lives in a particular region of the tropics: hummingbirds in the

The vivid orange tubular blossoms of a tropical mistletoe (Psittacina), *on oaks in Costa Rica's cloud forests.*

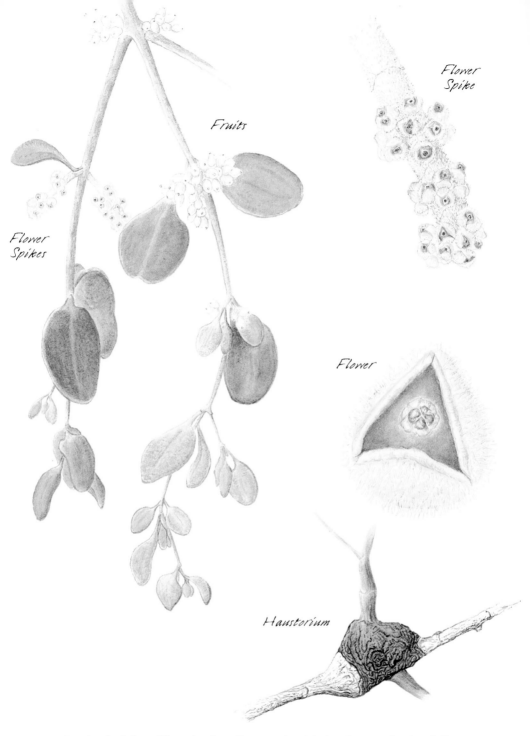

A sprig of mistletoe (Phoradendron flavescens) *with tiny flower spikes (top left) and a swollen haustorium, a mistletoe's entry into an oak twig (bottom right).*

Flower
Spike

Fruits

Flower
Spikes

Flower

Haustorium

59

Americas, sunbirds in tropical Africa and Asia, and honey eaters in tropical Australia and Southeast Asia.

The white, red, or yellowish berries that mistletoes produce are also tempting morsels of food for birds. As they sit high on an oak limb feeding on this bounty, birds attempt to get rid of the sticky seeds by wiping their beaks against neighboring twigs. All mistletoe seeds are liberally provided with a viscous glue, and as soon as they're fastened in place, the bird's job is done. The seeds rarely touch the ground, where they would surely fail. Fortunately for the oak, many mistletoe seeds don't find a way to penetrate, so they soon perish. But if there's some breach in a twig, the mistletoe is quick to find it and take advantage of the oak's break in its armor. A few plants on a healthy tree do little damage, but on old and weakened oaks, mistletoes can flourish, sickening the oak and helping to hasten its end.

A TOUR
AROUND
A LEAF

 eaves are truly the crowning achievement of trees. They are the center of energy production through photosynthesis; the synthesizers of vibrant green, yellow, or red pigments; and the nexus for prodigious transpiration of water. Whether tough, leathery, and evergreen, or delicate, thin, and deciduous, leaves are borne over the life of a large oak by the hundreds of thousands, even by the millions. They are changeable creations, quickly unfurling from tiny blades inside buds to full-sized leaves in a matter of days, then just as quickly curling up and changing colors in autumn.

The main part of the leaf is a flattened blade whose main purpose is to photosynthesize. Common to all green plants, photosynthesis provides the basis for all the food that feeds the planet. Photosynthesis is a complex set of interacting chemical steps, but, to give a simplified overview, the plant uses the energy from sunlight to combine carbon dioxide (carbon and oxygen) from the atmosphere with water from the soil. The result is the simple sugar glucose and the gas oxygen. Glucose tastes sweet, like table sugar. (Table sugar, or sucrose, is only a slightly more complicated sugar; it consists of glucose hooked to fructose, or fruit sugar.)

This chemical slight-of-hand requires large amounts of energy. Plants capture the energy from sunlight using the green pigment we call chlorophyll. Chlorophyll is packaged into spherical or football-shaped green bodies known as *chloroplasts.* Chloroplasts are so tiny that they can only be seen through a powerful microscope, but they're also so abundant that they color leaves green. Chlorophyll catches the sun's violet and red rays and converts this light energy into chemical energy in the form of a molecule known as ATP (*adenosine triphosphate*). The energy stored in ATP makes the manufacture of glucose possible. Without ATP, life as we know it would be impossible, for ATP carries and stores the energy that fuels all the thousands of chemical reactions inside living cells. ATP is a universal currency of energy, occurring in bacteria and insects, fish and humans, and algae and oaks. The role of ATP in photosynthesis is to supply the burst of energy a plant needs to build glucose from carbon dioxide and water. Building complex substances from simple ones always requires a greater overall input of energy.

During the production of glucose, oxygen is given off by splitting water. This oxygen is released into the air where it adds to the atmosphere's oxygen supply. Photosynthesis can be summed up by this chemical shorthand:

$$6CO_2 \;+\; 6H_2O \;\xrightarrow[\text{Chlorophyll}]{\text{Light}}\; C_6H_{12}O_6 \;+\; 6O_2$$

(carbon dioxide) (water)   (glucose)   (oxygen)

Though this simple representation is elegant, it does not illustrate the full significance of glucose. Besides immediate use for respiration to produce energy, glucose can also be stored for later use—usually in the form of starch in roots and acorns—or converted into a multitude of other chemicals that build cells, defend leaves and wood, or create new genetic material. Every living organism ultimately depends on this never-ending source of glucose for all of these uses. Despite the seemingly simple scheme of photosynthesis, even the most clever human chemist has not managed to recreate this feat.

The importance of photosynthesis can hardly be overestimated. To begin with, the release of oxygen into the atmosphere revolutionized the world by creating breathable air. Earth's first simple organisms were poisoned by oxygen, which is actually highly flammable and corrosive. As oxygen accumulated in the atmosphere from photosynthesizing cells, organisms either survived or perished, and those that survived evolved the new mechanism of aerobic respiration, a process in which oxygen is the key ingredient. Aerobic respiration burns sugars and other foods in a closely controlled way, producing abundant ATP for metabolic energy. Sugars are broken down into their original starting materials, water and carbon dioxide. By contrast, the earth's first organisms carried on a much less efficient energy-producing process called anaerobic respiration ("without air"). Not only did the net gain from burning sugars this way yield far less ATP, but sugars were incompletely broken down, producing carbon dioxide and ethyl alcohol or carbon dioxide and lactic acid. Both alcohol and lactic acid are toxic. So photosynthesis has made possible the evolution of all the complex organisms, from oak trees to humans, through the doubly beneficial combination of producing sugars for food and oxygen for energy. Without the abundance of these two essential ingredients, the earth's organisms would have remained small and simple indefinitely.

Every detail of a leaf's structure assists photosynthesis. The outer surface of every leaf is enveloped by a layer of cells called the epidermis. The epidermis is covered by a waxy exudate called the cuticle, which keeps the leaf from drying out. Since leaves must "breathe" to obtain carbon dioxide, the epidermis on the leaf's underside is perforated by thousands of tiny holes called stomates. Stomates are the only entry point for carbon dioxide, yet they represent a decided weakness, as they're large enough to allow great quantities of water to escape through evaporation. The location of stomates on the cooler, bottom surface of the leaf helps cut down on water loss, but nonetheless, this innovation does not altogether prevent it.

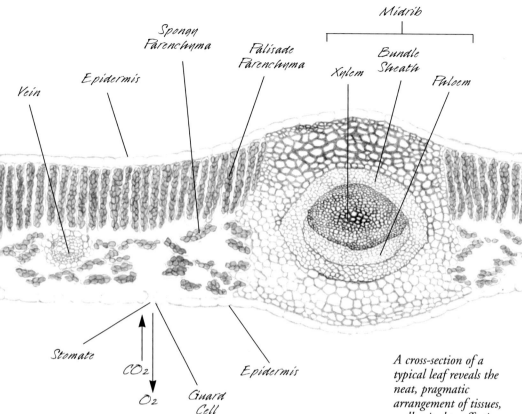

Vein

Epidermis

Spongy
Parenchyma

Palisade
Parenchyma

Midrib

Xylem

Bundle
Sheath

Phloem

Stomate

CO₂

O₂

Epidermis

Guard
Cell

A cross-section of a typical leaf reveals the neat, pragmatic arrangement of tissues, well-suited to effective photosynthesis. The central midvein carries water and minerals from the soil to the leaf and carries away sugars made by the leaf.

Stomates are bordered by a pair of guard cells that swell soon after the sun rises, pulling away from each other to create the stomate, and then shrink as the sun sets, coming together to close the stomate. So stomates open and close according to the sun, in a dance that coincides with photosynthesis, which, of course, is also driven by the sun. Despite the disadvantage of being open during the warmest part of the day, when water evaporates most rapidly from leaf surfaces, stomates allow carbon dioxide into the leaf at a time when photosynthesis reaches its peak because of the available sunlight. Leaves must always balance the need for making food through photosynthesis against the risk of desiccation by rapid water loss. If transpiration were to cease or slow to a near halt, the water stream that carries mineral nutrients from the soil would also fail. And without nutrients in the leaves, their chemical factories would shut down.

Palisade parenchyma fills the upper layers of the leaf just below the epidermis, in tubular columns that stand side by side in vertical files. They brim with the green chloroplasts that efficiently intercept most of the sunlight hitting the leaf. Below the palisade layer are irregularly wrinkled cells intertwined with their neighbors in an intricate pattern of channels and spaces. These spongy parenchyma cells also contain chloroplasts, so that any last bit of light that passes through the palisade parenchyma gets soaked up. The channels and spaces allow for the diffusion of water, oxygen, and carbon dioxide throughout the leaf.

Spread midway between the upper and lower surface of the leaf is a vascular web consisting of a central midrib, outlying veins, and myriad tiny veinlets that carry water to every nook and cranny of the leaf. These veins and veinlets are to the wood's vascular tissue what twigs and branches are to the oak's trunk. The phloem lies just under the xylem in each vein. It whisks away sugar made during photosynthesis, delivering it to all those places where growth is active: to flowers that are being pollinated, to acorns that are ripening, or to the roots to be stored for later use in fall and winter. The pattern of leaf veins is a genetic stamp that helps distinguish one genus of plants from another, and often one group of species from another. In fact, an entire subgenus of oaks—*Cyclobalanopsis*—is differentiated from all other oaks by the subtle patterns of its tiniest veins.

It seems amazing that leaves can vary so much with such success. Leaf design has a long evolutionary history, during which leaves have been shaped and reshaped through adaptations to changing habitats. The original gene pool from which various oak groups evolved may have limited the options for leaf design within certain definite parameters, but these parameters are broad enough that oak species have had leaves with numerous variations.

There are some basic features shared by all oak leaves. Each consists of a slender stalk—the petiole—attached to a thin green blade. At the base of the petiole are a pair of ephemeral stipules—slender, narrow, pointed, pale green appendages that remain on the twig for a brief time, then fall. The shape of the leaf blade varies from a narrow lance to a broad oval with a pointed tip to a wide ellipse. The margin of the leaf may be flat or turned down and curled under. It can be smooth and unbroken

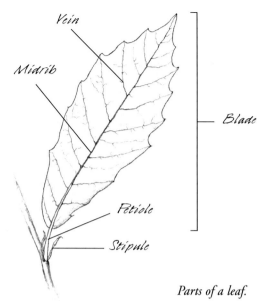

Parts of a leaf.

(entire), finely to coarsely toothed (serrate or dentate), or shallowly to deeply scooped (lobed). Lobes may be no more than a brief suggestion of an indentation, or they may delve deeply into the blade and run nearly to the leaf's central midrib. Lobe tips may be blunt, gently rounded, or tipped by slender bristles.

The veins are arranged in a pinnate, featherlike pattern which branches from a substantial and obvious central midrib. These veins themselves rebranch into bewilderingly complex patterns that vary from one oak group to another.

What oak leaves are not is perhaps just as important as what they are. For example, oak leaves are never compound—they never have separate leaflets arranged in various patterns to comprise a single leaf. And no oak leaf would ever be long, narrow, and needlelike. The basic genetic program for oaks as a whole precludes these (and many other) possibilities.

Oak leaves can also be identified by their two-five phyllotaxy (*phyllus* means leaf; *taxis*, arrangement). If you look at a twig from its base to its tip, you'll count five leaves attached to the twig, and you'll find that they describe two complete turns around the twig. In other words, there are five leaves—each at a

2/5 phyllotaxy
of oak leaves.

different level—making two imaginary spirals around the twig. Each kind of tree or tree group has its own phyllotaxic formula; this is the basic one for oaks.

Oak twigs are shaped into rough pentagons, and each of the five leaves of the two-five formula are attached to a different angle of the pentagon. This arrangement prevents neighboring leaves from getting in each other's way. When a leaf begins a new two-five rotation, it is a considerable distance from another leaf placed at a similar angle competing for the sun. Such careful placement guarantees that you can have a crown full of many twigs, and that most of the leaves of that crown won't crowd each other or interfere unduly with one another's attempt to trap sunlight.

Of course, you can have too much of a good thing. If every branch kept all of its leaves permanently, there would be such a welter of leaves—a veritable leaf jungle—that the innermost leaves would be deprived of light and air. Deciduous oaks have solved this problem by simply shedding all their leaves at the end of the growing season in fall. They make a new set in spring, and the twigs that bear the new leaves only grow a certain length in one season and only produce so many leaves. But the tropical, subtropical, and Mediterranean-climate oaks—what we call live oaks—keep their leaves through the winter; they have another solution to the problem of too many leaves. If you carefully scrutinize a live oak twig, you can usually tell how many years leaves have been growing on it. Starting with the end of the twig, follow the leaves back along the twig until you come to a place where there's a small gap; this will be one year's growth.

Continue back from this gap, repeating the process until you come to a place where there are no more leaves on the twig.

The number of years of leafy growth seldom exceeds three, and is often no more than two. The difference between live oaks, then, and deciduous ones is mainly that live oaks hold onto a given set of leaves for at least a full year and grow a new set of leaves before shedding the old. The old are discarded after a few years simply because maintaining them would be wasteful and unhealthy. The farther back on the twig leaves grow, the more shaded (and less efficient) they are, until a point of dysfunction is reached.

But leaf design has more to it than simply how leaves are arranged on their twigs or how long they're kept on the tree. Those factors depend partly on the need for sunlight. But remember that the way leaves are constructed also means they lose great quantities of water, simply because their stomates are wide open during the day. Leaves that receive the full brunt of the hot summer sun are especially vulnerable, as are leaves exposed to forceful winds or the chill of frigid winter days, both of which can also dry out leaves. The waxy cuticle and the location of stomates on the bottom surfaces of leaves help protect against water loss, but oak design dictates that leaves also drop when water is unavailable.

Deciduousness is an effective way to deal with excessive winter cold, when frigid air dehydrates leaves and water is frozen solid in the soil. This undoubtedly is why deciduous oaks are so widespread in colder temperate climates, such as those found in eastern and midwestern North America, in central and northern China, throughout Japan, and in central and northern Europe. Deciduousness also has its uses in climates with long, hot, dry summers, such as those in the foothills of California and the mountains of Texas and Arizona. There, deciduous oaks—most of which have ancestors from cold-winter places—lose their leaves especially early, sometimes by summer's end.

Oaks must balance this method of dealing with hot, dry summers against the cost of making a whole new set of leaves the

Winter in California's inland foothills is a good time to see the contrast between the evergreen coast live oak (left) and the deciduous blue oak (right).

next year. New leaves take energy to produce and need water to fill new leaf cells, costs that could be avoided if a tree already has a set of serviceable leaves. This is not to say that live oaks don't make new leaves each spring, but in springs that follow rain-poor winters, the number of new leaves is minimal. So in places with summer drought, some kinds of oaks simply make tough leaves that resist water loss and keep them throughout the year. The proof of the effectiveness of both strategies is seen in Texas, Arizona, and California, where deciduous and live oaks grow side by side, or at least within a short distance. There is more than one way to solve the same problem of little water!

Additional adaptations to minimize water loss include small leaves, as they have less surface area from which to lose water. Surface area is also reduced when leaf edges are rolled under.

Unusually glossy leaves, the result of an extra-thick waxy cuticle, provide a highly protective coating comparable to a layer of varnish. Bluish green leaves deflect the hottest, most energetic of the sun's rays, resulting in cooler leaves. Thick, tough leaves, made that way by extra stone cells (thick cells that are heavily lignified), don't collapse on hot days and allow recovery from wilting when more water is pumped into leaves during the night. Leaves are often covered by hairs of many kinds—from straight and single, to starbursts, to curly and wooly. Most hairs are on leaf undersides, where they retard evaporation. Whitish hairs reflect away excess heat by deflecting most of the sun's spectrum. Some hairs also secrete sticky substances that retard desiccation, and epidermal exudates in the form of waxy flakes may further insulate the inside of the leaf from water loss.

Some oaks, instead of preventing water loss, have leaves that accomplish just the opposite: they waste prodigious amounts of it. Why? In order to have highly efficient sun-trapping abilities. Such oaks live in climates where it rains a lot in summer. Oaks from the Great Smoky Mountains of North Carolina and Tennessee have leaves that are up to eight inches long and four inches wide. Because summer days are often cloudy, leaves have to be more efficient at absorbing light by being broad and thin, attributes that also make them vulnerable to rapid water loss. The leaves can afford this water loss because their roots have access to plenty of water to replace what is lost through evaporation.

Some oak leaves have large surfaces that are broken up into many parts; in other words, they are lobed. Lobing, a feature that has evolved in many unrelated species of oak from similar habitats, ensures a maximum surface deployed to the sun. While it's true that a large, unbroken leaf surface could absorb just as much or more light than a lobed leaf would, consider the overall picture: indentations between lobes allow bits of light to pass through and be absorbed by a lobe on the leaf just below, like a jigsaw-puzzle.

Lobed leaves, it turns out, are sometimes found on oaks that inhabit summer-dry places, where maximum sun exposure would not normally be desirable. California's magnificent valley oak (*Quercus lobata*) survives by living in places with a guaranteed, dependable water supply, along the banks of meandering rivers and streams, and in well-watered valley bottoms. In these places, the valley oak's broad, deeply lobed leaves lose large amounts of water to evaporation, which cools the leaf surface much like sweat cools our skin. Without such a mechanism, the fierce summer temperatures, which regularly top 100 degrees, would fry delicate leaf cells full of precious chloroplasts.

The leaves on the lowest branches of forest giants and on shaded saplings seldom become stressed by high temperatures, but they do have great difficulty obtaining enough sunlight. And the sunlight they are exposed to has often been "filtered" by the chlorophyll contained in the leaves above. Chlorophyll is green because it reflects those wavelengths of sunlight that we see as green. (It also reflects yellows and oranges, but the eye sees green because the green overwhelms all else.) Only the reds and blue-violets are absorbed by chlorophyll and turned into chemical energy. So every time light passes through a layer of leaves, the leaves take the red and blue-violet rays, and allow the rest to pass on. By the time the light arrives at the branches closest to the ground, there is precious little red or blue-violet light left, so for such leaves the light is far dimmer than we might imagine.

Upper Leaf

Lower Leaf

How do leaves cope? Most expand their surface to the maximum allowed by their genetic programming. Unlobed oak leaves don't suddenly grow lobes—that evidently is beyond their capabilities—but they do increase their surface area by as much as four times more than leaves in the tree's top canopy.

California's magnificent valley oak, (Quercus lobata), *growing near a stream course in California's Sierra Nevada foothills.*

Oak leaves exposed to direct sunlight look very different from those that grow in shade, even on the same tree.

Part of the fascination with oak leaves is the intriguing changes they undergo from bud to death. Buds sit prominently on trees all through the winter. As spring warms the air, they swell and then burst open in a green shower of tender new leaves. The leaves quickly expand, orient themselves to the sun, and take on their mature color. The procession may finish with a flourish of color in autumn, when deciduous leaves fall.

Buds are the repositories for all future leaves. If you were to split a bud lengthwise down the middle, you wouldn't see much—the view would be so obscured with densely-packed parts that the details would remain hidden. Yet the bud's structure is

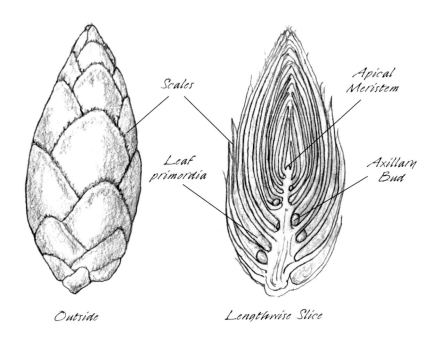

Scales

Apical
Meristem

Leaf
primordia

Axillary
Bud

Outside   Lengthwise Slice

The simple buds of oaks sport several rows of tough bud scales on the outside (left). A lengthwise slice (right), reveals the apical meristem, new leaf primordia, and preformed axillary buds.

elegantly revealed if you take a firm hand and make a paper-thin, lengthwise slice straight down the middle.

The exterior of the bud is wrapped in thick, triangular scales that are often neatly arrayed in stacked rows rather than in twisted spirals. Unlike many trees, oak bud scales are dry, not sticky. They may wear furry coverings or be rather plain and smooth, depending on the species. Oak bud scales create an impervious layer that acts as an insulating jacket around the delicate contents of the bud. By trapping innumerable minuscule pockets of inert air, scales protect the vulnerable living cells of the bud from temperature swings and desiccation, much like foam insulation protects the occupants of a house.

Just inside the bud scales lie a series of thin, upward-arching appendages that are white or the palest green. These leaf primordia are tightly packed against one another and attached to a gradually tapered central stalk. With a clear view, you can see warty lumps at the bases of the leaf primordia on the central stalk. These lumps are destined to become the next round of buds—they're called axillary buds because they sit in the angle between the leaf and the stem's axis. The tip of the central stalk is rounded or dome-shaped, and contains a cluster of tiny cells known as the apical meristem. Through cell division, the apical meristem adds more leaf primordia and adds to the length of the stalk beneath, producing the fodder from which the shoot ultimately grows.

Each bud is a perfectly preformed miniature shoot, provided with leaves, a stalk, and an apical meristem, all wrapped inside a protective envelope, awaiting a change in season. Winter buds remain protectively ensconced within their scales, dormant, meristems shut down.

As leaves expand, they push back the bud scales and unfurl. Leaves enlarge at an accelerated rate, so that within a few days, they've gone from tiny nubbins inside bud scales to full-blown blades extended to the warm spring sun. During this period, oak leaves also change color dramatically, for at first they are nearly colorless. Some oaks have such vividly colored young leaves that the tree appears to blossom with flowers. The California black

The new leaves of California black oak (Quercus kelloggii) *wear a frosting of pink hairs.*

oak (*Quercus kelloggii*) produces new leaves that wear a velvety frosting of pink hairs. So vividly colored are these first leaves that it looks as though the tree were in glorious flower, deceiving the observer into believing it is some exotic tree straight from a tropical rainforest. Those hairs are soon shed as the burgeoning leaves assume mature stature and begin to manufacture more chlorophyll. The pink hairs, however, are not merely decorative; their brilliant color deludes potential browsers into believing that these leaves may be bitter and distasteful, perhaps even downright poisonous. In the plant world, such bright flashes of color act as a warning sign against chewing on leaves, even when the toxins that often accompany these colors are not actually proffered. In the case of the oaks, it is sufficient to hang out a warning sign.

The color of most oak leaves deepens to an emerald green during the summer, but oak leaves from droughty habitats may take on a blue tint like California's blue and Engelmann's oaks

The bluish cast of blue oak leaves (Quercus douglasii) *reflects the heat of the summer sun.*

(*Quercus douglasii* and *Q. engelmannii*) and Mexico's blue oak (*Q. oblongifolia*). Living in the California coast range, the Sierra Nevada foothills, and the southwestern desert mountains where the mercury may exceed 100 degrees for many days on end, the leaves of these oaks assume a distinctive blue-green coloration from the extra-thick wax that coats and protects them. Even from a distance, blue oaks are readily identified by this "cool" color. The coolness is no illusion, for a blue leaf is reflecting the highly energetic wavelengths of the blue end of the spectrum that would otherwise heat up and dry out the leaf.

In the fall, the evergreen live oaks seldom signal a change, except to quietly jettison their oldest set of leaves some distance back on the twigs. These old leaves lose their green chlorophyll, turn brown, dry up, and fall.

For many deciduous oaks, events unfold differently. The first sign that things are about to change is a gradual loss of the leaves' chlorophyll. Chlorophyll needs ample water to keep functioning; when water is in scarce supply, leaves dry out, and chlorophyll splits into smaller pieces that lose their light-trapping abilities along with their green color. The green color of chlorophyll is manifested only when the entire molecule is intact, with its highly stylized shape and spatial arrangement. Sometimes this chlorophyll loss occurs so abruptly that the entire leaf turns brown and falls immediately, but often there is a lag between the time the leaf dries out and when the chlorophyll deteriorates. The reason for this lag and its consequences, the leaf "turning color," are still poorly understood. Change in day length, accompanied by chilly nights that alternate with warm days, seems to be the key, transforming leaves from green to golden yellow, yellow brown, or vivid red.

Inside every green leaf of every plant—regardless of kind—is a set of *accessory pigments* responsible for this dramatic change of color. Without the masking overlay of green chlorophyll, these pigments would paint forests a kaleidoscope of shades from the warm end of the spectrum. The exact kinds and amounts of these pigments are specific to each kind of plant. Accessory pigments

After drying out and turning brown, deciduous oak leaves fall to the ground.

aid chlorophyll in capturing more light, for they are able to absorb light from the orange, yellow, green, and blue-green parts of the spectrum, which chlorophyll cannot absorb. The yellow and orange pigments are called *carotenoids;* other reddish or brownish pigments are called *xanthophylls.* The leaves of California black oak (*Quercus kelloggii*) contain lots of carotenoids, so we see vivid flashes of yellow, gold, or yellow brown in the autumn in California's Sierra Nevada. The leaves of the scarlet oak (*Q. coccinea*) of eastern hardwood forests are rich in xanthophylls, so there we see gaudy splashes of scarlet red. Oaks play a masterful role in the beauty of fall foliage in the hardwood forests of the world's Northern Hemisphere, from the Atlantic seaboard of eastern North America to the Pacific slope's Sierra Nevada, from the mountains of Japan to the foothill forests of France and Germany.

Like so many other key processes, the simple fall of a leaf is determined by hormones manufactured by the buds at the tip of each twig. When leaves finally dry to a crisp, hormones signal cells to sever the connection of leaves to twigs, allowing the leaves to fall. The layer of cells responsible for this severance is called the *abscission layer*. Some oaks obstinately hang on to their leaves using the tough strands of vascular tissue that pipe water from stems to leaf veins, and the leaves sway to and fro in gentle fall breezes until winter gusts finally rip them from their moorings.

Leaves on the ground play significant roles in maintaining the forest's health. A carpet of dead leaves provides a fascinating interface between the dry air above and the moist soil below. This rich mulch holds in moisture, interferes with competing seedlings, and provides a home to the minute grazers and browsers from the soil's topmost layers. Dead leaves furnish a rich organic salad that will be attacked by ground-dwelling beetles, foraging fungal strands, and battalions of microscopic bacteria. These microorganisms and insects are responsible for the final act of reducing leaves to *frass*—a humusy powder—helping to recycle nutrients to the soil. Leaf frass adds nutrients to soils and ameliorates their textures. The last hold-out in the process of decomposition is the firm skeleton of veins that was each leaf's plumbing system and framework. In the winter, beautiful leaf skeletons are testimony that the process of decay is not yet complete; it may take months before the veins are finally demolished.

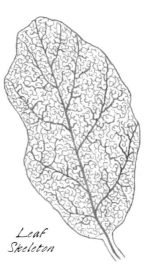

Leaf
Skeleton

The pace of leaf decomposition varies from forest to forest. In northern hardwood forests— at the limits of where hardwoods can survive—the entire process may take more than a year; in Mediterranean climates, it can be several years; in tropical rainforests, it may move to completion so swiftly that at any time only a few leaves can be found intact on the dark, dank forest floor.

Just as oaks provide shade and shelter for a wide variety of animal life, so are their leaves irresistible morsels of food to many pests and diseases. Perhaps oaks have become the target of so many opportunistic prospectors because of their long tenure on earth or because of their wide range over diverse habitats. Or possibly it's because they have plenty of good-tasting young leaves. Even though oak leaves are later laced with chemicals such as tannins, predations on oak leaves may weigh heavily on the growth rate of the tree and diminish its chances of success. Most attacks occur when newborn leaves have first opened to the world; older leaves are tough and hard to consume, having accumulated fibers that lend them substantial stiffness and having manufactured bitter tannins that interfere with browsers' digestion. (Tannins combine with proteins in a way that prevents their effective absorption.) The vulnerability of new leaves indicates that metabolic energy is required to make the fibers and tannins that defend leaves, and that the energy needed to do so isn't available until

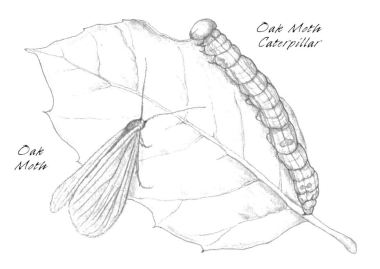

Oak Moth Caterpillar

Oak Moth

leaves have had a chance to photosynthesize in the sun. After turning sunlight into chemical energy, oak leaves can stockpile their arsenal of defensive chemicals.

The most striking example of outright attack on leaves is from the oak moth. In years when abundant egg production and favorable weather coincide, record crops of new caterpillars hatch and set to work right away, devouring the year's flush of new growth. During such attacks, oaks are literally stripped of all new leaf blades before their defenses can be readied. But just when devastation seems assured, oaks undergo a miraculously rapid recovery. Evergreen oaks have last year's set of leaves to draw upon, which are already prepared for attack. Deciduous oaks have all those axillary buds—previously initiated but inhibited by hormones from growing until this moment.

Most plants, including oaks, have a tiny axillary bud in the crotch between each leaf and the twig to which it's attached. If every axillary bud were to grow—each major branch carries dozens of them—the resulting morass of brushy side branches would encumber the plant with more leaves than it could use. Dense branches compete with one another for light and impede air flow through the living leaves, create nexuses where diseases can flourish.

Oaks avoid this dilemma through the careful orchestration of hormones. Each species has a unique genetic blueprint that controls the production of hormones in the twigs' terminal buds. These hormones control many key processes, including the direction of growth, the dormancy or activity of buds, and the shedding of leaves. The concentration of hormones determines exactly what their effects will be. In large quantities, hormones may entirely arrest a bud's development, while in trace amounts the same hormone may encourage and speed growth. The farther hormones travel from their point of origin, as they move from the branch's tip toward its base, the more dilute they become. When leaves are stripped by oak moths, the hormonal balance changes. Many axillary buds will now have just the right amount of hormone to stimulate their growth in a tightly controlled manner. The new twigs don't grow into long side branches that resemble the branch they're attached to, rather, these twigs remain short and stubby, covered with dense clusters of new leaves to replace the old. And as those new leaves appear—one after the other in quick succession—each carries at its base a new axillary bud in reserve, in the event that even more growth will be called for.

Each crop of leaves from axillary buds gets progressively smaller, for until leaves fully expand and photosynthesize for a while, new food sources are in short supply. Food is kept in reserve for just such emergencies—cached in trunks and roots for safekeeping. Moth predations take a heavy toll, costing the tree a great deal of energy to repair the damage, but seldom do they kill oak trees outright.

The oak leaf blotch miner (*Cameraria agrifoliella*) and live oak ribbed casemaker (*Bucculatrix albertellia*) are two more culprits that feed on oak leaves when they are young. Both are moths and follow a moth's fascinating life cycle: eggs that hatch into wormlike larvae, larvae that pupate into a protective cocoon when ready to undergo transformation into an adult, and short-lived, winged adult moths that emerge from the cocoon. In both cases, the early caterpillar stage is a green larva that feeds exclusively on the softer leaf tissues, such as palisade and spongy parenchyma, and is confined entirely between the two epidermal layers of a leaf blade. Neither organism does damage to the extent that the oak moth does, but they're highly visible because of the complex silvery traces they leave behind as they eat their way about in an apparently haphazard manner. Close examination reveals that these paths are anything but haphazard, for they represent routes around major veins. To these tiny larvae, the veins loom as armored obstacles in their paths. Each vein is engirdled by a *bundle sheath* that contains tough *sclereids*—thick-walled, irregularly shaped, stonelike cells—and so stand as formidable obstructions to the caterpillars' progress. By contrast, the labyrinths of air passages in the spongy parenchyma provide easy routes for the peregrinations of the miners.

After feeding in the leaf, the leaf blotch miner spins a cocoon that actually protrudes through the top of its leaf tunnel, and the moth that emerges flies away unfettered by the confines of the leaf. The live oak ribbed casemaker, by contrast, emerges from the interior of oak leaves to feed on leaf surfaces as it grows, skeletonizing the leaves with its voracious appetite. It pupates inside white, cigar-shaped cocoons that are suspended from the oak tree's trunk.

Butterflies also victimize oaks. We often fail to realize that the leaf damage caused by the caterpillars of butterflies is necessary if we are to enjoy these winged beauties. Adult butterflies are very selective about where they lay their eggs, and in the case of the vibrant, royal purple hairstreak (*Quercusia quercus*), whose scientific name is so evocative of its larval food plant, it is oak leaves alone that will feed its ravenous caterpillars.

Fungi are also oak leaf exploiters comparable to their oakroot-consuming counterparts. Mildews are among the most obvious,

These young coast live oak shoots are already covered with white powdery mildew conidia, which can infect other vulnerable growth.

proliferating and reproducing with abandon when tender new growth is subjected to humid conditions. Mildews may cover all leaf surfaces with a white powder. Under a strong magnifying glass, one can see that this powder consists of tiny balls—*conidia*—that are pinched off from long chains. The main vegetative feeding body of the mildew stays inside leaf tissues, continuing to digest them, while the breezes spirit the conidia away to other vulnerable leaves.

On an entirely different scale of magnitude, there are many mammals that make oaks an integral part of their diets: deer, cattle, sheep, monkeys, and agoutis, to name a few. The same chemical defenses that make leaves taste bad to moth larvae also work at this level—that mature leaves will be shunned while young leaves may be gobbled up. New oak leaves are just as vulnerable to deer browse as they are to oak moths, and the first flush may be entirely stripped from the twigs. This is fine for a mature oak, with innumerable branches high beyond the reach of the tallest deer, but for saplings, deer browse takes a heavy toll. It may take saplings many years to become tall enough to be spared this harmful stripping and grow to full potential. Severe browsing is especially striking in places with summer-dry climates, such as California's foothills, where young oaks look as though they had been pruned by some mad topiarist into distorted vegetal sculptures.

Cattle, too, pose a threat to oaks, but that threat is reciprocated. The first new leaves do not harm cattle, but when cows depend on mature foliage, devastating poisoning can result. The amount of oak browse on rangelands is of considerable concern to range managers. Many conservationists, however, are taking the oak's perspective into account and are growing concerned about oak regeneration where cattle browsing has long been a fact of life. The fear is that young oaks, unable to make it through the first critical years, will fail to replace old trees as they die. This same concern also extends to bloated deer populations. Since the near-elimination of cougars, deer predation has dropped close to zero. As a result, deer have multiplied to such an extent that they

Not the work of a mad topiarist, the top of this young oak has finally reached a level where deer can no longer browse it.

consume more browse than the land can reasonably support and have a major impact on oak saplings. But because the long-range consequences of predation on oak saplings will not become dramatically obvious until all the old oaks die off, it may take some time before the problem is fully appreciated.

In addition to the buildup of tannins in sapling leaves as they mature, some oaks also protect themselves from predation with large, prominent, hollylike teeth along the leaf margin. Oaks whose mature leaves carry scarcely noticeable teeth may begin to produce obvious, palpably sharp teeth when they are subject to excessive browsing. Even toothless oak leaves produce feeble bristle tips on the ends of their lobes, which frequently misleads the newcomer to oak identification. (Presence or absence of bristle tips can be a crucial feature in separating species.) Just how effective these teeth are varies according to the power and hunger of the browser involved; leaves armed with the tough holly-type teeth are bound to discourage all but the strongest, most ardent browsers.

On oaks like California's goldcup oak (*Quercus chrysolepis*) and interior live oak (*Q. wislizenii*), holly-toothed leaves sometimes join company with absolutely smooth-edged leaves on the same branch. This is especially confounding to the novice taxonomist, for it appears as though leaves from two species had been glued to the same branch! When this occurs, the sharply toothed leaves appear toward the branch tip—the location where leaves are most likely to be exposed to browsers.

Among all the organisms that interact with oak leaves, there is a prolific group that doesn't fit neatly into any other category: the gall makers. Galls are unusual deformations and outgrowths of plants caused by a wide variety of organisms, including bacteria, viruses, fungi, and insects. The actual gall is made by the oak, but it is caused by complex interactions with the other organisms in a story quite unlike any other. Whether galls harm oaks is uncertain; their prominence on weak trees suggests that possibility, although most studies don't implicate galls in the death of oaks. This notwithstanding, heavy infestations may further weaken trees that are already stressed.

Galls occur on any plant part—leaves, buds, twigs, flowers, and fruits. And they affect a wide range of different plants, from roses to alders, sagebrush to coyote brush, junipers to acacias. Some resemble fat vegetative buds, some mimic cones or flowers. Despite the widespread appearance of galls on many different kinds of plants, oaks harbor more kinds of galls than all other plants combined. One highly specialized group of insects—the cynipid wasps (family Cynipidae)—is responsible for the majority of oak galls. Cynipids and oaks share a long evolutionary history, and oaks have influenced the diversification of these minute, stingless wasps. Fully 82 percent of all cynipid species use oaks for a home. Many kinds live on only one or a few oak species

Pink urchin galls heavily lade the branches of this blue oak. Blue oaks are noted for the diversity of galls they carry.

and are restricted to one particular part of the tree at one particular time of the year. Galls can be found on every conceivable part of oaks, even on roots and acorns—some acorn galls are revealed only when the acorn is opened! White oaks host the greatest numbers of gall species. And among white oaks, *Quercus douglasii,* the California foothill species called blue oak, harbors the most lavish diversity of them all. Blue oak leaves wear galls that look like ornamented dunce caps, multi-colored starbursts, rose pink sea urchins, and buttonlike cups and saucers. The explanation for such diversity probably resides in the chemistry of oak bark and leaves.

Cynipid wasps have fascinating life histories, full of unfamiliar and unexpected details. For these tiny insects—the adults are measured in mere millimeters—the galls provide food and home for most of their lives. Cynipids have become poor competitors in the outside world, and the oak has become their protector and benefactor.

Life for a cynipid begins as an egg laid in the young, active meristematic tissues of twigs, buds, leaves, or flowers. Meristems, such as those described for root tips and bud apices, are places where cells actively divide to add new growth. Because the newly formed cells have not yet taken on any specialized mature form—they do that later—they are able to accept new "programming." This is what cynipid hosts provide.

The first step is for the mature wasp to lay one egg in a place that will later become the brood chamber. Next, the egg hatches and grows into a minuscule larva, which looks like a tiny worm. The larva releases chemicals from its saliva while it feeds. These chemicals activate genes in the oak's meristematic cells that, in turn, direct production of the gall. Controversy rages over just what it is in the saliva that has such a profound effect on the plant tissue. Some scientists have extracted hormones from the wasps' saliva that resemble the plant hormones that regulate so many growth processes. Other scientists contend that there are actually nucleic acids—the building blocks of the genetic code— in the saliva, and that these acids interact with the meristematic cells to produce extremely complex galls. Some researchers have even gone so far as to suggest that there may be actual bits of DNA from viruses in the larvae's saliva. Viral DNA can replace the genetic machinery of host cells, completely reprogramming them and their activities, though how and why these viruses would have entered into such a specific relationship with the larvae is not clear.

Whatever the cause, the malleable plant tissue is reprogrammed to do the bidding of the larva. The chamber in which the larva develops is often ensconced in a wad of protective cells, sometimes suspended by threads inside a larger, multilayered structure of wondrous engineering. Each gall announces the identity of its owner by form, color, and texture; there are galls that resemble Russian minarets, miniature artichokes, mush-

A tiny gall wasp beside a millimeter ruler.

rooms, hats, caps, wooly marbles, prickly instruments of torture, exquisite vases, and, of course, the famed oak apples and potatoes. Some measure less than a centimeter across, while others span five or six inches.

The timing of all these activities—from the depositing of the egg to development of the mature gall—has to be exact, for the stage of development of the tissue in which the egg is laid is critical if the wasp is to prosper. If the egg is laid in late spring to early summer, it will hatch into a female wasp, without exception. The wasp gradually passes through her metamorphoses inside the gall, all the while munching on food provided by her host, until she is finally ready for a brief life on her own. Summer has come and gone and fall is in the air before the wasp burrows her way out, leaving a tiny hole as evidence of her former occupancy. She may then wait until the following spring before laying her own eggs. Some females actually extend their stay inside the gall through fall and winter before emerging. In a very few cases,

Oak Galls

Ruptured twig gall of
Callirhytis perdens
on *Quercus wislizenii*

Mushroom gall of
Heteroecus sanctaeclarae
on *Quercus chrysolepis*

"Spotted beaked" gall of
Disholcaspis plumbella
on *Quercus berberidifolia*

"Yellow wooly" gall of
Heteroecus dasydactyli
on *Quercus chrysolepis*

Potato gall of
Andricus quercuscalifornicus
on *Quercus lobata*

"Porcupine" gall of
Andricus crystallinus
on *Quercus douglasii*

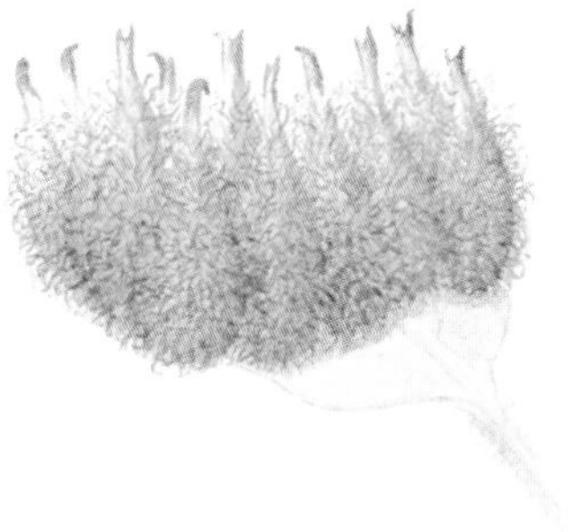

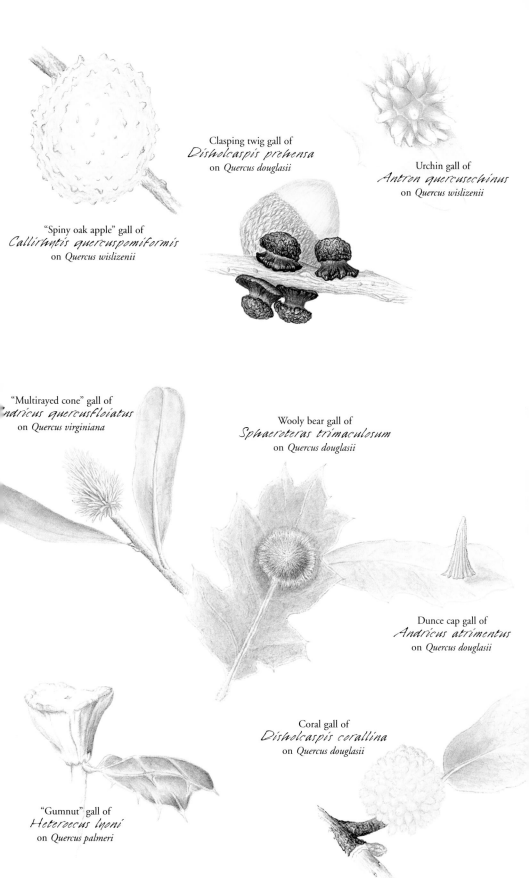

"Spiny oak apple" gall of
Callirhytis quercuspomiformis
on *Quercus wislizenii*

Clasping twig gall of
Disholcaspis prehensa
on *Quercus douglasii*

Urchin gall of
Antron quercusechinus
on *Quercus wislizenii*

"Multirayed cone" gall of
Andricus quercusfloiatus
on *Quercus virginiana*

Wooly bear gall of
Sphaeroteras trimaculosum
on *Quercus douglasii*

Dunce cap gall of
Andricus atrimentus
on *Quercus douglasii*

Coral gall of
Disholcaspis corallina
on *Quercus douglasii*

"Gumnut" gall of
Heteroecus lyoni
on *Quercus palmeri*

cynipids may remain for more than a year in their particular gall, perhaps awaiting just the right set of outside conditions before their final emergence.

A surpassingly strange aspect of these female wasps is that they never mate, for they are endowed with the power to lay their eggs parthenogenetically. In *parthenogenesis,* eggs develop without fertilization, and this situation is found in many other species of insects. Perhaps even more astonishing is what follows, for when the nonmating female lays her eggs, the larvae that hatch grow into male or female wasps that eventually do mate. Thus, cynipids have an *alternation of generations.* The mating generation generally develops during the spring months, completing its short life span by spring's end, when a new round of nonmating wasps are hatched.

Mating and nonmating generations of the same species produce offspring and galls that look so different from one another that they scarcely seem to belong to the same species. Early observers were frequently fooled into classifying the two generations as entirely different species. Spring galls are seldom so fanciful or conspicuous as summer galls, perhaps because they last a shorter time and need less fortification against winter chill. One fascinating variation on this basic life cycle makes matters even more intriguing: some species of cynipids consist exclusively of females that always lay their eggs parthenogenetically; mating pairs have never been seen.

Life histories of cynipid wasps vary in wonderful and unsuspected ways. For example, the hedgehog gall of the eastern white oak (*Quercus alba*) forms on leaves when the female wasp (*Acraspis erinacei*) lays her eggs on the young leaves in spring. These green, spine-encrusted galls are round to oblong and develop on both sides of the leaves. The larvae slowly grow inside, eventually reaching the pupal stage. When the adults emerge in fall, they look immature and helpless and only have vestigial wings. This nonmating generation hardly needs wings because they live just long enough to lay their eggs in oak buds, after the oaks have lost their leaves and the twigs are bare. The original leaf

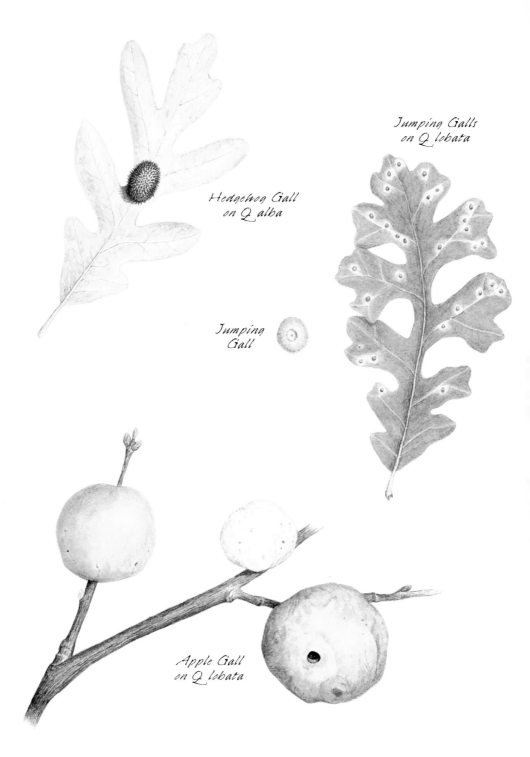

Jumping Galls
on Q. lobata

Hedgehog Gall
on Q. alba

Jumping
Gall

Apple Gall
on Q. lobata

91

gall has dried and turned brown by the time the wasp emerges. The tiny galls that develop on the bud scales appear in May and are shaped like a long oval cocoon. When winter ends and buds are swelling, the new mating generation emerges. These adult wasps look quite different, are male and female, and have larger, functional wings. Their wings allow them to fly to the leaves of new trees, where after a brief mating, they deposit their eggs and renew the cycle.

Jumping galls demonstrate a bizarre innovation. Although not related to the famed Mexican jumping beans, which involve caterpillars that live inside seeds of the spurge family, jumping galls behave in much the same way. There are several jumping galls in different parts of the United States. California's magnificent valley oaks (*Quercus lobata*) are host to one of them, *Neuroterus saltitarius* (translation: vein-wing jumper). Appearing on leaves in May, these tiny, glossy brown spherical galls are small enough to overlook unless they occur in large numbers. And unlike most galls, they complete their development on the ground, falling off oak leaves by September. There, the galls jump about each time the larva inside flips its body. Such erratic hopping movements may serve to bury the galls deep in the leaf litter, away from parasitic insects roaming the surface of the litter, on the lookout for these tempting morsels. Despite the abundance of life in the litter layer, few insects harmful to cynipid wasps live within the litter itself. The galls winter under the leaf duff until the warm spring days return; then the minute nonmating females exit the galls to lay their eggs on new leaves. These eggs develop inside tiny greenish blisters that gradually turn brown as their inhabitants get ready to leave a month or two later. The emergence of male and female wasps occurs very precisely, in the wee morning hours just as the sun is rising. The newly hatched wasps soon mate and lay eggs, giving life to another generation of "jumpers."

In stark contrast to these minute galls are the large, conspicuous oak apple galls that occur on many members of the white oak alliance. The life cycle of the wasp *Andricus californicus*

This chalcid wasp, (Torymus californicus), *parasitizes the larvae inside galls by laying eggs on them.*

provides an example of the development of one of the larger galls. The cycle begins when a nonmating female lays her eggs on a young twig in fall. Throughout winter's storms and bluster, there is no sign of the eggs inside, but come spring, the twig ruptures under the pressure of the developing gall. Soon the gall has become apple-shaped, glossy green with blushes of red and intensely bitter to the taste. The gall's high tannin content may put off creatures looking to make a meal of these succulent-looking "fruits." Inside the gall, the larva is slowly developing in a central chamber suspended by a series of slender threads that radiate from the outer casing. As summer approaches, galls turn whitish and resemble pallid potatoes. As fall comes once again, the galls dry and become brownish. Still, the wasp inside may not emerge, for she can remain safely encased inside her gall for more than a year. When she is finally ready to crawl out, she does so by biting a round hole. The reason *Andricus californicus* gestates for so long is because of her size. In keeping with the gall's conspicuous size, the mature wasp herself is also unusually large, measuring up to four millimeters in length.

As oaks are magnets to hordes of organisms seeking food and shelter, so, too, are their galls. A wide variety of other animals—mostly predacious insects—find cynipid wasps a fine meal. The acorn woodpecker raids the gall's larder, supplementing its steady diet of oil-rich acorns with protein-rich wasp grubs. Galls may host filbert worms and other wasps, some of which parasitize the host wasp, while others eat the food stores of the gall itself. Other wasps often have no qualms about lunching on their distant relatives.

Gall wasps, of course, have come up with some ingenious ways to assure that their own lines continue. One solution to predation is to use and amplify the oak's natural defense chemicals: tannins. While cynipids are able to neutralize tannins and render them harmless, they can also program galls to produce unusually high levels of them to deter intruders.

Another trick is to deceive predators through clever gall design. Often the elaborate construction and attractive colors of galls are created to lure predators away from the location of the cynipid's brood chamber. Fanciful extensions of galls are often distant from the larva. False chambers may mislead the intruder once it burrows inside the gall.

Still another ploy is to entice aggressive insects to do battle with or at least discourage unwelcome gall visitors. Several galls exude a sweet honeydew, a high-sugar nectar that lures bees and ants, which will defend their food source against the predations of other insects. A strange twist in this tale is that honeybees are actually poisoned by certain chemicals in the gall honeydew and so in the end are killed by their visits. Why this poisoning occurs is uncertain, but it is probably a biological "accident." The pugnacious ants suffer no such poisonous effect; they benefit from the honeydew and are efficient at scaring off predators. Many insects are dissuaded by the aggressive stances and formidable bites of such ants.

Just as gall wasps are master manipulators of an oak's genetic machinery, so oak leaves themselves are master chemists. We've already seen how photosynthesis is carried out in oak leaves, but we haven't seen all of what happens to the sugars made during photosynthesis. It is not all carried directly to storage areas, or

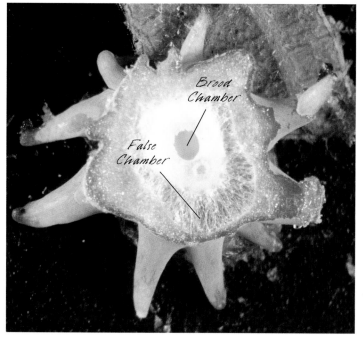

Brood Chamber

False Chamber

A slice through this oak gall reveals a large, conspicuous false chamber and a smaller, true brood chamber for its resident wasp. The false chamber is a ruse intended to fool invading parasites.

used to fuel active cell growth and flowering, or to create sweet exudates. By combining with the minerals carried up through the vessels from the soil, sugars are converted into a plethora of complex substances. All of the substances an oak uses to build all the parts of new cells get their start from the sugars produced by photosynthesis.

Many sugars are also converted into what old-time biologists called *secondary compounds* or *by-products,* meaning substances relegated to the category of "incidental" or "unimportant." We know today that most of these substances have great importance, for these are materials that defend oaks by tasting bitter, or being downright toxic. Tannins, of course, head the list here, for they occur throughout the oak tree in varying quantities at different times. Another chemical defense generated by oaks are *terpenes,* which occur in several forms in oak leaves and probably protect the tree against chewers.

But of all the substances produced by oaks, the chemical *isoprene* is the most puzzling. Automobile emissions also contain isoprene, and it has received considerable notoriety as a contributor to air pollution. Despite reductions in automobile exhaust, levels of isoprene are still high along the Atlantic seaboard, and the resurgence of oaks in eastern hardwood forests may explain the anomaly. Isoprene is a direct by-product of oak leaf photosynthesis. The hotter the weather in summer, the faster the rate of photosynthesis and the greater the quantity of isoprene produced, exacerbating an already difficult situation. No one knows why oak trees and other plants make isoprene, for it provides no known benefits to them. And in another odd twist of evolution, certain Mediterranean oaks fail to make isoprene at all.

Isoprene production is not a simple process and is unlikely to have accidentally evolved, for its biochemical pathway is different from those of other chemical by-products. Yet its role remains unknown, pointing out just how ignorant we are about oak leaf chemistry. Exactly how many substances are manufactured from the glucose sugar in oak leaves? Besides building the nearly infinite number of proteins and fats that make cell structure possible, beyond the assembly of the megamolecular enzymes that direct cells' activities, and beyond creating the doubly spiral molecule that carries the genetic code, what other substances exist? How many chemicals are required to attract, repel, deter, and poison? How little we understand this chemical pharmacopoeia.

THE OAK AS

AN ECOSYSTEM

 learly, there is an elegant simplicity to the overall design of oaks. Yet when we examine each part—roots, trunks, branches, bark, wood, leaves, and buds—we find miracles of unimagined complexity. That complexity is echoed by the resonance of each element with the world around it. Oaks are not only important members of greater ecosystems, but every oak tree is also a wonderful, infinitely complicated ecosystem unto itself.

Oaks have climbed a convoluted, evolutionary stairway from the earliest photosynthetic cells that lived over 3 billion years ago.

These simple blue-green bacteria were precursors to the ocean's algae that went on to radiate into thousands of varied forms. From this rich algal flora, a few species made a tentative venture onto land, adapting to the rigors of a dry atmosphere. The first land plants were simple, scarcely more complex than their algal ancestors. Soon they innovated and evolved new forms, including trees. Those first trees had single-veined leaves and reproduced by microscopic spores; the evolution of seeds came considerably later. From the first seed plants came various lines of trees—some with palmlike leaves and immense cones, others with seed-filled cups borne on fernlike fronds, and still others with broad leaves and flowers, the seeds enclosed safely inside the ovaries. The first flowering plants made ample, insect-pollinated flowers; only much later did wind-pollinated trees like oaks arise, with their highly specialized and much reduced flowers. Oaks have come through many, varied pathways to arrive at their present com-plexity—a complexity reflected by the stages of an oak's life cycle.

The Oak Life Cycle

*A*ll flowering plants follow a well-wrought, time-tested order in their reproduction. Hormones quicken the initiation of flower buds, which swell and open into flowers that set the stage for pollination. Each kind of flower is uniquely designed to lure pollinators—bees, beetles, butterflies, moths, or birds—that pick up pollen and transfer it to another flower. Pollination is complete when the pollen has been moved from one flower's stamen to another flower's stigma. But pollination is only a prelude to fertilization, during which pollen grains must send their pollen tubes into the ovary to release sperm for fertilization. The fertilized egg grows into an embryonic plant inside the seeds contained in the ovary; the seeds must ripen before they're shed to seek a new home. Wind, water, birds, mammals, and gravity are used by seeds as a means to reach a suitable home. With the proper mix of moisture and temperature, the mature seed germinates and grows into a seedling.

This is the essence of the life cycle for every flowering plant, yet the details vary in rich and wonderful ways. For example, most brightly colored garden flowers bear both the male and female parts on the same flower and are pollinated by insects or birds. But wind-pollinated flowers that lack colorful petals separate the male pollen-producing parts from the female seed-bearing parts by putting them in separate flowers.

Petunias provide an easy reference for the parts of a flower. Petunia plants sprout quickly from seed once the soil has warmed in spring. By the time summer rolls around, they are primed to bloom; the right mixture of temperature, moisture, and day length have acted in concert to produce flowering hormones, which stimulate flower buds to develop, swell, and finally open— a signal the flower is ready to entice bees for a visit.

Like most flowers, the petunia is composed of four clear-cut layers. The outer layer, forming a cup around the base of the flower, is called the *calyx*. In the petunia blossom, the calyx consists of five green and sticky *sepals*. Sepals protect the contents of the flower in bud and, in most cases, have already served their purpose by the time the flower is open for the business of pollination.

Just inside the calyx is the *corolla,* the collective name for the *petals*. The petunia has five velvety purple, red, pink, or white petals fashioned into a flared funnel. Bees are especially fond of purple, a color that along with blue, ultraviolet, and yellow, they see clearly. The ends of the petals provide a clear landing platform, and when bees land, they follow the petals' dark striped *nectar guides* to the base of the funnel to reach their reward of sugary nectar that oozes from the base of the pistil's ovary.

Inside the petals are the male organs, called *stamens*. Each stamen consists of a slender stalk—the *filament*—topped by a bulbous pouch—the *anther.* The anther consists of four sacs filled with microscopic pollen grains. To ensure that the pollen grains are picked up by bees, the anthers split open along zipperlike, vertical creases. Petunia stamens are short and sit just above the base of the petals' funnel so that bees must rub directly against the anthers as they make their pilgrimage to the nectar.

In the very center of the flower is the female organ, the *pistil.* Most flowers have a single pistil. In the petunia, it sits deep in the flower. The pistil consists of three basic parts. At the bottom is a green, saclike *ovary,* which contains tiny egg-shaped *ovules.* (These ovules will later grow into seeds, after pollination and fertilization.) A slender *style* protrudes from the top of the ovary,

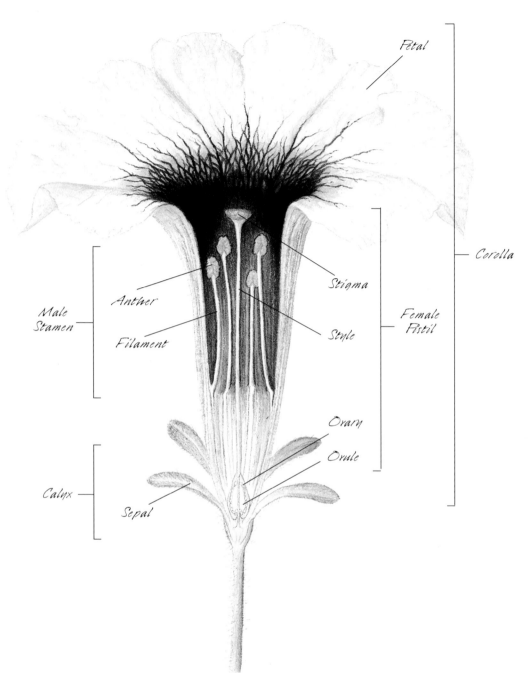

*A lengthwise slice of a garden petunia flower reveals its parts:
sepals, petals, stamens, and pistil.*

Sexing a Flower

The terminology governing how we speak about flowers' sexuality is confusing yet useful. For example, the majority of flowers are bisexual or perfect: they have both male stamens that produce pollen and a female pistil with potential new seeds. By contrast, imperfect or unisexual flowers have only one or the other: male flowers with stamens, female with pistils. Oak flowers belong in this category. Flowers with only one sex often occur in wind-pollinated plants, such as oaks and beeches. In order to prevent self-pollination, these plants use one of two ploys: either the flowers are borne on entirely different plants, in which case the plants are dioecious (Greek for two houses); or they're borne on the same plant and are referred to as being monoecious (Greek for one house). Monoecious plants, again exemplified by oaks, avoid self-pollination by timing events so that male flowers shed their pollen at a different time from when female flowers have receptive stigmas. In summary, oak trees have unisexual, imperfect flowers and are monoecious.

carrying at its tip one or more protuberances called *stigmas*. Stigmas are hairy or sticky to catch and hold pollen grains. Petunia styles are just long enough to place the stigma at the most strategic place to brush pollen off visiting bees.

Now the stage is set for pollination. In petunias, the anthers open first, discharging the pollen grains, followed later by the ripening and receptivity of the stigma. In other species of flowers, the stigma quickens first, then the anthers open. In both scenarios, stigmas remain receptive only long enough to receive pollen, and anthers release their pollen over a precisely timed period. Seldom do both stages occur simultaneously, because this would promote self-pollination. Cross-pollination is preferable because it encourages new genetic combinations. New gene patterns provide the grist from which natural selection can work, should conditions change.

Pollination is complete when a pollinator has carried pollen from the anther to the stigma. But pollination does not automatically guarantee that the ovary's ovules will ripen into seeds; each pollen grain must first send out a pollen tube that travels down the pistil's style all the way into the ovary. The pollen tube delivers two sperm to an unfertilized ovule; they are then released inside the ovule to fertilize its egg.

Once fertilized, the ovule grows into a *seed*. The fertilized egg inside each seed becomes a miniature plant, an embryo surrounded by a layer of stored food and a tough seed coat. Seeds enlarge and swell as their embryos burgeon. The ovary also expands, for it still contains the seeds and protects them from outside marauders. The now superfluous sepals, petals, styles, stigmas, and stamens fall away.

Seed ripening takes anywhere from one week to several months according to the kind of plant. As seeds mature, the ovaries change color and texture, growing into a mature *fruit*. Petunia ovaries turn brown, dry, and quickly open to release their many tiny seeds; oak ovaries grow into thick-shelled nuts; and tomato ovaries become fleshy, brightly colored, flavorful berries.

When oaks bloom in early spring, they are decorated with countless slender yellow trusses of petal-less male blossoms. Hidden behind the male catkins are very small female blossoms that might be mistaken for extra-plump buds. Oaks differ fundamentally from petunias by having separate petal-less male and female blossoms, pollinated by wind. Botanists theorize that the earliest flowers of 135 million years ago were bisexual and insect pollinated, but if that is the case, oaks have clearly left that path behind.

The summer before flowers appear, oaks are busily fattening their buds for the next year; the terminal buds swell as the tree discards its leaves for the season or, in the case of live oaks, as

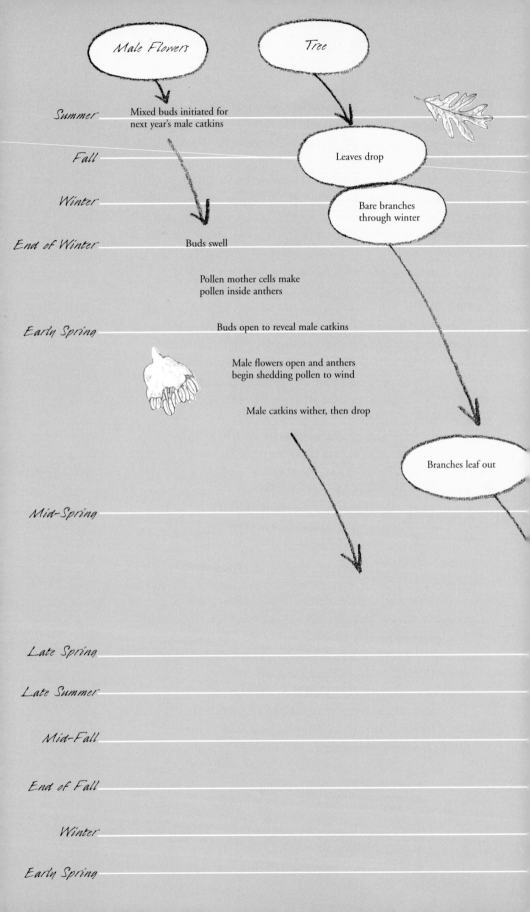

Male Flowers

Tree

Summer — Mixed buds initiated for next year's male catkins

Fall — Leaves drop

Winter — Bare branches through winter

End of Winter — Buds swell

Pollen mother cells make pollen inside anthers

Early Spring — Buds open to reveal male catkins

Male flowers open and anthers begin shedding pollen to wind

Male catkins wither, then drop

Branches leaf out

Mid-Spring

Late Spring

Late Summer

Mid-Fall

End of Fall

Winter

Early Spring

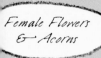

Female Flowers & Acorns

The Oak Life Cycle

For a typical white oak of E North America

Buds swell

Buds open, and female flower extends stigmas

Female flowers have finished receiving
pollen from another tree

Pollen begins to grow tubes
down to ovule inside ovary

Ovary makes ovules

Megaspore inside ovary's ovule
grows into an embryo sac

Pollen tube has completed its journey
and releases two sperms (white oaks)

Fertilization occurs: one sperm fuses with egg;
the other with two polar nulcei in the embryo sac

Ovule becomes a seed with
developing embryo inside

Acorns begin to grow larger and larger

Acorns have reached full size and embryo
is nearing maturity inside seed

Acorns signal their readiness to drop by turning
from green to brown; embryo is mature

Leaves drop

Acorns have dropped to ground, awaiting
collection and burial by some animal

Acorns may germinate immediately or
often await the spring thaw

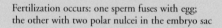

leaves go into a state of semidormancy. Through the long fall and across the short days of winter, oak buds are primed to bloom when spring arrives. Terminal buds hold male catkins, while axillary buds produced the following spring contain tiny female flowers.

LIFE CYCLE
OF THE OAK

Most oaks begin their new cycle of growth and bloom whenever early spring arrives. Each region has its own rhythm: early spring appears in the foothills of coastal California from late March to early April; in the Sierra foothills it may come in early May; in the Great Smoky Mountains, it will be late May to early June. Oaks from Southeast Asia, Mexico, or Costa Rica blossom according to subtle environmental cues that still elude us. They might include gentle swings in temperature and patterns between relative dry or wet periods.

The first rush of new growth neatly coincides with flowering, for the terminal buds at the ends of twigs are also *mixed buds,* which combine new shoots with male flowers. These unfolding buds burst through the bud scales to release tiny, preformed leaves held in close embrace, and male flowers precisely arranged in slender catkins. The timing of this mad rush is finely tuned to temperature. As frigid nights give way to warm spring days, hormones known as auxins promote bud burst by increasing the tree's intake of water. Some years, these events come unheralded in late winter; other years, oak buds may wait through a few weeks of an unseasonably cold spring.

Oaks' reliance on the vagaries of weather has advantages and disadvantages. Flowers and leaves are scorched and burned after an untimely bud burst when a winter warm spell is followed by a plunge into freezing cold. This is often mitigated by leaves that develop from buds held in reserve, but a close accommodation between weather and growth is advantageous most years. When plants rely solely on day length to determine bloom time, they risk encountering conditions out of sync with the best circumstances for growth.

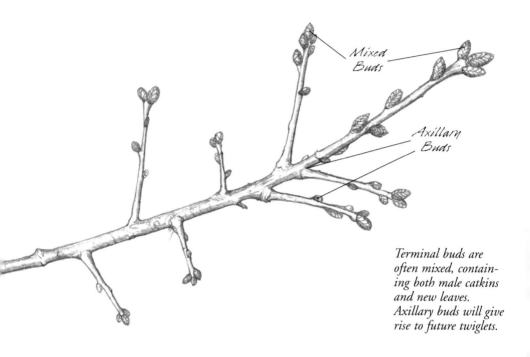

Terminal buds are often mixed, containing both male catkins and new leaves. Axillary buds will give rise to future twiglets.

Named for their resemblance to a cat's tail, *catkins* are chains of minute, wind-pollinated flowers that lack petals. The catkin consists of a long, pendulous stalk to which dozens of male flowers are attached. Catkins are found in plant groups that share the common denominator of wind pollination, including willows and cottonwoods, alders and birches, hazels and hornbeams, and walnuts and hickories. The catkin design evolved independently in many separate plant lines because it works so well for spewing pollen into the wind.

The whole catkin is contained inside the terminal bud, but each male blossom is also enclosed inside its own bud. Individual male flowers will not open until the catkin itself has begun its rapid elongation. Oak catkins are light and streamlined, swinging easily to-and-fro in the lightest breeze. Each flower couldn't be of simpler design: a small green umbrella of four to six green sepals at the base of four to ten slender stamens. Each stamen's filament firmly attaches to the middle of its anther; the threadlike filaments carry the anthers well beyond the sepals, exposing the anther's pollen to any passing wind.

Petals are conspicuously missing, unnecessary to the indifferent medium of wind. The production of petals requires extra food and energy that could be diverted to other needs, and since petals serve no purpose for wind-pollinated flowers, they've been eliminated. For this very reason, many people think oaks don't have flowers, as petals are what make most flowers so conspicuous.

Busy and important preparations precede the opening of male flowers. Inside each of the anthers' four parallel sacs is a dense stuffing of pearl-like *pollen mother cells*. Through a special process of cellular division called *meiosis*, these cells make daughter cells that are fundamentally different from their parents.

Meiosis is the magical dance in which tiny hereditary carriers—*chromosomes*—cross over and exchange pieces with one another, creating new combinations of genes that are passed on to the daughter cells. These daughter cells eventually produce sperm, which faithfully carry the new chromosome combinations, thus affecting the genetic heritage of the fertilized egg. Most plant and animal cells carry two copies of each kind of chromosome, but meiosis apportions only one copy of each kind of chromosome to every daughter cell. In order to do this, the pollen mother cells make duplicates of its chromosomes so that it has four copies of each of its chromosomes; it then divides into four daughter cells that carry a single copy of each chromosome.

The new daughter cells quickly develop into microscopic propagules called *pollen grains*. Individual pollen grains are so small they're invisible to the naked eye, but when pollen is massed together, we see it as a fine yellow dust. Every pollen grain is a complete, self-contained package, capable of growing a tube and producing sperm once pollination is successfully completed.

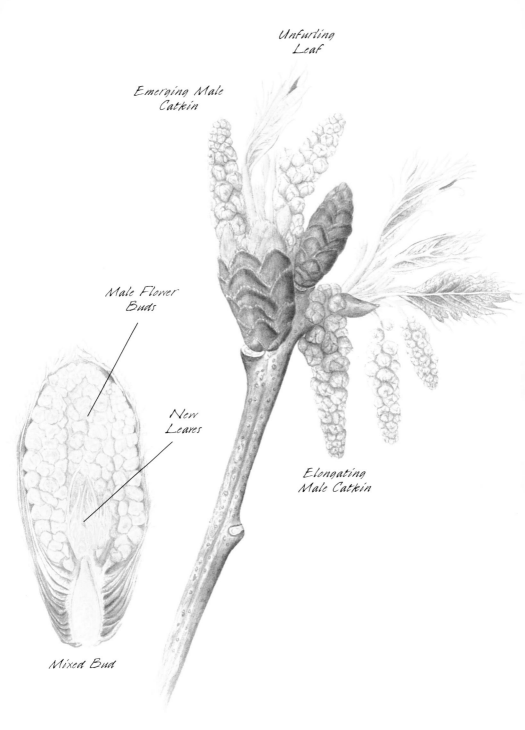

Unfurling
Leaf

Emerging Male
Catkin

Male Flower
Buds

New
Leaves

Elongating
Male Catkin

Mixed Bud

Mixed buds illustrate their purpose when cut lengthwise (left). The flower buds of male catkins are densely packed around a small clump of future leaves. This miracle of efficient packaging is quickly loosed (right) as buds open to warm spring days.

A branch of a deciduous black oak decked with yellow male catkins and the tiniest of new leaves.

The stage is set for a fine blustery spring day, when clouds of pollen emerge from catkins to ride air currents and cause misery to those who suffer from hay fever. The anthers' pollen sacs are filled with thousands upon thousands of pollen grains. As water pressure builds to a final explosion, the thin creases that run the length of the anthers suddenly tear, releasing the pollen in a rush. The anthers swing freely in the wind, liberating pollen in all directions and turning the air yellow with their profligate numbers.

Just before they discharge their pollen, many oak catkins are particularly colorful, especially when seen from a distance. The California black oak (*Quercus kelloggii*), for example, is adorned

Opening Bud

Partially
Open
Flower

Flower with
Pollen shed

As male catkins push out of the casing of bud scales, they go through rapid changes.

with wine red pollen sacs, while the scrub oak (*Q. berberidifolia*) wears a cascading mantle of bright pink. What advantage or disadvantage these colors provide—or indeed, whether they matter at all—is mostly speculation, but they impart an ephemeral beauty that must be witnessed to be appreciated. The display shifts to bright gold when the anthers open to rain their pollen.

One has to wonder why wind-blown pollen is yellow. Yellow is attractive to bees and other pollinators, luring them to flowers. Yellow pollen may be leftover from oaks' distant—and hypothetical—bee-pollinated ancestors. Or yellow may simply represent the original color of pollen from ancestral plants that preceded insect pollination. Wind-pollinated pines and other conifers predate flowering plants by millions of years, and their pollen is also yellow.

Oak pollen grains are microscopic, measuring about forty microns long—that is, about forty-millionths of a meter! Under the powerful eye of a scanning electron microscope, oak pollen looks like a puffer fish, but in cross-section, it is lumpily three-sided. Running down the angle where each of the three sides meets is a furrow, a thin area in the fabric of the pollen grain's covering, or *exine.*

The design for each pollen grain is exacting: the inner living contents of the grain—nuclei that will direct the growth of the fragile pollen tube and produce sperm—are delicate and quickly perishable, while the outer exine is tough and waxy, resistant to wear and tear. The exine is the only protection the nuclei have from the desiccating air, so it must be tough in order for pollen grains to survive their flight to the stigma of a female flower. Oak pollen's exine is slightly corrugated on the outside, with an intricate pattern

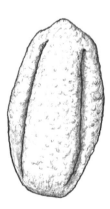

Pollen Grain

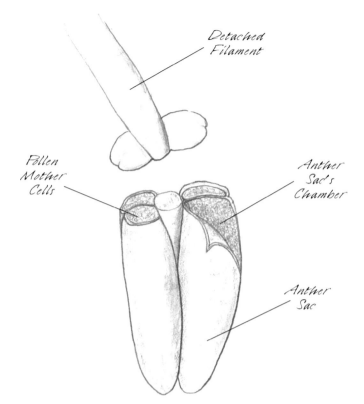

Detached
Filament

Pollen
Mother
Cells

Anther
Sac's
Chamber

Anther
Sac

Detaching the filament of the stamen from the anthers reveals the thousands of pollen mother cells that fill the anther's four chambers.

of tiny pimples that botanists refer to as *verrucate.* These minuscule bumps are probably remnants from a time when oaks' ancestors had a highly ornamented exine with protrusions that allowed pollen to easily cling to the bodies of pollinating insects. But in wind pollination, each pollen grain needs to go its separate way, so oak pollen has evolved a smoother exine that offers the least possible resistance to slipping gracefully through the air.

A larger evolutionary story is also embedded in the structure and pattern of oak pollen. While most flowering plants now use animals to move their pollen, a number of flowers have gone the other way, returning to the agency of wind. Several details suggest a progression from insect pollination to wind pollination. In many genera of closely related flowering plants, some species will display colorful petals, while others will produce drab flowers without petals. (Several different species of maples and ashes nicely illustrate this point.) And petal-less flowers often still grow tiny protuberances where petals would normally be attached, recalling ancestors with bright, showy blossoms.

Why are animal-pollinated flowers considered so effective? Animals have predictable, repeatable behavior that makes pollen transfer efficient. For example, honeybees visit many flowers of the same species when they forage for nectar. As they move from flower to flower, they inadvertently carry large quantities of pollen along with them, so that many pollen grains are transported from one flower's anther to another flower's stigma. The expenditure flowers make to produce colorful petals and potent perfumes is more than compensated for by this increased efficiency.

If this is so, it seems perplexing that oaks have returned to the wind. There are no easy answers, but there are strong hints. The fact that oaks are often tall trees that grow in gregarious stands is our first clue. Tall branches are often subject to strong winds, and these winds don't have to carry pollen very far to find a receptive neighbor. Oaks also bloom early in the new growing season, when winds and stormy, unsettled conditions predominate. So winds are readily available when most animal pollinators are lying dormant, since many bees and other insects hatch only when weather has warmed the air and soil around them. The energy oaks expend to make copious amounts of pollen must be balanced against the availability of strong, reliable winds.

After being released from the anthers, pollen doesn't move uniformly in all directions. Careful experiments show that wind-blown pollen follows a plumelike pattern caused by local convection currents that are commonplace in the spring. The ground warms unevenly because it is shaded by oaks in some places and hit directly by the sun in others. As the air above the sunny patch of ground is heated, it rises and is replaced by cooler air from the shaded patch, resulting in the localized eddies called convection

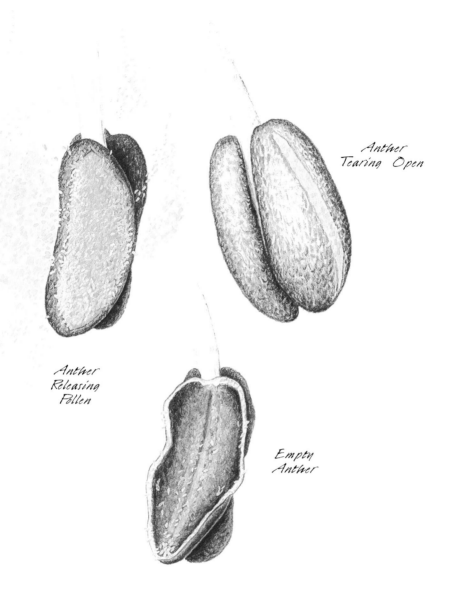

Anther
Tearing Open

Anther
Releasing
Pollen

Empty
Anther

The stages of pollen release (counter-clockwise from top right).

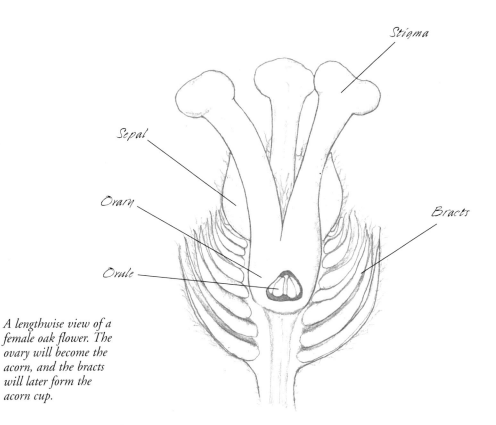

Stigma

Sepal

Ovary

Ovule

Bracts

A lengthwise view of a female oak flower. The ovary will become the acorn, and the bracts will later form the acorn cup.

currents. These convection currents provide most of the basic transportation for oak pollen. Only a small amount of pollen is buffeted to some distant place, away from immediate vicinity of the forest. Luckily, most oak trees grow in close proximity to one another.

To further the efficiency of wind, deciduous oaks delay fully deploying their new leaves until the male catkins have finished their job. Were those leaves to unfurl first, they would get in the way of pollen movement. Evergreen oaks always carry sets of old leaves, but their catkins lie in front of the old leaves, and pollen flow is scarcely hindered.

Soon enough, the show is over, and hay fever sufferers can relax. The pollen shower from any given tree lasts only a matter of a few days, or perhaps even hours if the weather turns hot. Cross-pollination succeeds only because the different trees in a forest are genetically programmed to spill their pollen or open their female flowers at slightly different times. Each oak tree is either in its pollen-shedding stage or in its pollen-receiving stage.

While all this hoopla is attached to the lavish production of male catkins and their pollen, the much less obvious female flowers have been quietly preparing for pollination and fertilization. They sit inside small *axillary* buds, which are found in the angle (axil) between a new leaf and twig. Older axillary buds often give rise to the growth of new side branches. So small are the female flower buds that you must watch carefully for the exact moment they open, or you'll miss the brief pageantry of the female flowers. A good time to look is when new leaves are opening behind the male catkins.

Female flowers occur singly, are arranged in clusters of two or three, or are sometimes borne along slender side branches called *peduncles*. Starting with the outside of the flower, there is a close-knit cluster of *bracts*—the future scales of the acorn cup. Enveloped inside these bracts, the top of the ovary peeks out. The ovary carries a minute cap of six green sepals, often inconspicuous at this stage, but obvious later as they are carried aloft by the growing acorn. The ovary's tip carries three styles that end in spherical or spoon-shaped stigmas. Some oak stigmas are short and abruptly bulge from the slender styles below; others gradually taper from the style to a thickened tip; still others are rounded spheres at the ends of slim styles.

The ovary is the birthplace of future seeds. The first event inside the ovary is the budding off of tiny egglike bodies called ovules. What's remarkable about oak flowers is their timing of ovule production. In petunias and many other flowers, ovules are well-formed by the time the flower opens; oaks, by contrast, may wait for a month or more *after* pollination to start producing ovules. This delay may well relate to the success or failure of pollination itself; if pollination fails, no extra energy is expended on useless ovules. The mature oak ovary has a single ovule that eventually will nearly fill the ovary's single chamber, but it starts with three chambers, each with two tiny ovules. These six ovules may persist for some time and—in at least some cases—do not abort until the winning ovule has been fertilized and starts growing its embryo. The three chambers evoke oaks' ancestors, which produced three fully functional chambers, with a total of six serviceable seeds to maturity. No one knows why oaks have evolved a genetic program that favors a single-chambered ovary with a single ovule, but one possibility is that a single large seed can store more food, allowing new seedlings in a shaded forest to get a head start.

Buried in the middle of each ovule is a single *megaspore mother cell* that behaves the same way pollen mother cells do inside anthers. The megaspore mother cell also divides by meiosis, producing four daughter cells with one copy of each kind of chromosome. But three of the daughter cells immediately perish. The surviving cell now starts growing into a minute embryo sac, totally contained inside and nourished by the ovary's ovule. The embryo sac, despite the fact that it represents a full-fledged individual with a single complement of chromosomes, never sees the light of day nor experiences life as a separate entity. Instead, it becomes something entirely unique, a microscopic, bag-shaped structure that produces the egg needed for fertilization. The original nucleus inside the embryo sac divides, producing two nuclei that in turn divide to produce four nuclei. These divide once more to produce eight different nuclei: one of these is the all-important *egg,* two more become the *polar nuclei,* and the remaining five have no obvious importance.

Under a strong magnifying glass, stigmas can be fully appreciated for their form and function. Oak stigmas work like fly paper: their tips are generously covered with a viscous glue. Because oak stigmas are relatively massive in design, they present a substantial wall for pollen grains to slam against. Impact against

Female
Flower
Bud

Blossom
Opening

Stigmas
Extended

Stigma
Detail

The stages of female flowers development from youngest (left) to oldest (right)
of the California black oak (Q. kelloggii).

This deciduous valley oak displays its new leaf canopy after pollen is released to the wind.

thick, sticky surfaces such as this are likely to stop pollen grains, for the grains can't easily change direction to flow around an obstacle the way air currents can. Even so, wind pollination is tremendously wasteful, and a large percentage of pollen grains never reach their goal. Many never even get close.

After the energetic activity of pollination, quiet initially prevails. Empty male catkins sway in the breeze before their final plunge to the ground. Energy is now being channeled into the rapid growth of the leafy canopy, for leaf expansion is essential to the tree's continued vigor, and soon a green blanket covers the oak. But all reproductive activity has not stopped; it's merely hidden.

Once pollen has landed on the stigma, a whole new chain of events is unleashed. Will pollen grains be able to grow their pollen tubes, or will they simply shrivel and die? For most plants, when the pollen comes from a different species—say, for example, rose pollen on an oak stigma—the question is moot. The chemistry is all wrong. But what about pollen amongst different kinds of oaks? Can the pollen from a holly oak (*Quercus ilex*) quicken on the stigma of an English oak (*Q. robur*)?

This question might seem absurd, but in fact, oaks are notoriously promiscuous. Oak hybrids abound in many areas, and they can confound the novice trying to sort them out. But not all oaks can cross with one another. The pollen of a scarlet oak (*Q. coccinea*) would suffer rejection at the stigma of an eastern white oak (*Q. alba*). These two oaks belong to different oak groups, and there are just too many incompatibilities between their genes to allow reproduction.

Pollen grains must grow delicate *pollen tubes* that bore their way down through the style to its ovary. In order to make this long journey, pollen tubes need food, which the tubes procure by releasing enzymes to dissolve bits of the style. If the wrong enzymes are released on the wrong style, nothing happens, and the pollen starves to death.

When the chemistry is in harmony, those thin creases running down the oak pollen grain are easily pierced by the pollen tube as it begins its lengthy decent. To give some idea of the memorable feat the tube is about to accomplish, imagine that a single pollen grain is the size of a marble. If that marble sat in a living room, it would have to send out a spaghetti-sized tube that would make a complete circuit around the room in order to reach its goal. The tube is guided by hormones released by the ovary to nudge the pollen tube in the right direction.

While the ovaries of most flowers produce several ovules, requiring a mad scramble from many contending pollen tubes, the oak has only six. All the pollen tubes descending from an oak stigma compete to reach these few ovules, a situation similar to human sperm all swimming toward one egg. Whichever pollen tube arrives first is the clear winner, for usually that now-fertilized ovule will develop into a seed with an embryo, precluding the successful development of the other five ovules. Oak stigmas

need only intercept a few vigorous pollen grains, for one successful grain will suffice.

The coordination of the rate at which the pollen tube grows
and the embryo sac develops inside the ovule is critical to successful fertilization. The fine tuning of these events is also controlled by hormones. For many oaks, the time required for the
pollen tube to reach the embryo sac is a matter of a month or
two. During this time another key event takes place: two sperm
are produced inside the lengthening pollen tube.

The white oak group typifies oaks with fast-growing pollen
tubes; most species progress from pollination to ripe acorns in a
matter of six to eight months. In the black oak group, the process
is more leisurely. At the end of the growing season, the pollen
tube simply stops growing, halting partway in its journey down
the style. Only when spring returns does the pollen tube finish its
travel. The lag in the pollen tube's journey is also mirrored in the
ovule's behavior, as the embryo sac doesn't finish growing until
the next spring. Thus, the time from pollination to acorn ripening has been extended from a matter of months in white oaks to
nearly two years in black oaks.

Why would black oaks prolong this process? Perhaps because
they first evolved in a place where the entire growing season was
unpredictably short, and it may have been risky to finish the job
when its end was fraught with the dangers of freezing temperatures and snow. Little extra energy is available when oaks go dormant. Today, many black oaks live in climates with long, favorable growing seasons and, in keeping with these changes, some
species have gone back to completing their acorn development in
a matter of months.

When the pollen tube at last nears its destination, it must
find a path into the ovule to reach the embryo sac inside. In the
majority of flowers, a tiny canal called the *micropyle* leads from
the tip of the ovule directly into the embryo sac. But oaks must
use a different strategy, because by some fluke in evolution, the
outer layers of the ovule block the entrance to the micropyle.
The last stage in its journey requires the oak pollen tube to bore

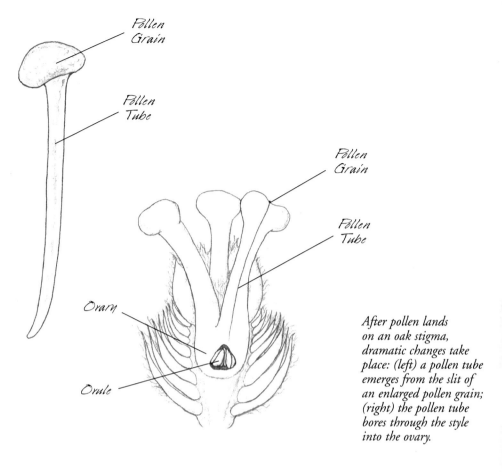

Pollen Grain

Pollen Tube

Pollen Grain

Pollen Tube

Ovary

Ovule

After pollen lands on an oak stigma, dramatic changes take place: (left) a pollen tube emerges from the slit of an enlarged pollen grain; (right) the pollen tube bores through the style into the ovary.

its way through the base of the tiny ovule, setting the stage for fertilization.

When the pollen tube reaches the embryo sac, its tip suddenly bursts, releasing two sperm. These sperm were the result of a division of the *generative nucleus* inside the tube. The sperm are delivered to exactly the right place since they're incapable of swimming on their own. In the embryo sac, one sperm fuses with the egg, the other with the two polar nuclei. This thrifty use of two sperm, called *double fertilization,* distinguishes flowering plants from other seed plants. It also sets in motion the next events: the fertilized egg grows into a new *embryo* plant, and the fertilized polar nuclei form the *endosperm,* a nutritive tissue

expressly designed to feed the embryo. One important consequence of fertilization is that one set of chromosomes from
the pollen parent and one set of chromosomes from the egg
parent combine to form two complete sets of chromosomes in
the embryo, restoring the full genetic complement necessary
for development of an oak tree. Because these two sets of
chromosomes come from plants with different genetic make-
ups—the consequence of cross-pollination—the embryo plant
has brand-new combinations of traits that are different from
either parent.

ACORNS

*A*fter fertilization, the miraculous drama of the
oak's life cycle continues. The embryo grows at
an exponential rate, forming a miniature plant
inside the new seed. At first, the embryo is nourished by the mushrooming endosperm tissue.
(It is also nourished by the stream of food and water piped in
through the plumbing system of the parent tree.) But almost
immediately a curious transformation takes place, and the
endosperm is transferred into the embryo's *cotyledons* through
digestion and absorption. In many plants, cotyledons function as
the first leaves when the embryo germinates. But in oaks, the
cotyledons are repositories of food and remain permanently confined inside the seed. Investing cotyledons with their own food
store for the embryo to draw upon helps spur rapid growth later
when the embryo germinates.

Acorns represent the oak's ovary, which contains a single seed.
The name *acorn* itself is telling: *ac* is old English for oak, and
corn or *cern* comes from the Greek for grain or kernel. These
acorns slowly swell as their seed packs away more and more food
in the form of starches, fats, and proteins. Once this course is
under way, the tree is programmed to successfully complete it.
Occasionally, new acorns may abort their development partway
through, but only if some drastic change in weather derails the
normal functioning of the tree. By fall, every green acorn has
reached its maximum size and is chockablock with food reserves.

Acorn within the Flower

Ripe Acorn

Green Acorn

Young Acorn

The acorn cup, derived from the bracts that engulfed the ovary back when the female flower first opened, has also matured into a receptacle that holds the acorn until it is ripe. Whether this cup carries out any other function is unknown. It's likely that the cup simply protects the young ovary from marauding, chewing insects. The details of the cup's architecture—whether it is covered with warts, scales, or rings—is an accurate means of identification.

The progress of an acorn from its birth inside an oak flower (left) to its brown ripeness inside the acorn cup (right).

The acorn's green color signals that it is not yet ripe. Most flowers start with green ovaries and change color when they are ripe. By midfall, nature's finishing touches turn acorns brown. Like everything else, this color change seems to have a purpose:

green acorns are not palatable and can contain substances that are downright toxic. The brown color, then, serves as a way of saying that acorns are ready for harvesting, whether by an acorn woodpecker, pig, scrub jay, wild turkey, gray squirrel, bear, or human. All respond to the same signal.

The seed's transformation is reflected in its overall architecture: within its brown shell is a parchmentlike seed coat, the *testa*. In many plants, the seed coat is comparable to the exine of the pollen grain, creating a protective barrier between the outside environment and the embryo plant inside. But in oaks, the seed never leaves the confines of the tough shell of the ovary, so its seed coat doesn't need to be particularly thick, nor does it serve a protective role.

Inside the seed coat, the entire space is occupied by the embryonic plant. The actual areas of future growth are still small: there's a short *radicle* toward the pointed end of the acorn that will grow into the taproot. Above it, the cylinder-shaped *hypocotyl*, or future stem of the seedling, ends in a minute tuft of colorless leaflets, the *epicotyl*. This epicotyl will ultimately become the bulk of the above-ground oak tree. Attached to the end of the hypocotyl, just below the fragile epicotyl, are two oversized, plump cotyledons joined at their base and filled with ample stores of rich food.

The acorn's shell provides strong protection to the seed. It has a multilayered construction like the complex layering of quality plywood—different layers of variable strengths are carefully joined to create a tough and pliable whole. A stratum of waxy cells help shed water and prevent rot; other strata of tough fibers give strength for protection and prevent drying out; and still other strata of softer cells stiffened with clusters of stone cells offer extra reinforcement. These softer layers may very well regulate water pressure as the acorn swells in preparation for its germination.

Seeds of all plants need to find appropriate new homes. Plants with the least specialized means of dispersal simply scatter

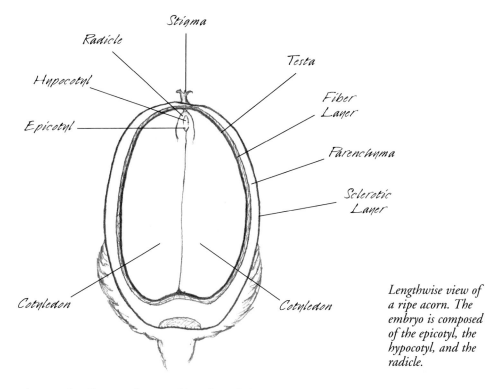

Stigma

Radicle

Hypocotyl

Epicotyl

Testa

Fiber Layer

Parenchyma

Sclerotic Layer

Cotyledon

Cotyledon

Lengthwise view of a ripe acorn. The embryo is composed of the epicotyl, the hypocotyl, and the radicle.

their seeds, allowing them to fall pell-mell from seed pods that split open. More highly adaptive plants bear seeds that are winged or have tufted hairs and are borne away on gusts of wind. Still other plants have exploding ovaries that forcibly eject their seeds as though they were sprayed from a hose under pressure. Many plants package their seeds inside the tempting wrappings of brightly colored, flavorful fruits, to be eaten, then excreted. Oaks and their kin—chestnuts, beeches, and chinquapins—have chosen a different pathway: their nutlike fruits are designed to be carried to new places and stored for later consumption by various animals.

Plants hedge their bets in their reproductive strategies. Some, for example, have succeeded well by producing numerous ovules in several-chambered ovaries. With such a vast number of potential seeds, the plant need only be minimally invested in making each one of them food-rich. Orchids best exemplify this: their ovaries may contain up to a million ovules. Orchids have opted to produce huge numbers of seeds without stored food, with the truly minuscule chance that one seed will find a way to survive. Oaks represent the other end of the spectrum, where each ovary contains a single ovule, but that ovule is richly endowed with nutriments for a maximum chance of survival. Oaks generally live and reproduce in a forest or woodland with other trees, where this strategy pays off handsomely. Large, food-rich seeds not only have more to sustain them when they leave the parent tree, but they also have the resources to grow rapidly once they germinate. Fast growth, in turn, helps give saplings a head start in reaching the light and competing well with their neighbors by establishing vigorous roots. Many of the oaks' companions in the forests—buckeyes, bay laurels, sassafrases, hickories, walnuts, chestnuts, and filberts—offer similar strategies with their seeds.

The shaping of this particular fruit design—what we call a nut—probably happened 100 million years ago, a long time even as flowering plants are reckoned. So deeply imprinted is this pattern on the entire genetic stock of the beech family that it has been largely unaltered, save for details of shape. Owing to the relative antiquity of oaks and their widespread dominance across the Northern Hemisphere, this system of provisioning large, meaty nuts has become finely balanced in a profusion of places, times, and habitats. Yet despite this seemingly straightforward strategy for successful reproduction, the acorn is surprisingly vulnerable to predation and outright thievery.

Nonetheless, many acorns manage to get buried, both by accident, when they fall from the tree into the thick leaf duff on the forest floor, and by design, when rodents and birds, seeking acorns for food, bury them for later retrieval. Such food caches are commonplace among animals preparing for their winter needs, and they also help meet the oak's needs. Animals forget where they've stashed some caches, are killed by predators, or simply don't use up their entire store. The longer acorns lie buried, the greater their chances for successful germination.

Why are acorns such tempting morsels? Many plants begin life with a reserve of starch to speed their growth, but oaks' seeds

These abundant Engelmann's oak acorns testify to a mast year.

possess a wider spectrum: in addition to starch, the acorn's food reserves are comprised of 20 to 30 percent fat and 6 to 8 percent protein. Such bounty does not go unnoticed by the outside world. It might even be argued that the food reserves of acorns are an intentional provocation, since oaks depend on animals to seek out, collect, and bury their acorns.

All creatures need a balance of carbohydrates, fats, and proteins. Carbohydrates (sugars and starches) are widely available from many sources, but fats and proteins are harder to come by. While oak acorns are liberally endowed with all three, their proteins are not readily available to most acorn eaters, as they are chemically bound to bitter substances called tannins. Widespread in many plant groups but especially abundant in oaks, tannins guard the proteinaceous foodstuffs for the embryonic plant's use.

Some oaks, probably because they have a lower overall protein content and thus do not need tannins to safeguard their

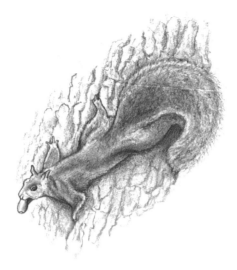

food stores, have acorns that are pronounced sweet (that is, without bitter tannins). Such sweet acorns, surprisingly, were not always favored by various tribes of Native Americans, because the bitter acorns had other advantages: they were oilier and thus tastier, and they kept better. And so the long leaching process of removing bitter tannins was considered an essential part of food preparation for these staples of everyday Native American life.

Even without available protein, an acorn's fat content is more than enough to nourish a very wide array of different animals. Though all acorns are considered high in fat, some contain roughly twice the fat of others. Generally speaking, acorns of the black oak group have the most fat; those of the white oaks have less. Perhaps this makes a difference in which kinds of animals visit different species of oak.

It is probably no accident that oaks and the communities they create—from montane forests, chaparral, woodlands, and mixed evergreen forests to savannahs, scrublands, tropical cloud forests, and rainforests—are so rich in animal life. Likewise, it is no accident that the success of these communities allows them to dominate huge expanses of land, for the ecological web of interrelated organisms that live on, browse, eat, or destroy oak trees has endured for a long time. No other tree group, save possibly pines, holds comparable sway in the wooded places of the Northern Hemisphere.

Many oaks have years with bumper crops of acorns followed by years when they're nearly devoid of fruits. This periodicity is all the more enigmatic because one kind of oak may be producing an acorn bonanza, while another species growing in the same woodland may be barren. This lack of synchronicity in acorn crops precludes the idea that fruitful years are necessarily related to external circumstances such as long growing seasons, abundant rainfall, or especially warm days.

When trying to solve puzzles such as this, it's always a good idea to look at other factors in the local ecosystem, such as other organisms that interact in the local food web. If we do so, we find consumers and opportunists whose activities shape the reproductive chances of oaks. In a year when consumers are especially plentiful, the acorn supply may be exhausted without giving oaks a chance to establish new saplings. If, however, the acorn crop plummets some years, the population of the consumers may also fall, leaving behind few progeny to plague the following year's crop of acorns. So when good years are followed by bad, the trend for opportunists to continue their unmitigated success is interrupted, and the balance between oaks and exploiters returns to a more normal routine. At least for a time.

Another important consideration is that different oak species in the same forest may bloom at different times. A harsh, blustery windstorm or torrential downpour may strip male catkins before they shed pollen in one species, but leave another species that has not yet begun its outpouring of pollen unaffected.

The list of organisms that feed on acorns is encyclopedic and includes minute weevils that drill holes in acorns while they're still ripening on the tree, snails that feed on the remains of rotting acorns on the ground, large birds and mammals, the microscopic fungal threads of molds, and ravaging millipedes. Every kind of acorn in every ecological niche hosts an incredibly rich ecosystem. That a few acorns make it through this maze of biological hazards is remarkable, but the prodigious output from a single tree—referred to by the old English word as mast, from meat—guarantees that in most years there are acorns to spare. A mast year is one of bountiful acorn production and harvest.

Current studies are assessing how effective oak regeneration is in places that may have suffered from human activities and impacts. Results suggest that when we curtail practices destructive to oak environments—by preventing overgrazing and keeping deer populations under control—or restore oak habitats, acorns still grow into new oaks as they have always done. It doesn't take many new oaks to replace what's normally lost to old age and death, for oaks live for a long time.

Many oaks are what ecologists call *keystone species*. This term is particularly apt, because it implies that without such species, the vast web of interrelated plant and animal life in the ecosystem would soon unravel. As the keystone species disappears, so do others that depend on it; as the secondary species decline, a whole array of tertiary species succumbs. Healthy forests owe their vitality to a continuing sequence of young, mature, and old individuals of the keystone species. Every age counts.

The list of animals associated with acorns is far too long to detail here, but a look at a few species affords insight into how thoroughly dependent the many participants are, from fungi, mites, ants, weevils, and moth larvae to jays, squirrels, woodpeckers, turkeys, and bears. Let's begin with the animals that benefit oaks by dispersing their acorns. The most important among these are rodents and birds, which harvest acorns for food but bury them in caches for later use. Of these creatures, the jays of the Northern Hemisphere (including Mexico and Central America) play one of the most precise and interesting roles in the life of an oak.

Jays represent a special subfamily of the Corvids—medium to largish birds that display quick intelligence, scavenge for food opportunistically, and promptly adapt to new circumstances. An ancient bird group, jays are thought to have originated in Central and South America, where they diversified early on, then radiated into western North America and across the Northern Hemisphere. A secondary area of diversification appears to be in Southeast Asia, but a couple of species—the common jay of Eurasia and the blue jay of North America— also have wide distribution through the forests of those regions.

Jays provide an important key to acorn success because many species make nuts the main staple of their diets. These nuts

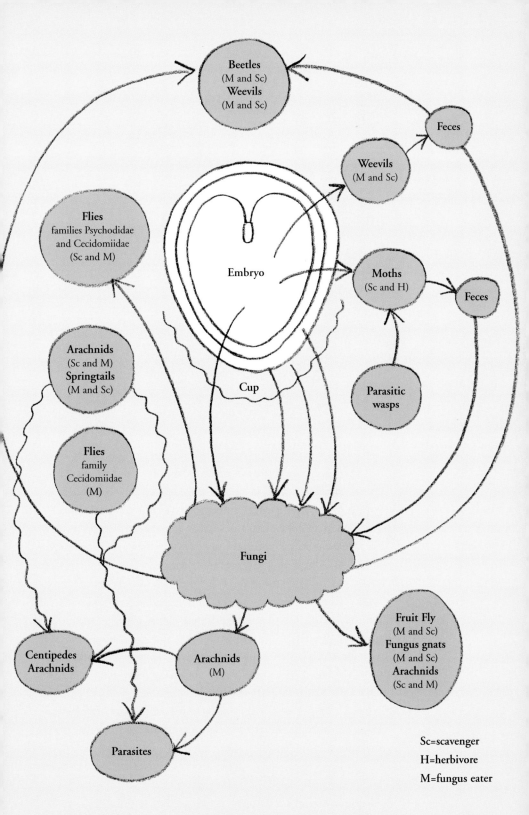

The web of predators, consumers, and decomposers of eastern United States oak acorns.

The burying and caching behavior of scrub jays is an effective way of dispersing and planting acorns. Many acorns are not retrieved and will succeed in germinating.

generally include acorns—and, for a few species, pine nuts—that are harvested over two or more months in the fall and are stashed in strategically located places for retrieval in winter and early spring. Some jays, such as the scrub jay of southwestern North America, may depend on the success of an acorn harvest for rearing its young in the spring. A poor harvest may mean no brood. The distribution of jay species and their diversification coincides closely with the distribution and diversification of oaks. The two areas of the world most noted for their great variety of oaks, Southeast Asia and the highlands of Mexico, are also areas of great jay diversity.

These facts present us with many intriguing questions, especially regarding the possibility of jays giving oaks a competitive edge by dispersing their acorns to new places. Could it be that jays have shaped oak evolution? Is it at least possible that jays are largely responsible for the present distribution of oaks? Did oaks diversify where jays did?

One such parallel certainly seems to exist between jays and their primary food plants. In the case of the pinyon jay of northern Mexico and the southwestern United States, there is a close fit between the bird's feeding and gathering behavior and the distribution of pinyon pines—a group of pines adapted to the arid uplands of that part of the world. In harvesting the large, nutrient-rich pinyon nuts, the pinyon jay shows purposeful and thoughtful behavior. It evaluates the seeds by color, weight, and the sound they make when they are vibrated in the beak. Only the nuts that pass these tests are gathered and stored; these are the seeds that haven't suffered the ravages of insects and other invaders. Could there be a comparable situation between scrub or other jays and the acorns they gather? It seems highly likely.

Other animals, including cattle, pigs, deer, wild turkeys, bears, peccaries, agoutis, monkeys, and acorn woodpeckers, may play less positive roles in the life of oak trees. A notable example is provided by the acorn woodpecker. Acorns play a major role in the social order and survival of acorn woodpeckers, yet these birds seldom return the favor. In areas with up to five species of oaks, well-established populations of acorn woodpeckers are marked by their impressive granaries: old trees and trunks riddled with thousands of carefully drilled holes, each occupied by an acorn. Everyday life and a complex social order revolve around these granaries, for they provide stability to these birds, just as humans' agricultural fields give people a sense of permanence and home. Since the acorns are stored well above the ground and diligently pounded into the holes of the granary, they are seldom able to fall out and germinate, so they lose any opportunity to grow into new trees.

Acorn woodpeckers seem to need a diversity of oak species to ensure a plentiful harvest. When one species is experiencing a barren year, another may be groaning with acorns. Seldom do all five kinds fail to provide sustenance in any given year. And despite the prodigious number of acorns gathered by these woodpeckers, their take is a small percentage of the overall crop, on the order of 1 percent in any given place.

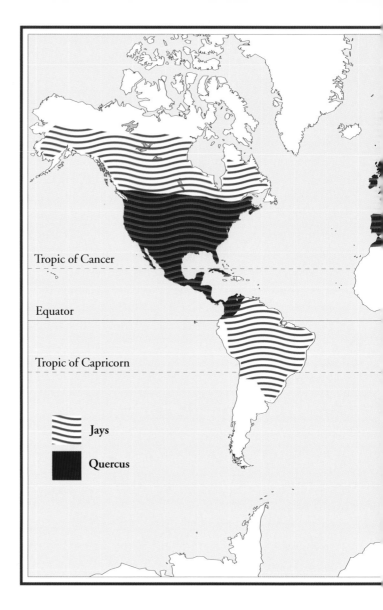

Tropic of Cancer

Equator

Tropic of Capricorn

Jays

Quercus

Larger mammals also take advantage of an oak's acorn bounty, but whether they seriously threaten oak reproduction depends
upon whether they have lived with their particular oaks over the
eons, evolving together, or whether they're newcomers on the
scene. Newcomers thrive courtesy of human activities. For example, cattle now graze in many lands where they never occurred
naturally, and deer give birth to fawns with abandon because
mountain lions, who once so effectively culled deer populations,

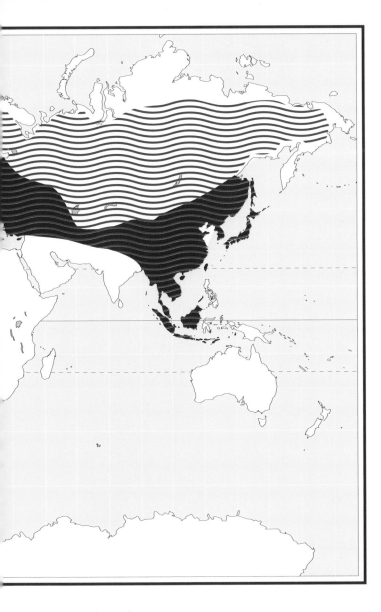

The hatching on this map reveals the overlap between oak and jay distribution. Jays likely have been instrumental in the successful spread of oaks across the northern hemisphere.

have been hunted to near extinction.

Human impact on the delicate balance between consumer and acorn is vividly illustrated by the feeding habits of wild boars and pigs. In the Old World, boars and pigs slowly evolved with oaks. They don't overburden oaks with their determined rooting activities in fall; in fact, they may possibly aid some oaks by burying their acorns more deeply as they plow through the moistened leaf litter. By contrast, their introduction to the New World has been recent and devastating. Acorns here are already under attack from many native predators, and the final insult to an oak's abilities to withstand onslaughts on many fronts can be fatally compromised in places where pig populations are burgeoning.

The fate of acorns provides a look at how the lives of many seemingly disparate organisms depend on one small environment for survival. Each contestant wins its prize at a different time. Some organisms attack acorns while they're still firmly attached to the tree; others begin only when the ripe acorn has fallen to the ground; others wait until the acorn has already been split open; still others move in when only the acorn shell or tatters of the shell remain. Studies on oaks in the eastern United States offer a glimpse into the richness of these dramas; watch what happens, for example, when a still-green acorn is first attacked by the acorn weevil (*Curculio proboscideus*).

When acorn woodpeckers pound an acorn into a hole they've made in a dead tree, there is little chance for the acorn's germination or survival. The dead tree serves as a granary for retrieving food throughout the upcoming year.

An acorn weevil deposits an egg into an acorn by drilling through the shell with its rasplike snout.

Using its long snout, which has rasping teeth that twirl back and forth like a miniature drill, the weevil bores a long, cylindrical hole into the heart of the acorn. To add insult to injury, the weevil then lays an egg in this hole and passes on to the next acorn for a repeat performance. Soon a fat, wormlike larva hatches, surrounded by abundant food. As it feeds, though, it may trigger a reaction in the acorn's connection with its twig, and the acorn may be dropped prematurely, thus conserving for the tree food and water that otherwise would have been invested in a now-worthless acorn.

After the acorn falls to the ground, the larva eventually shoves its way out, having fattened up for the next stage of its life. If the acorn has not been completely consumed during this process, it is likely to fall prey to a second round of assaults—the acorn moth (*Valentina glandulella*) may lay its eggs on what's left of the acorn's embryo. The exit hole from the previous occupant provides a ready entrance for the new intruder. Sometimes the larvae from these eggs overwinter inside the acorn, staying in their snug home until inclement weather has passed, in the spring. Often, the larvae last only long enough to crawl from the acorn; they too die, victims of parasitic wasps that lay their eggs in the larvae's bodies. But if they are lucky, the moth larvae eat their way out and proceed to their next stage of development before winter sets in. At this point, it's a certainty that the acorn embryo has died from the ravages of its invaders.

Now the scavengers move in. These include several tiny snails and the truly minute beetle mites, both of which feast on the acorn's rotting remains. Various fungal spores also make their way into the holes of the acorn's armor, growing at an accelerated rate in the dampness of winter. While the detritus-seekers are busy feeding, predators of the forest floor are on the prowl. Centipedes and fungus gnat larvae (family Mycetophilidae) make a good living feeding on the unwary snails, beetle mites, and fungi there. At last, when all the soft material has been eaten out or eroded away and the acorn shell lies empty, the last round of visitors appears—many ants begin new colonies inside these snug and waterproof homes. So it goes, until, at last, even the acorn's shell has been abraded, fragmented, and broken down into nutrients that bacteria and fungi in the forest's soils will return to the tree's roots.

Let's suppose that an acorn somehow manages to find its way to a cozy hole in the ground, perhaps put there by some animal for the duration of the winter. How does that acorn fare as compared to a companion that may have lain forgotten on the surface of the forest floor? Acorns that simply land on the leaf litter face stiffer conditions, for if they germinate after a brief rain that is followed by a drought—a sequence common in the fall months before winter storms come in earnest—the new sapling may perish, unable to strike water with its root. Unburied acorns may also perish by freezing. A well-buried acorn, on the other hand, is secure among a carpeting of old leaves and rich organic duff that helps seal in moisture and keep it comfortably humid. If it germinates ahead of schedule, it has a much greater chance of survival.

The need for acorns to be snugly buried beneath the leaf litter has recently been chronicled by people studying earthworms in some Atlantic seaboard hardwood forests. Some earthworms are widely acclaimed as superb aerators and enrichers of soils in gardens. But despite their positive impact on garden soils, some earthworms are not native to this part of the world, and when they multiply in native hardwood forests, they are not beneficial to oaks. The thick carpeting of autumn leaves that provides a nurturing environment for acorns becomes a delectable salad for voracious earthworms. Without this blanket to nestle under, most acorns will perish. In their place, the winged samaras (fruits) of maples grow and flourish, producing a virtual carpet of baby maple seedlings. (In the absence of earthworms, these samaras would usually be consumed by litter-inhabiting fungi and bacteria.) And so the forest composition changes, becoming poor in oaks and rich in maples.

Because acorns die if they become dehydrated, the timing of germination varies widely in accordance with the time when water is plentiful and temperatures are mild enough to allow growth to take place. Where autumns and winters are frigid, acorns remain dormant, coming to life in the spring after snows thaw. In milder climes, such as those of the piedmonts of the southeastern United States, the hammocks of Florida, and the foothills of California, acorns may actually germinate in late fall or early winter, if rain is plentiful and temperatures mild. Even deciduous oaks may bear leafy seedlings then, under the protection of the forest canopy. In the tropics, acorn germination follows more nebulous environmental cues, and new seedlings appear throughout the year, as long as rains are frequent.

As soon as the thick shell of the acorn has become sodden, it softens, swells, and bursts open at the pointed end. Water easily passes across the flimsy, papery seed coat to swell the nascent embryo. As more water moves in, the embryo inflates like a balloon. The water moves primarily into the radicle, hypocotyl, and epicotyl; the food-containing cotyledons remain tightly ensconced within the acorn's shell while the rest of the embryo shoves through. In many plants, cotyledons are justifiably called seedling leaves—they're the first green structures to emerge when the seed germinates. And they usually do function just like leaves, even though their shape may differ sharply from the shape of all other leaves to come. But in oaks, the cotyledons' job is to remain embedded within the acorn shell and serve as a food source to spur the growth of the rest of the embryo. Oak cotyledons never become leaflike, but instead, gradually shrivel inside the acorn's shell as food is withdrawn.

The plunging downward of the new root and the thrusting upward of the new shoot announce the successful germination of the baby oak. As with so many other processes from birth to death, the growth of roots and shoots is governed by specific concentrations of hormones. Much of the initial energy goes into the seedling's root before the epicotyl begins its rapid elongation toward the sun. The quick-growing root draws on the food stored in the cotyledons, accumulating the mass necessary to become a secure anchor and be able to probe for deeply buried water sources. Then the new leaves—slow to enlarge and proliferate at first—undergo a dramatic transformation. Inside the seed they were colorless, but now, as light strikes them, they quickly turn from white to pale green to deep green. The pigment—chlorophyll—cannot be synthesized by the plant without sunlight.

SEEDLINGS espite all the hazards to successful germination and growth, so many acorns *do* germinate that there is keen competition for the prime commodities of light and water. After germination, seedlings engage in a mad dash to grow as rapidly as possible. As soon as the days lengthen, the pursuit of light and water quickens. In addition to a deep, strong taproot, it is equally important for the seedling oak to make as many leaves as possible, so that the young tree can begin converting the sun's energy into food. If either pursuit falls short during the spring, the seedling is doomed. Not all seedlings will survive their first full

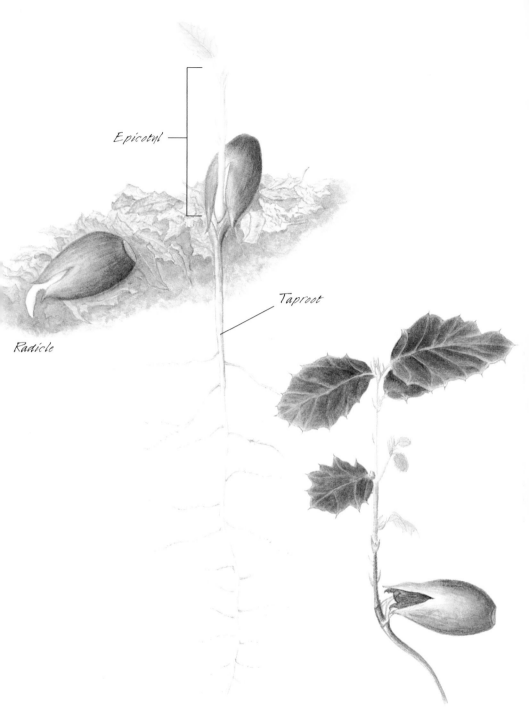

Epicotyl

Taproot

Radicle

Stages of acorn germination: (top left) an acorn first sends out its radicle; (middle) the radicle develops into a taproot while the epicotyl pushes upward; (bottom right) the young oak now displays several healthy leaves.

season, but those with a slightly more rapid growth or a modicum more leaf surface will likely end up the victors.

The second set of hurdles for seedling survival comes during summer. In summer-dry climates, such as those of the arid Mediterranean basin, the rugged mountains of Texas, or the rolling foothills of California, progressive drought challenges the new seedling. The young taproot may need to be supplemented by a horizontal spread of surface roots that trap any remaining moisture. In eastern hardwood forests, another challenge presents itself: the gathering of sufficient light as the forest canopy grows ever denser. Though the first stirrings of spring are met with a new flush of growth, leaves don't completely cover tree crowns until the long days of summer arrive. So while many saplings can gather enough light in the spring, summer's deep shade may overchallenge their abilities. Either way—increasing drought or deepening shade—summer spells a time of hardship for new seedlings.

Throughout this process, there are the ever-present dangers of invaders and intruders. Many fungi have protracted life spans and are avidly opportunistic. They strike when seedlings are most vulnerable, often just as they first extend their new roots and shoots. If the skin protecting the new embryo is breached through abrasion or contusion, fungal spores can enter and consume vulnerable cells at a frightening pace. These fungi grow right into the new plumbing system, destroying the root's ability to move water to the tender top shoot. The shoot falls over as it wilts and dries. This phenomenon, called *damping off,* is usually quick and dramatic.

If the young seedling survives in its new home, the new leaves close to the ground present an alluring meal to creatures, such as caterpillars, deer, leaf miners, and stingless wasps. While some consumers merely weaken the leaf, others eat enough to destroy the young seedling. As a consequence, the leaves of young oaks carry their own form of armament. Many are laced with the same bitter tannins that protected their acorns; in fact,

This eye-level view shows a coast live oak (Q. agrifolia) *acorn thrusting up its epicotyl into a brand new leafy shoot.*

it's likely that some of the tannins already in the acorn simply get transferred to the new leaves. Tannins stored in the acorn are not the only source of this protective substance, for oaks at all stages of life are capable of manufacturing tannins, but the initial dose from acorn stores gives seedling leaves an extra boost. The leaf margins of oak seedlings also carry their own version of defensive design. Even those oaks whose adult leaves lack bristles or spines often wear them on the edges of their young leaves.

Life as a sapling is seldom easy: there is water to compete for; there are nutrients to capture in sufficient quantity to assure healthy growth; and there is the never-ending need for light to fuel photosynthesis. During the first critical years of growth, many saplings succumb to competition with other oak saplings or other species.

But not all do, and some saplings grow into strapping new oak trees, passing through their youth in the understory to emerge as mature trees. Somewhere just after youth but well before middle age, another milestone is reached: the age of flowering and fruiting. Exactly when that age is depends on the genetic programming for each species in concert with a mix of environmental factors such as water supply, the effects of competing vegetation, and the impact of browsing. Most oaks make a tentative venture into reproduction between ten and twenty years of age. If all goes well, the output of flowers and acorns will increase thereafter for many years, eventually reach a plateau, and finally taper off in old age.

Some oaks have a way of reproducing that doesn't involve pollination, fertilization, or acorns. These oaks multiply through an underground system of stems or roots, using a process called *vegetative reproduction.* The new oaks created this way are exact genetic copies of their parents.

While most oaks are incapable of vegetative reproduction, a few have made a specialty of it. Such oaks—mostly low-growing, semiscrubby oaks—find this an efficient way to co-opt more of an environment to which they have become well-suited. Vegetative reproduction allows these oaks to proliferate in their immediate neighborhood without requiring the extra time and energy to make flowers, seeds, and seedlings. And because the original oak parent has proven itself well-adapted to its particular growing place, vegetative reproduction ensures that genetically identical new plants will have the same successful adaptations.

Oaks that promote themselves by vegetative means sometimes have many low-lying, horizontally trending branches. When their branches get buried, or when the branches plunge inadvertently just beneath the soil's surface, they quickly root and send out a new set of branches. A large colony of interconnected individuals results. You can see this behavior in two very different North American oaks, Gambel's oak (*Quercus gambelii*) of the Rocky Mountains and turkey oak (*Q. pumila*) of the sand plains along the Atlantic seaboard. The turkey oak has developed its

Gambel oak's (Q. gambelii) *vegetative reproduction results in a close-knit line of trees, seen here in autumn.*

vegetative reproduction to such an extent that it sends out special runners—slender horizontal stems that skim just below the soil's surface—to bind and hold the loose, blowing sands of barren coastal pine forests. Other oaks have hard lignotubers (swollen, woody, underground stems) that sprout into vigorous new colonies.

How many times during their existence have oaks repeated their basic life cycle? Perhaps the number of repetitions is in the billions. That's an impressive testimony to the efficiency of that life cycle, for it has withstood millions of years of changing environments and evolving animal life. While it is generally acknowledged that oaks have been around a very long time, just how long is highly controversial. But regardless of the exact figure, one thing is very apparent: the overall pattern of the oak life cycle has probably changed very little. To understand how important this idea is, we will turn next to the origins of oaks and their evolution.

AN OVERVIEW

OF THE

LIFE CYCLE

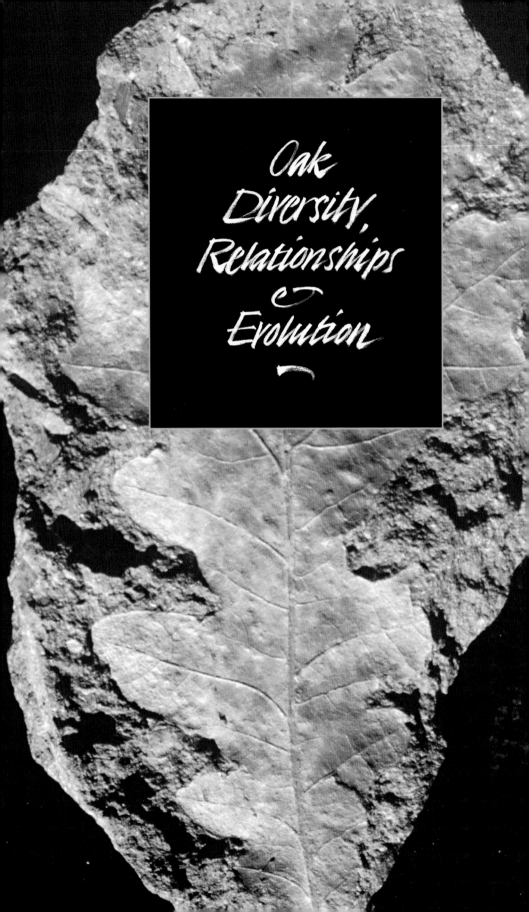

Oak Diversity, Relationships & Evolution

S ince humans first evolved language, they have been naming objects in the world around them. It's not surprising that this propensity for naming has embraced the natural world. Many aboriginal peoples have incredibly complex systems for naming the creatures and plants in their homelands. For scientists, though, *taxonomy* is the formal science of naming these natural entities. Taxonomy has evolved from the earliest concepts of the ancient Greeks, who arranged plants into basic convenient groupings such as trees, shrubs, and nonwoody, herbaceous plants. Taxonomy has come a long way since then, and today's classification system, with its precise rules for naming, attempts to reflect the relationships between plants and their evolution. As the system is refined with every addition of new knowledge, we hope to perfect our view of the natural world. We need to remember, though, that we are the ones imposing order on an inherently chaotic system. Nature seldom draws sharp boundaries around her creations, as anyone who has wrestled with the intricacies of oak classification readily acknowledges.

A quick overview of the modern classification system will help elucidate the order of groups in which plants are arranged. The largest category within the plant kingdom is *division* (what zoologists call a phylum). The division Anthophyta represents the most major assemblage of plants, encompassing the 300,000 or so kinds of flowering plants. Divisions are split into *classes*, which are in turn separated into *orders*. Below order is *family*, a fundamental grouping of plants that share several usually obvious features. Examples of easily recognized families include the grasses (family Poaceae), daisies (family Asteraceae), mustards (family Brassicaceae), and peas (family Fabaceae). Large families such as the beech family (Fagaceae), to which oaks belong, are often sorted into *subfamilies*, which contain one to several genera (singular, *genus*, from the Latin word for people or race) that have features but differ in those features from other subfamilies. The beech family has three major subfamilies: the beech subfamily (Fagoideae), the chestnut subfamily (Castanoideae), and the oak subfamily (Quercoideae). The genera themselves are more tightly defined than families or subfamilies; they often intuitively reflect a group on which we have already bestowed a common name. Oaks, for example, belong to the genus *Quercus;* beeches to the genus *Fagus;* chestnuts to the genus *Castanea.* There is sometimes only one kind, or *species,* in a genus, but in large genera, such as those that oaks and pines belong to, there are many different species. Large genera are often divided into *subgenera, sections,* and *subsections*—in descending order of size—as a way of categorizing related species. In *Quercus,* for example, we recognize at least four subgenera: white oaks (*Quercus*), black oaks (*Erythrobalanus*), golden oaks (*Protobalanus*), and ring-cupped oaks (*Cyclobalanopsis*). Sometimes a single species may vary a lot; for example, the tree and shrub form of Garry oak (*Q. garryana* var. *garryana* and *Q. garryana* var. *breweri*) belong to the same species, so sometimes we recognize *subspecies* or *varieties* in such situations.

How and where do oaks fit in to the vast host of 300,000 species of flowering plants? It may surprise you to learn that despite our long acquaintance with oaks and their relatives, there is considerable controversy over oaks' lineage.

An oak tree provides an apt metaphor for the evolutionary arrangement of flowering plants. The massive trunk of the tree stands for the first wave of early flowering plants. The boles and limbs that depart from the trunk represent the several evolutionary lines that diverged from those earliest flowers. Branches diverging from limbs depict individual families; where branches depart close to one another, the families share a common ancestor. The beech family Fagaceae is one small branch of that tree, and the twigs that extend from that branch represent the genera.

Oaks are a major twig by themselves, alongside one other tiny twig, the genus *Trigonobalanus*. Together those two genera form their own branchlet or subfamily, the Quercoideae. Other genera in the family include beeches (genus *Fagus*), southern beeches (genus *Nothofagus*), chinquapins (genus *Chrysolepis*), chestnuts (genus *Castanea*), evergreen chestnuts (genus *Castanopsis*), and tanbark oaks (genus *Lithocarpus*). Those genera belong to two other branchlets of the family: beeches and southern beeches to the subfamily Fagoideae; chestnuts, chinquapins, and tanbark oaks to the subfamily Castanoideae.

We've already examined oak architecture and reproduction. But just what is the essence of being one of the 300 to 400 species of the giant genus called *Quercus?* This large number of species is equalled or surpassed by only a handful of other flowering plant genera, placing oaks squarely at the forefront of prominence and diversity.

Throughout this book, we've seen how scores of different traits help define oaks, yet so far no single feature has distinguished them from all other groups. When taxonomists look at oaks, they put great emphasis on traits that involve reproduction, such as details of male catkins, stigmas, ovaries, acorns, and acorn cups. Modern taxonomic practice delves deeply into the tiniest details and probes the seemingly inconsequential aspects of reproduction: the development of ovules and seeds inside the ovary; the development and shape of the ovule's tiny embryo sac; the route the pollen tube travels to reach the ovule's egg; the shape and sculpting of pollen grains; the patterns and details of leaf veins; and the shape and number of chromosomes.

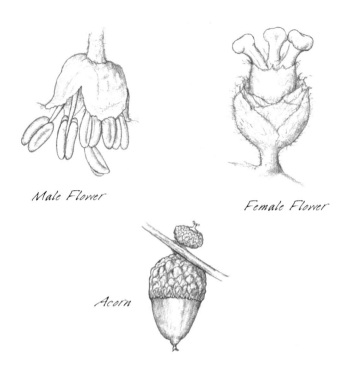

Male Flower

Female Flower

Acorn

Why is such weight given to this one slice of oak life? The answer is simple: reproductive traits show relationships much more clearly than do vegetative traits such as bark, leaves, and roots, because reproductive traits evolve much more slowly. If flowers and acorns did not resist change, devastating mutations could ruin the whole process of making new oaks. Mutations that make rash alterations in the reproductive machinery are dealt with harshly, for oaks that carry these traits perish immediately. Leaf or bark mutations are much less likely to affect an oak's ability to make viable seeds.

But we don't need to list all of the technical details that botanists look for in oaks. Knowing a few very basic features will suffice. True oaks always bear dangling male catkins that release their pollen to the wind. True oaks always produce tiny, inconspicuous female flowers with three stigmas, and the male and female flowers are separated from one another both in time and space. Finally, true oaks always bear an acorn that sits in a distinctive scale-covered cup. If a tree or shrub displays all of these traits, you can be sure it's an oak; if it displays only two out of four, it's some other kind of plant. For example, alders, birches, walnuts, willows, and cottonwoods also produce male catkins, but none of them produce acorns. Any time one or two characteristics alone are used for identification, you run the risk of misidentification.

In addition to the key features just listed, there is another way to know true oaks: by their great diversity of leaves, bark patterns, acorns, and acorn cups. Rather than being the same for all oaks, these parts reveal their intriguing and beautiful variety, and you can imagine what is possible and not possible within the mold for true oaks. As we illustrate this diversity, you'll also grasp the necessity to group oaks into comprehensible subgenera within the genus.

olor, shape, size, vein pattern, margins, and leaf hairs offer a wealth of information about oak leaf design. For leaf shape, we can talk about the outline of the leaf, whether the leaf is lobed or not, and the shape of the leaf tips and bases. Despite the temptation to use size to separate oak species, the size of the leaves is not a particularly useful taxonomic tool, since it varies tremendously in accordance with environmental circumstances, age of the tree, and position of the leaf on the tree, but it can tell us much about the tree's condition and its locale. Leaf color is no less diverse, especially as no two people perceive color in quite the same way. The subjectiveness of color vision hinders rather than aids in precise descriptions, just as distinguishing odors is a tricky and unexplicit pursuit; nonetheless, leaf color offers a subjective, personal way to know a tree. Some oaks are distinguished by their bicolored leaves, which display different colors on their upper and lower surfaces. Vein patterns are harder to describe; they diverge in rich and complex patterns that challenge explicit descriptions. Leaf margins vary from flat and smooth to tightly curled downward and sharply toothed. Teeth may be tiny and inconspicuous,

Q. tomentella
Island Oak
California

Q. stellata
Post Oak
SE United States

Q. palmeri
Palmer's Oak
California

Q. engelmannii
Engelmann's Oak
California

Q. marilandica
Blackjack Oak
SE United States

Q. montana
Chestnut Oak
E United States

Q. phellos
Willow Oak
SE United States

Q. alba
White Oak
E United States

Q. durata
Leather Oak
California

Q. coccinea
Scarlet Oak
E United States

Q. gambelii
Gambel's Oak
Rocky Mountain Region

Q. robur
English Oak
Europe

Q. arizonica
Arizona White Oak
S Arizona, N Mexico

Q. ilex
Holly Oak
Mediterranean

Q. oleoides
Encino
Central America

Q. rugosa
Mexican Netvein Oak
SE Arizona, Mexico

Q. suber
Cork Oak
Mediterranean

Q. frainetto
Hungary Oak
SE Europe

Q. crassifolia
Thick-leaved Oak
Mexico

Q. variabilis
Asian Cork Oak
Japan, Korea

Q. acuta
Acute-leaved Oak
SE Asia

Q. elmeri
Elmer's Oak
Malaysia

Q. faginea
W. Mediterranean

Q. chrysotricha
Golden-haired Oak
Malaysia

Q. dentata
Diamyo Oak
China, Japan, Korea

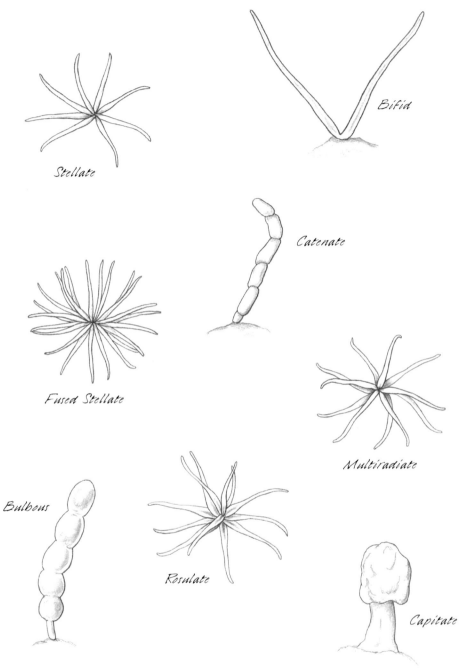

Stellate

Bifid

Catenate

Fused Stellate

Multiradiate

Bulbous

Rosulate

Capitate

Variations of oak leaf hairs.

156

large and obvious, fine and numerous, coarse and scattered, spinelike or blunt, bristle-tipped or tapered to a point.

While the variety in the macroscopic world of leaves is easily seen by the unaided eye, the microscopic world is apparent only with the aid of a magnifying glass or microscope, divulging a magnificient array of leaf hairs. Hairs are visible to the naked eye as fuzzy or wooly coverings on leaves, but when they're magnified, they reveal their particular form. Hairs may be simple and straight; wavy, interlaced cobwebs; multirayed starbursts; or have enlarged, rounded, glandular tips. Different hairs offer different kinds of protection: white hairs reflect hot sun to cool the leaves' surfaces; densely-matted hairs help retard water loss from leaf stomates; sticky hairs deter tiny chewing insects from making inroads into soft leaf tissue; and red hairs serve as signals to stay away from young leaves.

Even within what appears superficially to be a single kind of hair, close examination at twenty magnficiations with an ordinary dissecting microscope reveals even greater variation. For example, starburst-patterned hairs can be subdivided into large starbursts, wavy starbursts, one-sided starbursts, and dwarf, densely aggregated starbursts, to name a few. Such "splitting of hairs" can help clarify differences between closely related species of oaks. Different patterns of starburst hairs help separate the bewildering welter of look-alike scrub oak species in Southern California.

Oak hairs also help elucidate the relationships of oaks to other members of the beech family, Fagaceae. Hairs found on oak leaves may also occur in other members of the family, but some patterns of hairs are unique to oaks, while other patterns may identify other genera.

Oak bark is starkly conspicuous on deciduous oaks in winter. Several major oak groups, such as black oaks and white oaks, derive their names from the color of their bark, though these color designations can be misleading, since black oaks don't always have blackish bark and white oaks often fail to have pale

Q. engelmannii

Q. agrifolia

Q. sinuata

Q. gambelii

Q. lobata

Q. kelloggii

Q. suber

Q. palmeri

Q. variabilis

Q. macrocarpa

Diversity of oak bark patterns.

gray to whitish bark. To further complicate matters, heavy growths of lichens may give the overall impression of white bark, even on black oaks. And bark color changes with the age of the tree.

Besides color, there are more palpable differences in bark, for each kind of oak shows its own particular bark pattern. Oak bark is relatively smooth on young trees, or even on mature trees from tropical Southeast Asia. The bark of other oaks flakes in thin strips, checkers, or other shallow designs. Many writers have remarked on the thin, flaky bark of white oaks, but alas, this trait is not consistent. Sometimes white oaks' bark is deeply fissured. The bark of the famed cork oak (*Quercus suber*), which has been used for centuries to stopper the world's finest wines, is the most striking example of this.

Acorns are without peer as a reliable, stable feature by which to identify any given species of oak. Once you learn the acorn's size, shape, color pattern, and, most importantly, the nature of the cup it sits in, you'll easily identify the oak from which it came. Acorns can be miniatures, less than an inch long, or giants of three to four inches. They can be pencil thin or plump. Acorns can be a solid tan or bronze or appealingly striped with darker lines and rays. Acorns can be broader than they are long or taper elegantly from base to tip.

Because of its beauty, precise construction, and conspicuous presence, the acorn cup is arguably the most interesting feature of oaks. The reasons for its various and esoteric permutations have not been clarified, but nonetheless, specialists use the distinctiveness of acorn cup design—in particular the way the bracts (scale-like appendages) are shaped and arranged—to divide the broad groups of oak species into subgenera, sections, and series. Acorn cups can have thin, shinglelike, pointed scales or thick, warty scales; the scales may be brown, tan, or powdered with gold; and the scales may sometimes be spinelike or fused into concentric rings.

*I*n order to make sense of the rich diversity of the genus *Quercus,* botanists have split this prolific lot into subgenera, sections, and series, in descending order. Even though many people intuitively group oaks according to whether they're trees or shrubs or whether they're evergreen or deciduous, botanists base their groupings on details of reproductive features, because these features better reflect the true relationships among oak species. For example, within a single oak species, we may have both a shrub and tree form that are genetically distinct, as in the case with Garry oak and Brewer's oak (Garry oak, *Q. garryana* var. *garryana* is a tree; Brewer's oak, *Q. garryana* var. *breweri,* a shrub). Yet Garry and Brewer's oaks are alike in their leaf design, bark color and pattern, and acorns. By contrast, separate species such as the goldcup oak (*Q. chrysolepis* from the golden oak subgenus) and interior live oak (*Q. wislizenii* from the black oak subgenus) both live in the dry foothills of California's Sierra Nevada and both display leaves that are tough, evergreen, narrowly lance-shaped, sometimes smooth-margined, and sometimes lined with prickly, hollylike teeth.

Quercus, the White Oaks

Quercus is not only the name of this subgenus, but the oak genus as well. Alternate names often used for this group are *Leucobalanus* (*leuco* means white) and *Lepidobalanus* (*lepido* comes from the Greek word for scaly; *balanus* means oak in ancient Greek).

There are more than 100 species of white oaks. They are abundant in Europe and the Mediterranean region, prolific in temperate mountainous Asia, and rich and varied across North America from the Pacific coast to the Atlantic seaboard. White oaks are missing only from tropical Southeast Asia. A sampling of white oaks from around the world might include eastern North America's magnificent white oak (*Q. alba*), the southern United States' graceful live oak (*Q. virginiana*), the stalwart European English oak (*Q. robur*), Spain and Italy's drought-tolerant cork oak (*Q. suber*), the half-deciduous Asian cork oak (*Q. variabilis*), California's

Q lamellosa
Scale-ringed Oak
Himalayas and Tibet

Q gaharuensis
Sarawak Oak
Sarawak, Borneo

Q kingiana
King's Oak
Thailand

Q kerangasensis
Keranga Oak
Malaysia

Q gemelliflora
Cup-flowered Oak
Malaysia

Q oleoides
Encino
Central America

Q faginea
W. Mediterranean

Q suber
Cork Oak
Mediterranean

Q variabilis
Asian Cork Oak
China, Japan, Korea

Q cerris
Turkish Oak
Mediterranean

Q. rugosa
Mexican Netvein Oak
SE Arizona, N Mexico

Q. marilandica
Blackjack Oak
SE United States

Q. phellos
Willow Oak
SE United States

Q. lyrata
Overcup Oak
E United States

Q. chrysolepis
Goldcup Oak
California

Q. lobata
Valley Oak
California

Q. palmeri
Palmer's oak
California

Q. agrifolia
var. *oxyadenia*
Peninsular Ranges
California

Q. turbinella
Desert Scrub Oak
SW United States

Q. agrifolia
var. *agrifolia*
Coast Live Oak
Coastal Ranges
California

Hairless Inner Shell
(White Oak)

Fuzzy Inner Shell
(Black Oak)

chaparral-adapted scrub oak (*Q. berberidifolia*), and the multiple-trunked Garry oak (*Q. garryana*) from the Pacific Northwest.

The most obvious (but not necessarily consistent) feature of white oaks is their usually pale, whitish bark, which is the reason for the common name. The bark of white oaks is often shallowly flaky, rather than deeply fissured. Their leaves usually have rounded or blunt lobes for the deciduous kinds or gracefully tapered tips for the evergreen species. White oak acorns ripen in one year and are carried in acorn cups with warty or lumpy scales.

White oaks are also identified by less obvious features, such as the seven to nine stamens per male flower, and short, broad, horizontally trending stigmas of the female flowers. (Remember that botanists like to scrutinize flower details!) One of their most important features, in fact, is not at all obvious: the inner lining of the white oaks' acorn shell is smooth and hairless. In order to see this feature, you must crack open the acorn's shell and peer inside.

Because the white oaks are so incredibly varied, botanists interpret them in many different ways; no general agreement prevails. Many specialists include the white oaks in other subgenera, recognizing such groups as *Macrobalanus,* with its somewhat different pattern of cotyledons, and *Cerris,* which possesses black oaklike traits such as female flowers with narrow styles and stigmas, and acorns that take two years to ripen. Recent proposals include elevating the Turkish oaks (*Cerris*) to the same level as white oaks because of the different leaf vein pattern and often bristly scales on the acorn cup. The conservative approach is to recognize a common ground for all white oaks, but divide them into discrete subgroups called sections and subsections. Obviously, there is a bewildering assortment of white oak subgroups, making them highly controversial.

Erythrobalanus, the Black or Red Oaks

Erythro comes from the Greek word for red; *balanus* means oak. Alternate names include *Lobatae* and *Rubre*.

Black oaks number around 200 species and are restricted almost entirely to North and Central America, with one species entering northern South America. Across this continent, black oaks have had great success, and they vie strongly with white oaks for a place in a wide variety of habitats. Black oaks are especially diverse in the mountains of Mexico. A sampling of black oaks might include California's stately, deciduous black oak (*Q. kelloggii*); the evergreen South American oak (*Q. humboldtii*); the low-trending, glossy-leaved scrub oak from Santa Cruz island (*Q. parvula*); Arizona and northern Mexico's bushy silver-leaf oak (*Q. hypoleucoides*); the blackjack oak (*Q. marilandica*) from forests of the southeastern United States; and the vividly autumn-leaved scarlet oak from eastern hardwood forests (*Q. coccinea*).

Black oaks are distinguished by their usually (but not always) dark gray to near black, deeply fissured bark. Their leaves often have bristle-tipped lobes for the deciduous species and spine-tipped teeth along the leaf margins for the evergreen kinds. Black oak acorns usually take almost two years to ripen, and their acorn cups are covered with several rows of thin, fish scalelike bracts. Some black oaks—notably those that have moved into mild climates—have changed their life cycles to accommodate those climates by ripening their acorns in a single year. Examples include California's coast live oak (*Q. agrifolia*) and several species of black oak from the mountains of Mexico.

The less obvious features for black oaks include male flowers with six stamens and female flowers with long, curved styles that gradually taper into spoon-shaped stigmas. The inner shell of black oak acorns is lined with wooly hairs.

Protobalanus, the Golden Oaks

Proto comes from the Latin word for early or first; *balanus* means oak. The group is also known as the intermediate oaks.

The golden oaks are a very small and specialized group, containing only six species, and are restricted to western North America, occurring chiefly in California, the southwestern United States, and northern Mexico. Species of golden oak include the multitrunked goldcup oak (*Q. chrysolepis*) from the mountains of the American West; the shrubby, mountain-dwelling huckleberry oak (*Q. vaccinifolia*) from the granitic mountains of California and southwestern Oregon; the narrow-crowned relict island oak (*Q. tomentella*) from California's Channel Islands; and the half-tree, half-shrub Palmer's oak (*Q. palmeri*) scattered through the dry mountains bordering California's southern deserts.

The name golden oak refers to the golden wax that powders acorn cups and young leaves of some species. Other obvious identifying traits include thin, pale gray bark; evergreen leaves that are lined with spiny teeth or are sharply tipped; and acorns that take two years to ripen. The scales of the acorn cups, in addition to their white hairs or gold powder, are usually thick and corky.

The more esoteric features of golden oaks include eight to ten stamens per male flower and short, broad stigmas in female flowers. The inner shell of the acorn has wooly hairs.

The identifying features for golden oaks neatly balance traits from the white oak and black oak subgenera. The golden oaks are thought to have an early origin in North America and may have a common ancestry with both black and white oaks.

Cyclobalanopsis, the Ring-Cupped Oaks

Cyclo comes from the Latin word for ring and alludes to the rings of scales on the acorn cup; *balanus* means oak.

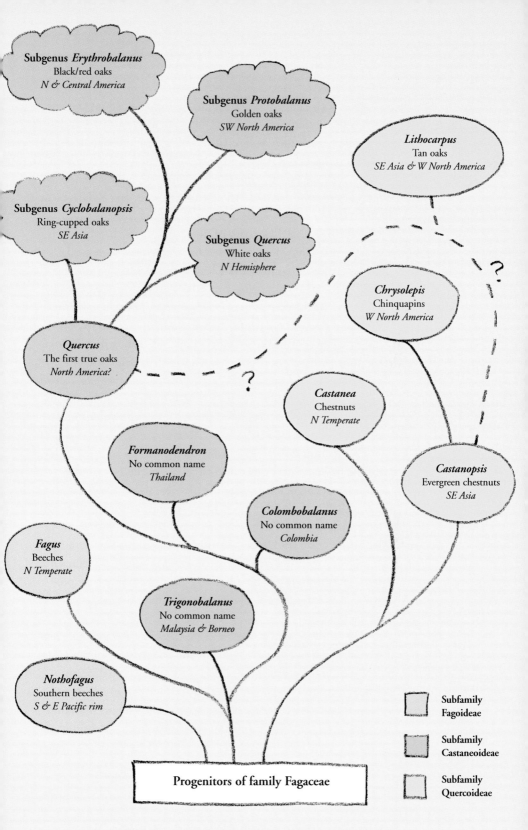

Hypothetical evolutionary scheme for the beech family.

The ring-cupped oaks are a mostly tropical and subtropical group of around forty species centered in Southeast Asia and adjacent islands such as Borneo and New Guinea. They also extend into India, China, and Japan. A handful are illustrated on these pages, including Elmer's oak (*Q. elmeri*), golden-haired oak (*Q. chrysotricha*), Sarawak oak (*Q. gaharuensis*), and Keranga oak (*Q. kerangasensis*).

The pale gray, flaky bark of ring-cupped oaks hardly stands apart from many white or golden oaks, but ring-cupped oaks' large, leathery, evergreen, ovate leaves readily distinguish them from most other oaks. Ring-cupped oak leaves are also characterized by what tropical botanists call *drip tips*. These long, narrow, pointed tips curve gently downward to allow water to roll off the leaves' surface instead of accumulating there during intense tropical downpours. Drip tips are a common adaptation of many species of tropical trees. Ring-cupped oak acorns take one or two years to ripen, but the cups they sit in are utterly different from the other subgenera, for their scales are fused into two or more rows of concentric rings.

Ring-cupped oaks have male flowers with six stamens and female flowers with head-shaped stigmas attached to slender styles. As with golden oaks and black oaks, the inside of the acorn shell is lined with wooly hairs. Ring-cupped oak leaves also have a pattern of veinlets along their margins that is fundamentally different from leaves in all other oak groups. This pattern, along with their distinctive acorn cups, clearly sets ring-cupped oaks apart from the other subgenera. Some botanists have proposed that ring-cupped oaks be placed in their own separate genus.

All four subgenera have varied features in common, and very few of these features can single out any one particular group. For example, each stigma shape is shared by at least two different groups, and the business of whether acorns ripen in one or two years is shared among as many as three of the groups. About the only trait that seems confined to one group alone is the unique ringlike arrangement of acorn cup scales and the distinctive leaves in the tropical ring-cupped oaks, *Cyclobalanopsis*.

Like most rules, those governing oak taxonomy are made to be broken. There are, of course, exceptions to the general statements we have made about the oak subgenera. For example, not all white oaks ripen their acorns in a year: the Turkish oak (*Quercus cerris*), which has many white oak features, matures its acorns in two years, as do several other oaks in this section of Eurasian white oaks. Also, some of these oaks have wooly hairs lining their acorn shells.

In fact, few of the signposts for these supposedly neat groupings hold up under close scrutiny. An honest and purely objective assessment of the features separating oak groups would blur the boundaries between them, producing hazy blotches in place of clear-cut lines. The only relatively consistent difference between our two biggest groups—white oaks and black oaks—is the presence or absence of bristles on leaf lobes and tips, and even that has exceptions.

Despite all the inconsistencies, one fact remains clear: we have not found hybrids between the species of these seemingly arbitrary groups; by contrast, different species within a subgenus often do hybridize. This suggests that there is some basis, after all, to substantiate these subgenera, a basis that actually may serve as a reliable estimate of relatedness.

Trying to sort through the bewildering patterns of life forms can be frustrating. Mother nature promotes diversity, and diversity is sloppy. In addition to promoting the continuance of evolution, diversity also makes for lively discussions among specialists, who usually agree to disagree about where to draw the necessarily arbitrary lines they need to make sense out of the jumble.

The dissection and regrouping of species aids scientific knowledge in two ways. First, it creates a framework, thereby providing a basis for comparison of species and subgenera, even when the edges of the frame are fuzzy and imprecise. Second, it provides a way to look at evolutionary trends within well-defined geographic areas.

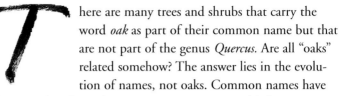

here are many trees and shrubs that carry the word *oak* as part of their common name but that are not part of the genus *Quercus*. Are all "oaks" related somehow? The answer lies in the evolution of names, not oaks. Common names have been conferred on plants since time immemorial. These names reflect a use, such as the hard wood of various ironwoods or the edible fruits of assorted plums; an association, such as heartsease helping the heart grow fonder; or a familiar pattern, such as the leaves of certain shrubs and trees resembling those of laurels. Often, common names intimate some obscure feature that has been forgotten; the lungwort's leaves once signified a medieval herbal remedy for healing lung diseases. Common names sometimes evolved from old, aberrant words or from fanciful allusions, as with Joe-pye weed and love-in-a-mist. The problem with common names is that they sometimes suggest close relationships on the basis of superficial resemblance between two unrelated plants. For example, poison oak (*Toxicodendron diversilobum*), a member of the cashew family Anacardiaceae, comes from western North America and is not related to true oaks. It is so named because of the resemblance of its leaflets (poison oak has compound leaves) to whole leaves of certain deciduous oaks. Its twig, flower, and fruit characteristics are all very different from those of true oaks. Poison oak makes chains of white, fragrant, bee-pollinated blossoms and greenish white berries attractive to birds. The twigs, stems, and leaves carry a skin irritant called urushiol.

Silk oak (*Grevillea robusta*), a member of the protea family Proteaceae, is a tree that grows in the rainforests of Australia's Queensland. Nothing about its outward appearance suggests oaks: it has highly dissected, fernlike leaves; bright orange, bird-pollinated flowers; and papery, boat-haped seed pods. The probable reason for its name is its heavy, oaklike wood!

She oaks (*Casuarina* spp.) belong to the strange family Casuarinaceae. Casuarinas are trees and shrubs native to Australia and other adjacent islands. Casuarinas are arguably the least oaklike of the lot: their jointed green twigs bear minute, scalelike

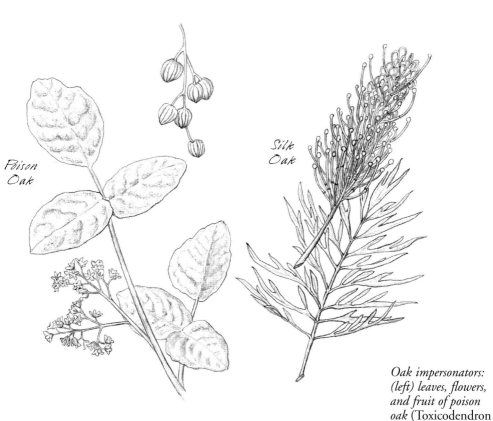

Poison
Oak

Silk
Oak

Oak impersonators:
(left) leaves, flowers,
and fruit of poison
oak (Toxicodendron
diversilobum);
(right) flowers and
leaves of silk oak
(Grevillea robusta).

leaves, and their branches resemble the plant called horsetail
(*Equisetum arvense*). The tiny male and female flowers are borne
in pine conelike structures on separate plants, and the seed pods
look like miniature pine cones that open gaping holes to shed
their seeds. She oak—also known as beefwood—is another hardwood species that shares the famed durability of oak wood.

Some so-called oaks outside the genus *Quercus,*
however, are related to them. Outstanding
among such "oaks" is the genus *Lithocarpus*
(*Litho* comes from the Greek word for stone; *car-*
pus from fruit; together, they refer to the hard
acorn shell). A single species (*Lithocarpus densiflorus*), often called
tanbark oak, grows in the Pacific Northwest. The lithocarps are
richly represented in tropical Southeast Asia by more than 100
species. So oaklike are the lithocarps, that early botanists

OAK

RELATIVES

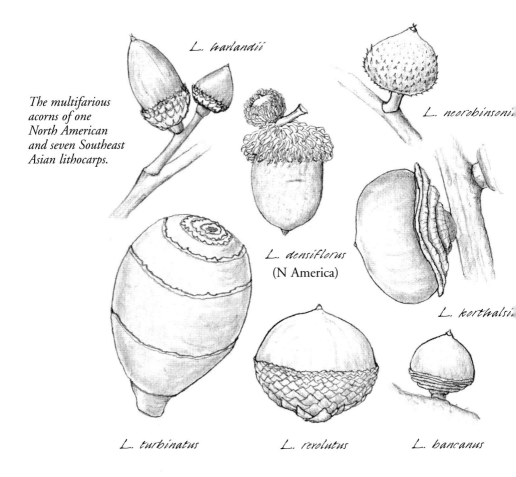

The multifarious acorns of one North American and seven Southeast Asian lithocarps.

L. harlandii

L. neorobinsoni

L. densiflorus
(N America)

L. korthalsi

L. turbinatus

L. revolutus

L. bancanus

classified many of them as species of *Quercus,* and some continue to do so to this day.

Why are lithocarps not true oaks? While true oaks always have hanging male catkins that are wind-pollinated, the catkins of lithocarps have stiff, upright male catkins that attract beetles, flies, and small bees. True oaks separate their male and female flowers, whereas lithocarps place their female flowers at the base of the male catkins so that they, too, are served by visiting pollinators. Both true oaks and lithocarps, however, bear acorns that sit in distinctive bract-covered cups. The two genera appear to be

A young tanbark oak (Lithocarpus densiflorus), *a close relative of* Quercus.

The stiff, white, insect-pollinated male catkins and associated acorns of Lithocarpus densiflorus.

very closely related, even though they consistently differ in their arrangement of flowers and modes of pollination.

Lithocarpus belongs to the chestnut subfamily Castanoideae and closely resembles other members of its subfamily because of the way they are pollinated. But they part ways with this group because of their acorn-in-a-cup fruit. Other members of the Castanoideae—chestnuts, evergreen chestnuts, and chinquapins—are distinguished by the (usually) viciously spiny, interlaced burrs that envelop the nuts, and by the nuts themselves, which are generally sweet and palatable, devoid of bitter tannins. Looking at the life cycle of a lithocarpus is like seeing the marriage of two disparate trees: chestnuts on the flowering and pollination side, and oaks on the fruiting and seed side. Although no one seems to have suggested it, it is quite plausible that at some unknown moment in the distant past, a chestnut relative and a true oak managed to exchange genes in a union that led to a whole new genus of trees, *Lithocarpus.* Another possibility is that *Lithocarpus* and *Quercus* evolved separately but developed similar-looking acorns in response to similar habitats.

To understand how fundamentally different the chestnut subfamily is from that of oaks, let's examine chestnut flowers and their mode of pollination. As with *Lithocarpus,* other chestnut relatives mix several female flowers among the usually upright white candles of male blossoms. Like the true oaks, male and female flowers are functional at different times to prevent self-pollination, but the proximity of male and female flowers draws pollinators close to both. The flowers, despite their lack of colorful petals, bear conspicuous stamens with stiff whitish filaments, and they make nectar or release powerful fragrances. This combination—white flowers and potent odors—draws in many beetles and flies. The smells may resemble semen or even dung, fragrances that achieve the desired effect of luring pollinators to the flowers.

The chestnut subfamily includes the genera *Castanopsis* (evergreen chestnuts), *Chrysolepis* (chinquapins), *Lithocarpus* (tanbark

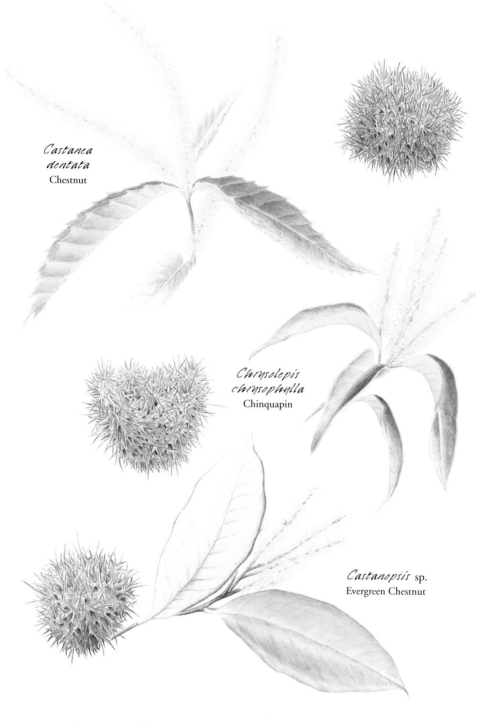

Castanea dentata
Chestnut

Chrysolepis chrysophylla
Chinquapin

Castanopsis sp.
Evergreen Chestnut

Comparison of the three genera of the chestnut subfamily (Castanoideae).

oaks), and *Castanea* (true chestnuts). The true chestnuts are
familiar and venerated trees of the temperate climes of eastern
North America, Europe, and eastern Asia. Although botanists
have steadfastly placed chestnuts in their own small genus, the
differences between *Castanea* and *Castanopsis* are relatively minor.
It's probable that the castaneas remain separate because of our
original acquaintance and enchantment with that group. After
all, the tropical evergreen *Castanopsis* species have only been well
known in European-dominated cultures for a short while.
Indeed, the generic name *Castanopsis* comes from *castanea,* Latin
for chestnut; and *opsis,* a suffix from the Greek word for
resemblance.

By far, the most diverse genus of the chestnut subfamily, next
to *Lithocarpus,* is the genus *Castanopsis,* which, for lack of a stan-
dardized common name, is best referred to as the evergreen or
tropical chestnuts. *Castanopsis* species abound in Southeast Asia,
where the lithocarps have also multiplied. In fact, the *Castanopsis*
species look very much like their lithocarps counterparts, and
many species of both groups occupy the same montane and
upland tropical forests. Often, it's only when the fruits fall to the
ground that the observer can confidently distinguish between the
two. *Castanopsis* species have evergreen leaves and bear spiny, bur-
rlike bracts around two, three, or four shiny, asymmetrical nuts.
Each nut has a rounded side and a squared off side that fits snugly against its neighbor within the burr.

Long ago, *Castanopsis* made the journey across the Bering
Strait to North America, along with *Lithocarpus* and true oaks.
Today, there are two species of these "outliers" in the montane
and coastal forests of western North America—the chinquapins,
whose name means "big fruit" in the Algonquian Indian language. Some botanists have chosen to separate these North
American chinquapins from their castanopsis brethren on the
basis of rather esoteric differences, placing them in a genus called
Chrysolepis (*Chryso* from the Greek for golden and *lepis* meaning
scale, for the golden scales on the backsides of leaves).

The only *Lithocarpus* that occurs outside of Asia grows in the same region of western North America that chinquapins do. Why have these species not ventured farther across this continent?

An approximation of the tanbark oak and chinquapin distribution between the mountains of China and Southeast Asia on the one hand and western North America on the other repeats itself in other plant groups. Probably these oak relatives migrated with many other flowers and trees across the Bering Strait's land bridge from Asia to Alaska when the earth's seas receded during one of the ice ages. As these trees moved into their new North American homeland, they were preadapted to cool, mild climates, but between their new home in the Pacific Northwest and other comparably appropriate climates (for example, the mountains of the southeastern United States and Mexico), there lie vast areas of cold desert that have been expanding over the last several thousand years—the Great Basin province of eastern Oregon, Nevada, Utah, Arizona, and southwestern Colorado. Such deserts have cut off any possibility for further migrations by chinquapins and tanbark oaks, restraining them from moving into new territory beyond North America's far west. Meanwhile, the climate north of the mild Pacific Northwest has grown increasingly cold, effectively isolating our few successful lithocarpus and castanopsis migrants and confining them to their present homes.

Lithocarps have diversified wonderfully in Southeast Asia, numbering more than 100 species, and despite the overall similarity of their tropical oaklike leaves and their universal production of white, candlelike male catkins in all species, they produce acorns of astounding variety. Lithocarpus acorn cups range from ringed bracts resembling the acorn cups of the oak subgenus *Cyclobalanopsis* to scaly cups like those of white oaks. Several species bury their acorns inside the cups, producing bracts that partially or entirely envelop the acorn. This incredible variety seems to have no plausible explanation. The lithocarp acorns of Southeast Asia are certainly not in keeping with what western North Americans consider typical for tanbark oaks!

The third subfamily in the family Fagaceae, the beech

subfamily Fagoideae, appears closely related to the Quercoideae via a series of intermediate plants often grouped under the name *Trignobalanus*. The beech subfamily consists of the familiar and much-esteemed beeches (genus *Fagus*), strong-limbed trees of the hardwood forests of Europe, eastern Asia, and eastern North America. There is currently only a handful of beech species.

The southern beeches (genus *Nothofagus*), are little known outside their homeland but are far more numerous than their northern counterparts. Southern beeches are richer in species and cover an impressive range in the southern hemisphere. The very existence of southern beeches, with their utterly unique distribution, confounds botanists and has provoked all sorts of conflicting opinions about the origin of the entire family Fagaceae. Southern beeches are found in a broad arc that starts in the rainy mountains of southern Chile and Argentina, skips across the southern Pacific Ocean to New Zealand, jumps its way up the eastern coast of Australia from Tasmania, and bursts into diverse species clusters in the rainforests of such Pacific islands as New Caledonia and New Guinea. Despite the geographical convergence of southern beeches, oaks, tanbark oaks, and evergreen chestnuts in the islands that lie between Australia and Southeast Asia, specialists question whether southern beeches originated there. They believe that southern beeches only recently reached those islands after a long migration northward. Perhaps the lineage that gave rise to southern beeches split off from the other members of the Fagaceae very early; the history of *Nothofagus* is shrouded in doubt. Wherever they occur, southern beeches dominate or codominate the hardwood forests they live in. Southern beech forests in the Southern Hemisphere are the ecological equivalent to the oak forests in the Northern Hemisphere.

Beeches and southern beeches both have small umbels or short tassels of male flowers with slender filaments, and both are wind-pollinated. A major difference between the two is that the male flowers of most beeches are in large, long-stalked, pendulous clusters, while the male flowers of southern beeches are

Nothofagus gunnii
Southern Beech

Fagus grandifolia
Beech

Comparison of the two genera of the beech subfamily (Fagoideae).

Southern beech trees (Nothofagus menziesii) in a New Zealand mountain forest.

single or in very small, upright, short-stalked clusters. Both bear separate female flowers in small clusters inside cuplike bracts covered on the outside with soft-tipped bristles. The small nuts of beeches and southern beeches are usually sweet. Although all northern beeches are deciduous, many southern beeches, especially those from the tropics, are thoroughly evergreen. All beeches and southern beeches bear similar-looking, simple, usually serrated leaves that are oval or lance-shaped.

Despite the superficial similarities between *Fagus* and

Nothofagus, microscopic examination of their pollen grains easily separates them so much that some botanists have suggested separate origins and even different families for the two.

There remains one tiny twig in the family Fagaceae, a genus called *Trigonobalanus* (no common name). (The name comes from *trigono,* meaning three-cornered, and *balanus,* meaning oak.) This genus was unknown until 1961, yet today three disparate living species are known in addition to fossil remains from North America. One species, *T. verticillata,* inhabits the hill country of peninsular Malaysia and the mountains of Borneo. A second species, *T. doichangensis,* from the mountains of Thailand,

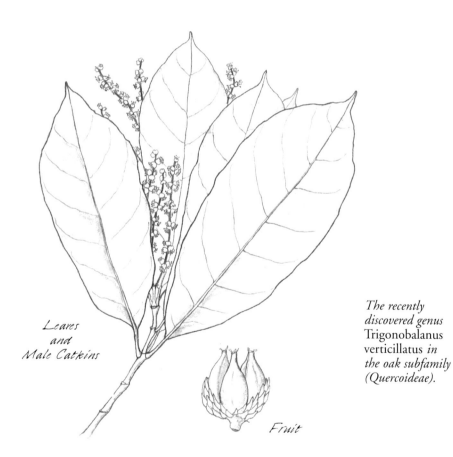

*Leares
and
Male Catkins*

Fruit

The recently discovered genus Trigonobalanus verticillatus *in the oak subfamily (*Quercoideae*).*

is now considered different enough to be placed in a new genus, *Formanodendron.* The third species, *T. excelsa,* isolated in the mountains of South America's Colombia, merits consideration for yet another genus, *Colombobalanus.*

The botanists who discovered *Trigonobalanus* describe it as a connecting link between oaks and beeches, for its wind-pollinated male catkins resemble those of true oaks, while its three-sided, acornlike fruit sits inside three scales that resemble the cuplike bracts of beeches. Does the trigonobalanus "complex" represent a series of closely related genera that once had a common homeland? Has this group diverged in ways that make it ancestral to the beech subfamily on the one hand and the genus *Quercus* on the other? According to certain fossil experts, there is evidence to suggest this scenario. The trigonobalanus group may be pivotal, showing the way evolutionary paths diverge from a group with a common ancestor from the distant past.

ORIGINS AND
EVOLUTION

n human terms, oaks are indeed ancient, for they had been on this earth for many millions of years before the first humanlike hominids appeared. But in terms of other flowering plants, oaks are relative newcomers. The oldest flower fossils extend back 135 million years (this is still relatively recent on the geological scale, since life may have first appeared as many as 3.5 billion years ago!); oak fossils arrived on the scene between 40 and 56 million years ago. But this vast timeline is approximate, for fossils are tricky to deal with, and interpretations of them remain controversial.

Plant fossils take a variety of forms. Some come from leaves that are laid down in ancient lake beds and then compressed among layers of sediments that are later turned into rock; others are remains of wood or bits of pollen, often encapsulated in coal. Still other fossils are mummified remains of plant tissue that have been preserved by immersion in peat bogs. Some fossils are even mineral deposits that gradually replaced the cells of leaves and wood as they decayed, or they are casts made by leaves or wood implanted in slowly hardening rock. Wherever they're found, fossils help us read the grand story of the evolutionary past. Eventually, we hope to find enough fossils from varied places and times that we will be able to piece together a coherent narrative of what happened in the past. At present, though, the story is far from complete, and we are forced to piece facts together like master detectives solving the world's most notorious whodunit.

Fossils are finicky things, and they don't always oblige. For starters, not all plant parts fossilize equally well. The softer parts are frequently consumed by bacteria and fungi, leaving only the wood, bark, pollen, and leaf veins intact. Complete flowers and other soft reproductive parts of fossils are rare, but since we rely heavily on flower details for classification, we're at a great loss to fill in the gaps. Some fossils have flowerlike seeds, for example, but we may never know if these seeds were associated with petals. Of course, in the case of oaks, we don't need petals, but the other soft parts of flowers—stamens, stigmas, and ovaries—are also poor candidates for preservation.

Often, a bit of a leaf will lie far from its former connection to a branch. Even the best specialists have great difficulty reconstructing whole plants from these bits and pieces, and their best assumptions remain educated guesses. Many fossils also stay deeply buried. Erosion along a stream bank or rocks revealed by a landslide may uncover a fossil bed by serendipitous chance, but we will probably never discover more than a small fraction of the fossils that exist. And for many plants, there are no fossils. The environmental conditions that allow fossilization have to be just right. Many plants have perished without leaving a trace behind.

There are two chief lines of evidence for dating fossils: geological data from the ordering of rock sequences and radioactive carbon dating. In the sequencing and dating of rock formations, the age of a particular layer of rocks can be judged by its relationship to other rock layers above or below it. Matching up different layers of rocks is like sorting out the pieces of a puzzle. When the pieces have been sorted, we can estimate age by extrapolating backwards in time from the most recent or uppermost layer. We can estimate the rate of sedimentation of the layers by measuring the rate of sedimentation taking place today. The multifaceted layers of rainbow-hued rocks from Arizona's Grand Canyon or Utah's Canyonlands vividly dramatize the enormity of the time sequences shown by these layered histories.

The process of carbon dating is more complex. Elemental carbon occurs in a stable form as well as an unstable form. The majority of the earth's carbon is stable; it doesn't change over time. But a tiny fraction is radioactive, that is, it is unstable, but it decays into a stable form over a measured period. The rate at which it changes from an unstable to stable form can be gauged very precisely. So if we measure the proportion of ordinary carbon to radioactive carbon in a fossil and compare that to a ratio found in similar material now, we can date the fossil very accurately.

How does fossil evidence illuminate the story of oaks and their relatives? Some paleobotanists insist that leaves and pollen from the family go back to the early Cretaceous, between 70 and 120 million years ago. Others insist that these fossils have been misinterpreted and that incontrovertible remains of the first Fagaceae only go back to the Paleocene, around 60 million years ago. All agree, though, that by the time fagaceous plants appeared, other flowers had exploded onto the scene in great diversity. There is little doubt that there were great pulses of evolutionary change at least twice in the history of flowering plants.

We believe now that the first pulse of evolutionary diversity brought forth most of the oldest plant families, lines that have been tried and remain true, despite their "primitive" status. Among these are the rose alliance, the magnolias, the buttercups and their cohorts, the barberries, the myrtles, the laurels, and a number of wind-pollinated trees, including maples and possibly beeches. The second wave ushered in the more "advanced" and specialized families, the flowers noted for intricate, precise design intended for specific pollinators. Among these were the ubiquitous grasses and grains, the sophisticated orchids, the multifarious composites and daisies, the intriguing snapdragons, and the fragrant mints. Although the beech line probably began during the first wave of evolution, the question remains as to precisely when the more specialized true oaks came along.

More than 200 million years ago, when the supercontinent Pangaea—the ancient, giant conglomerate that contained present-day continents—was being pulled asunder, the first flowering plants probably had not yet appeared, but the lack of obvious fossils may represent a hiatus in the fossil record. Even though Pangaea separated into a northern continental land mass, Laurasia, and a southern giant, Gondwanaland, there was still interchange between the two from time to time, and the straits that separated parts of the two supercontinents remained narrow. The first flowering plants may have lived in western Gondwanaland, where they could still readily cross those narrow straits of water, or they may have already evolved—though the fossil record doesn't show it—before Gondwanaland and Laurasia fully separated. Many of the ancient lineages of flowers either adapted or perished as climates changed with the ever-changing positions of the continents. As the continents moved, the first truly immense explosion of floral evolution began.

We can only conjecture that perhaps the fagaceous lineage had begun by then. Already Gondwanaland may have possessed the ancestors of its southern beeches (*Nothofagus*); Laurasia may have had true beeches (*Fagus*) and *Trigonobalanus*.

While Gondwanaland seems to have received only a small piece of the fagaceous empire—only the southern beeches were there at the beginning—the corner of Laurasia referred to as Malesia (tropical Southeast Asia and associated islands) became a cradle fostering many ancient flower groups. This part of Laurasia has remained rainforest for more than 100 million years, which is uncommon in the history of the earth's ecosystems. Malesia includes southern Thailand, Malaysia, Indonesia, and New Guinea. Among the well-adapted flowering plants in this ancient realm was a large chunk of the fagaceous evolutionary line, which early on diverged in several different directions. Of course,

Malesia may really represent a refuge for fagaceous plants from a time when many genera were widespread across the Northern Hemisphere. Some fossils from North America hint at this possibility.

Around 60 million years ago, another major explosion in floral diversity struck. The ancient lineages that had survived developed into a whole new array of forms. This is likely what happened to our fagaceous line, for now there were not only beeches and *Trigonobalanus,* but all sorts of new variations leading to the chestnut and oak subfamilies.

When we speak about these evolutionary explosions of flowering plants, we're speaking in relative terms about the evidence before us. Most often the fossil record is fragmentary. And fossils are also interpreted differently by different people. Fossils that were first believed to be beech or chestnut leaves may turn out to be something entirely unrelated and different. Many other hardwood trees had similar leaf shapes, and detailed studies of some of these early fossils shed doubt on the identity of these purported fagaceous fossils, because the leaf vein patterns don't really match those of living beeches or chestnuts. And even when there is a resemblance, it may lead to erroneous conclusions. Some resemblances are typical of a phenomenon known as parallel evolution, in which unrelated plants may develop similar forms in response to similar ecological situations. For example, many unrelated lines of woody plants bear palmately lobed, maplelike leaves because, like the maple, they live in moist forests. Among these maple look-alikes are sycamores (*Platanus* spp.), currants (*Ribes* spp.), and thimbleberry (*Rubus parviflorus, R. neomexicanus,* and *R. odoratus*).

Another problem with interpreting fossils is that they are often fragile. Fossilized pollen, for example, is widely subject to reinterpretation, especially when preserved grains do not reveal all of the details that fresh pollen might. (The outer sculpting of the pollen's exine is often highly abraded by long exposure to the surrounding environment.) Since pollen is frequently the only fossil remnant we have, it is hard to verify that the oldest caches of

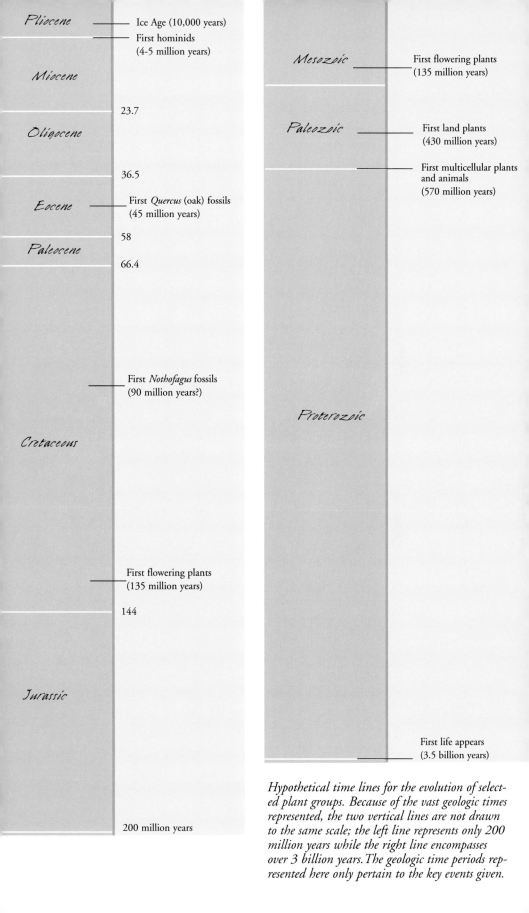

Pliocene	— Ice Age (10,000 years)
	— First hominids (4-5 million years)
Miocene	
23.7	
Oligocene	
36.5	
Eocene	— First *Quercus* (oak) fossils (45 million years)
58	
Paleocene	
66.4	

Mesozoic — First flowering plants (135 million years)

Paleozoic — First land plants (430 million years)

— First multicellular plants and animals (570 million years)

Cretaceous

— First *Nothofagus* fossils (90 million years?)

Proterozoic

— First flowering plants (135 million years)

144

Jurassic

— First life appears (3.5 billion years)

200 million years

Hypothetical time lines for the evolution of selected plant groups. Because of the vast geologic times represented, the two vertical lines are not drawn to the same scale; the left line represents only 200 million years while the right line encompasses over 3 billion years. The geologic time periods represented here only pertain to the key events given.

pollen are what they appear to be.

Different interpretations are also given to models of continental movement. As new geological evidence accrues, we're learning more about strange movements that glue pieces of continents onto distant land masses. These continental fragments, called *terranes,* are not well understood, but ultimately they may offer a far more complicated picture of the earth and its movements than was hitherto imagined. As we gain insight into land movements, we also come to understand more about plant distributions. Terranes may elucidate seemingly inexplicable distributions of families and genera, such as the current occurrences of *Trigonobalanus* in Peru, Borneo, and Thailand.

Floral evolution is another field subject to dispute. Specialists who hold different views take the same facts and interpret them very differently. Some botanists give more weight to certain floral features, for example, leading to a different basis for evaluating relationship and evolution. No sane scientist would dare say that his or her evolutionary scheme was actual fact. Instead, theories are based on carefully calculated comparisons and carefully constructed interpretations. Given enough ingenuity, a scientist can make practically any scheme sound plausible.

Nature seldom gives her creations clean, easy-to-apply boundaries. Plants are always changing, and there is no way to say precisely what defines a scarlet oak (*Quercus coccinea*) or a blackjack oak (*Q. marilandica*) from one moment to the next. Few individuals are genetically identical, so the population of scarlet, blackjack, and all other oaks changes every time an old tree dies and a new one is born. Boundaries imposed by classification can only give a rough idea of what defines any group—family, genus, or species. The more inclusive the group we define, of course, the more likely we are to succeed in defining the parameters of the group and in clearly separating that group from all others.

And so, tracing oak evolution remains fraught with problems. Such an immense group as oaks is difficult to define even in its present state; the estimate of how many species of oaks exist varies widely. But weaving together the twisted skeins of evolution—lines of evidence and some reasonable conjecture—it is possible to suggest a hypothetical scenario for oak evolution.

The triad of living species in the *Trigonobalanus* complex and the North American fossils of the group suggest that it may have once been more diverse, with some species giving rise to beeches and others to true oaks.

The earliest remains of a plant that is undeniably *Quercus* don't seem to extend as far back in time as those of southern beeches or chestnuts, so it appears that true oaks are a more recent offshoot of Fagaceae. Uncontrovertible signs of oaks occur some time in the Eocene, between 40 and 56 million years ago. From these modest beginnings, the indication that oaks had hit upon a successful design is told by their unquestionably rapid, far-reaching distribution and multiplicity of forms.

The earliest known oak fossils come from North America, yet the present-day cradle of the fagaceous diversity lies in the mountains of southern China and Southeast Asia. Most of the genera in the family occur there today. All but chinquapins, northern beeches, and true chestnuts are found in Malesia. Of these genera, *Castanopsis* and *Lithocarpus* have their species diversity centered in this region. Malesia is also the ground where the only Southern Hemisphere genus, *Nothofagus,* meets its Northern Hemisphere relatives. Nearby China also has a tremendous variety of fagaceous plants, including a still-unknown number of true oaks, lithocarps, and evergreen chestnuts along with true chestnuts and beeches. Southern China, Japan, and Malesia are the center for the unique, ring-cupped oaks of the subgenus *Cyclobalanopsis,* with its concentric, rimlike series of scales on its acorn cups. So different from other oaks is the overall appearance of these ring-cupped oaks—their broad, simple leaves are hardly oaklike and their acorn cups are highly distinctive—that they seem only distantly related to other oaks. (Some botanists separate ring-cupped oaks from all others as a subgenus, then relegate the other oaks to sections instead of subgenera.)

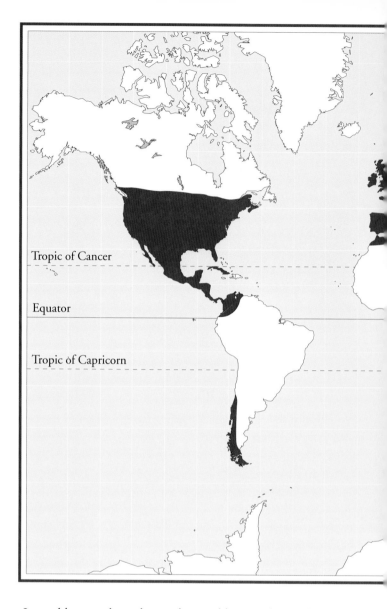

Tropic of Cancer

Equator

Tropic of Capricorn

It would seem, then, that we have a dilemma about where *Quercus* first arose. Could it be that North America was the original homeland where oaks diverged from possible trigonobal-anus-like ancestors? Perhaps China and Malesia appear to be the center of diversity simply because conditions in those regions have changed less over the past several million years than they have elsewhere. We know that extensive glaciations and drying trends in climate have caused many European and North

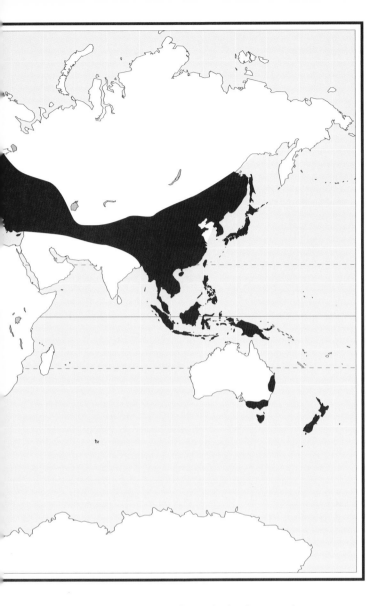

Global distribution of the beech family (Fagaceae).

American plants to vanish from the landscape.

If North America was indeed the cradle for oak evolution, oaks may have moved in several directions as they diversified. Some may have crossed the Atlantic Ocean (which was much narrower then) to arrive in Europe and the Mediterranean. Others may have crossed the periodic land bridge over the Bering Strait to spill into northern Asia and China. Many undoubtedly migrated southward into the mountains of Mexico, Central

Tropic of Cancer

Equator

Tropic of Capricorn

America, and northern South America before and during the Ice
Ages. Of course, this scheme doesn't explain the ancient diversifi-
cation of the distinctive ring-cupped oaks in Southeast Asia.
There are still many gaps to fill in the story.

The origin of at least the vast white oak group in North
America helps explain the origins of some other major groups.
For example, the black oaks probably had a white oak ancestor
and, since black oaks are exclusive to the New World, their

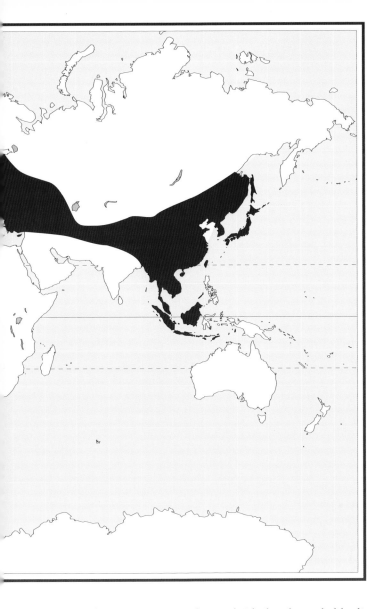

Global distribution of the oaks (Quercus).

restriction here is easier to understand. Black oaks probably diversified with the changing conditions of glaciation and drying
trends that swept across large parts of temperate North America.
Likewise, the golden oaks (*Protobalanus*) may have also arisen
from white oak ancestors that already had some black-oaklike
traits. Perhaps they splintered off from an ancient white oak line
established in the American Southwest as conditions there grew
more arid.

193

When the white oaks reached Europe and Asia Minor, some diversified in new directions. Perhaps the holly oaks were already preadapted to an arid life as tough-leaved evergreen oaks from their ancestors in the southern United States. Deciduous species similar to some from eastern North America proliferated in the temperate parts of Europe, including the English oak (*Q. robur*) and the sessile oak (*Q. petraea*). Still others assumed different forms, such as the Asian and Mediterranean Turkish oaks (*Cerris*), with their unusual life cycles, leaf vein patterns, and acorn cups.

For both black and white oaks, rapid speciation has been augmented by changing climates. Two well-documented trends in climate change over the last several million years illustrate this. First, many climates have grown more arid where uplifted mountains have created rain shadows, or where the jet stream has changed position, carrying storms to new places and leaving other places without much precipitation. The results are exemplified by the Mediterranean cork oak (*Q. suber*). Second, the building of high mountains has created new upland climates and microclimatic niches into which oaks could move. The Sierra Madre Occidental and Oriental of Mexico, California's Sierra Nevada, the mountains along the northern edge of the Mediterranean Sea, and the Himalayas of eastern Asia provide a few dramatic examples of new habitats into which the lowland species of subtropical oaks could migrate and adapt. Because many mountain-building episodes and changes in aridity have been relatively localized, oaks have evolved into clusters of related species often restricted to particular locales. Thus, we see the proliferation of black oaks such as interior live oak (*Q. wislizenii*) and coast live oak (*Q. agrifolia*) in California's arid foothills. Despite the fact that white and black oaks have widespread distribution, the particular series to which these species belong are often locally confined.

Much of this diversification has resulted from related oaks exchanging genes in the process we call hybridization. Oaks are a promiscuous lot, and many oaks do indeed exchange genes on

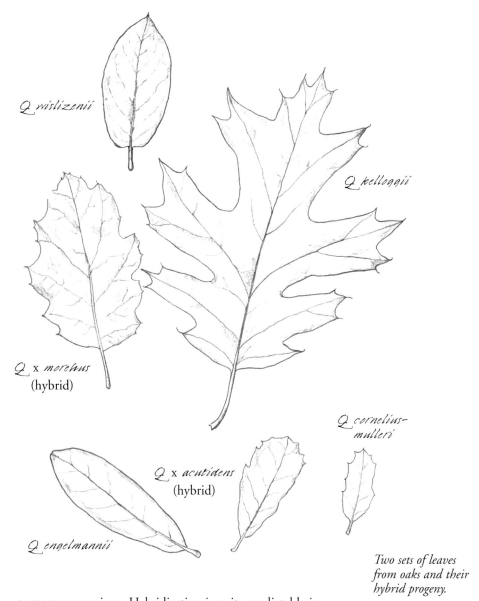

Q. wislizenii

Q. kelloggii

Q. x *morehus*
(hybrid)

Q. cornelius-mulleri

Q. x *acutidens*
(hybrid)

Q. engelmannii

*Two sets of leaves
from oaks and their
hybrid progeny.*

numerous occasions. Hybridization is quite predictable in
habitats where two different species' ranges overlap. For example,
California's blue oak (*Q. douglasii*) is common on steep, dry hills,
whereas the related valley oak (*Q. lobata*) prefers valleys with
high water tables. Along the edges of these valleys, where conditions are transitional between hilltop and valley, hybrids between
blue and valley oaks appear. These hybrid trees may combine the

bark pattern of one parent with the leaf shape of the other, which makes oak identification even more confounding.

Another example of hybridization is dramatically revealed by two very different-looking black oaks—interior live oak (*Q. wislizenii*), which has tough, evergreen, toothed leaves, and California black oak (*Q. kelloggii*), which has thin, deciduous, deeply lobed, bristle-tipped leaves. The resulting Morehus oak hybrids not only have intermediate-sized leaves with shallow lobes, but the leaves are half deciduous!

Some oak hybrids are limited in distribution and seldom reproduce themselves vigorously or abundantly. Nonetheless, there are regions where widespread and broad-based hybridization allows oaks to blur the line between species and provides a continuing source for evolution into new forms. These wide-ranging hybrids are sure to challenge the most ardent student of oak classification and provoke endless conjecture about just where species lines should be drawn. What is most interesting about this free gene exchange between species and central to our understanding of oak evolution is that species from different subgenera—white and black oaks, for example—are not known to cross.

WHERE IS OAK EVOLUTION HEADED?

Whenever a group has existed for several million years, still dominates so many niches in the earth's ecosystems, and spins off so many variations, there is little question of its evolutionary reach. If we look to oaks, we will see no end to the places where they thrive, no end to the complexities of their variation, and no end to their continued hybridization. In the botanical world, hybridization is an important fabric from which new forms are created. All of this strongly suggests that oaks are here to stay for a long while—although we need to factor in human interference in oak habitats. Oaks are seldom the profligate opportunists that weedy species are, and so, don't flourish where conditions are heavily disturbed—they cannot abide degraded soils, heavily grazed areas, or conditions of heavy pollution. We must pursue a strong conservation ethic to ensure that today's beautiful oak lands remain intact, since oaks have already lost ground in many places. When you read about oak habitats in the next section, you'll visit places where oaks still reign supreme in natural, healthy environments. What a pity it would be to lose these places to the unthinking degradations that humans impose upon the natural environment. We must not only prize the places still left but attempt to restore as much habitat that has suffered neglect and malignment as possible. We can only do this when we look at the impacts of our civilization; our dependence on certain elements of our lifestyles may affect the environment in subtle and not-so-subtle ways through mining, felling of forests, overgrazing pastures, and poisoned soils and waters.

Oak
Habitats

aks hail from areas as widely disparate as the steamy rainforests of Malaysia; the cool, piney Sierra Madre of Mexico; the hot, tropical coastal plains of Costa Rica; the dense mixed hardwood forests of China, Japan, and the eastern United States; the sunny summer-dry Mediterranean climates of foothill California and the Mediterranean basin; and the rugged high desert mountains of Texas and Arizona. That oaks can live in so many situations is testimony to how malleable they are. This chapter offers snapshot visits to diverse oak habitats around the world.

The Abundant Tropics: Visiting the Rainforests of Malaysia

Perhaps the greatest surprise is that oaks occur in the tropics, where many of us would expect trees with vividly colored blossoms. Most of the year, rainforest trees display infinitely varied shades of green, and despite the flashes of vibrant blossoms, the overriding impression is of green lushness. Malaysia's forests are no exception: from the lowland rainforests to the upland montane forests, the overall look is a solid green wall.

Since they receive plentiful rains year-round, the trees stand crown by crown and crown over crown, vying vigorously for space in the sun. The composition of this forest—once solid and unbroken from seashore to mountaintop—changes subtly from the foothills to mountain heights, despite its similar appearance from a distance. Only when you see the upper reaches—where trees become stunted atop sheer cliffs—do you realize that the montane forest is less diverse, less tall, and more intimate than the hot, steaming lowland forest. Wherever you go, oaks, tanbark oaks, and evergreen chestnuts are to be found. The middle elevations represent the best oak habitat; here, the rounded crowns of oak trees may soar to 100 feet or more, dominating the forest in company with laurels, podocarps, myrtles, tea relatives, and myrsines. The oaks are even more noticeable today than fifty years ago, for many of the giant forest dipterocarps (a distinctive family of tropical trees from Southeast Asia), which once topped 150 feet in height, have vanished to the greedy chainsaws of loggers.

Within these forests—and especially along their borders—you encounter the true exuberance of the tropics: layer upon layer of terrestrial ferns, tree ferns, and epiphytic ferns grow in the company of lush cushions of mosses, liverworts, and lichens. Punctuating the scene are the hanging trusses of brightly hued orchids, the velvety leaves and exotic flowers of gesneriads and begonias, and luminous flashes of golden impatiens. Perched higher in tree crowns are more orchids, vivid scarlet masses of tropical parasitic mistletoes, and, in the uplands, trumpets of pink, red, yellow, or white rhododendrons along with the other-worldly black, red-splotched, or green urns of tropical pitcher plants in the genus *Nepenthes*.

When you walk within a montane forest here, the impression is one of dimly-lit chaos. Trails are crisscrossed with shallow, widely diverging tree roots, and they are quickly blocked by lean-ing trunks and limbs hung with thick tapestries of mosses and ferns. By chance, a bright fleck of color from a fallen blossom may speckle the ground, or a monsoonal rain may have brought down boughs from above, adorned with orchids, ferns, and flow-ering epiphytes. Looking up, you'll see massive canopies thickly covered with crowded leaves, so that little light leaks through and the individual leaves are hard to make out. Looking at the ground, you may find old discarded leaves and fruits, though they quickly decay. Even if you do, Malaysian oaks—like most of

The view from
Mount Brinchang,
Peninsular Malaysia,
shows rugged moun-
tains clothed in lush,
evergreen cloud forest.

The showy blossoms of
an epiphytic rhododen-
dron are typical of the
colorful flowers in a
Malaysian cloud forest.

the trees here—do not have leaves that readily reveal their identity. Most rainforest trees have thick, evergreen leaves several inches long, unlobed and little toothed, whose overall shape ranges from a lance to a pointed oval. About the only way to learn that there are oaks is to look for their fruits. Often, a woody peduncle bearing clusters of acorns or old cups that held acorns will lie suspended in the leaf duff. These acorn cups vary from the familiar and comfortable scaly affairs, which most of us know from temperate climes, to cups that bear circle upon circle or rim upon rim of ringlike flutings. Of these latter, only some come from *Quercus* spp. The lithocarps here are the ones with varied acorn cups, some suggesting the scaly patterns found on the cups of temperate oaks, and others reminiscent of the ring-cupped oaks in the subgenus *Cyclobalanopsis*.

Sometimes you'll chance upon the fruits of a close oak relative—the evergreen chestnut *Castanopsis*—looking exactly like a tropical oak, except for its fruits. Evergreen chestnuts produce spiny burrs enclosing the shiny nuts. Individual seeds look just like glossy acorns, but they are flat-faced on one side—an indication that two or more seeds have shared a common space inside their protective covering.

Sometimes you'll see the crown of an old oak along a road and spy narrow white candles of male catkins decorating the tops; these are not true oaks either, but close relatives that belong to the tanbark oak genus *Lithocarpus*.

A Stroll along North Carolina's Blue Ridge Parkway

Though a montane rainforest in Malaysia and a temperate hardwood forest in the Appalachian Mountains of the southeastern United States may seem disparate, they are remarkably similar. Appalachian forests are temperate equivalents of tropical rainforests—in fact, a continuous zone of forest once joined the great tropical forests in the south with the temperate hardwood forests in the north. Shifts in rainfall pattern and heavy logging have changed this irrevocably, so that now only patches of forest are left in North America.

The spring foliage of the varied hardwood trees in the Great Smoky Mountains.

Colonies of pink moccasin flowers (Cypripedium acaule) *are one of the late-spring delights of Appalachian forests.*

Despite these similarities, there are differences between rain- and hardwood forests. Hardwood forests have seasonal changes that bring autumn color, winter bareness, and spring flushes of new leaves. And the hardwood Appalachian forests lack perched epiphytes; here, the forest floor receives enough light during winter and early spring, when the trees are leafless, that smaller plants are able to form a thick carpet.

Like their rainforest counterparts, Appalachian woods are also diverse in trees. As you stroll through, you'll be struck straight away by this diversity, for each tree here clearly bears its own stamp of identity. In this corner, the squared-off leaves with coarsely toothed sides belong to a tulip-poplar (the magnolia relative *Liriodendron tulipifera*). Close by you may see the palmately lobed leaves of a maple (*Acer* spp.); the mittenlike leaves of a sassafras (*Sassafras albidum*); the long, narrow needles of a white pine (*Pinus strobus*); the oversized, lopsided ovals of a linden (*Tilia heterophylla*); the doubly serrated, rounded leaves of a birch (*Betula* spp.); the pinnately compound, pealike leaves of a black locust (*Robinia pseudoacacia*); or the varied leaves of an oak.

The forest understory is a changing tapestry. As winter bluster turns to bursts of warm sunshine in earliest spring, new shoots push through the dense leaf mold to reach the sun. There is a mad rush, in fact, to put on new growth and unfurl flower buds before trees have filled out their canopies. All the drama of spring is compressed into a few short weeks, with a constant change in the floral pageant: shy purple violets (*Viola papilionacea*), yellow trout lilies with mottled leaves (*Erythronium americanum*), mats of fragrant, pale pink trailing arbutus (*Epigaea repens*), and pink and pin-striped white blossoms of spring beauty (*Claytonia virginiana*) are replaced by the pink-chevroned petals of painted trillium (*Trillium undulatum*), the curious, striped brown purple spathes of jack-in-the-pulpit (*Arisaema triphylla*), the white froth of foam flower (*Tiarella cordifolia*), and palest purple petals of fringed phacelia (*Phacelia fimbriata*). In turn, these give way to the stately pink moccasin flower (*Cypripedium acaule*), vivid blue violet spiderwort flowers

(*Tradescantia virginiana*), shocking red carnation-like blooms of fire pink (*Silene virginiana*), and pale pink saucers of mountain laurel (*Kalmia latifolia*).

By the end of the spring show, oaks have completed their leaf canopies, finished pollination, and are set for a long summer of photosynthesizing sugars, building acorns, and adding new wood to their trunks and branches. Although these are all deciduous oaks, there is a fascinating variety in the details of leaf shapes, from the widely scooped-out lobes of scarlet oak (*Quercus coccinea*) to the outlandish, fat, upside-down, pear shape of blackjack oak (*Q. marilandica*), and from the deeply rounded lobes of white oak (*Q. alba*) to the shallow, bristle-tipped lobes of red oak (*Q. rubra*).

Driving through Mexico's Sierra Madre Occidental

Perhaps nowhere does change in elevation reveal such dramatic variety in climate and vegetation as in Mexico's northwestern mountain spine, the Sierra Madre Occidental. You can easily experience the scope of these changes by driving a well-paved road from just south of Mazatlan over the mountain crest to the inland city of Durango. You start at sea level and ascend to 9,000 feet, passing from the wet side of the mountains that faces the Pacific Ocean to the dry, lee side turned towards Mexico's arid central plateau.

The vegetation starts as a stunted woodland of well-spaced, deciduous, spiny trees that lose their leaves during the annual drought of spring and early summer. After summer and fall rains, these trees are transformed by great flourishes of vivid, exotic blossoms. No oaks live in this zone.

As you gain altitude, the trees grow taller and closer together, but still reflect a dry-season pattern. Here, too, there is springtime deciduousness and later bursts of floral exuberance, as well as giant forms of plants we usually consider nonwoody flowers, such as tree morning glories (*Ipomoea arborea*) and tree poppies (*Bocconia* spp.), but still no oaks.

It isn't until the road climbs into the middle montane

regions, where canyons yawn as they plunge to distant river gorges, that you enter a world of thick forest. This middle region—from 3,500 feet to well over 7,000 feet—is the heart of Mexico's pine-oak forests, which cover all of Mexico's higher ranges from the Sierra Madre Oriental in the east to the southern mountain heights in the state of Chiapas, just north of the Guatemalan border.

The hushed shade of these thick forests lends the rugged mountains a softness they otherwise would not possess. Each time the road winds higher and opens to new vistas, the canyons are revealed on an even more stupendous scale. Many plunge to depths exceeding those of Arizona's renowned Grand Canyon. Their steepest walls show layer upon layer of red rock without any intervening plant cover, but the more moderate slopes wear the varied mantle of oak, pine, and fir trees. These forests are home to a greater variety of oaks and pines than any other place on earth.

The reason for this diversity can be explained by looking at the recent events of geological history: as glaciers swept down over much of North America during the last ice ages, they wiped out the diverse forests living there. Trees slowly migrated southward, ending in the uplands of Mexico's mountains, where they found a hospitable refuge. Among these trees were many kinds of pines and oaks that began a new round of evolutionary speciation fueled by the numerous varied microclimates. The oaks, in particular, diversified not once but twice—as new kinds of oaks arose, they often hybridized with other kinds, to the bewilderment of all who now attempt to sort them out. Some botanists have named hundreds of species and varieties from Mexico's mountains!

On a quiet walk through an upland forest, you'll discover all sorts of fascinating plants. Mexican oaks are hosts to many mistletoes, including those with bright scarlet flowers, and oak bark may be patterned with large clumps of epiphytic orchids and bromeliads. Underneath and along the forest edge grow assorted ferns, succulents, wildflowers, shrubs, and vines, many

A panoramic view of the canyons and mountains of Mexico's Sierra Madre Occidental, framed by a pine and an oak.

The vividly-colored, tubular flowers of cupheas are typical of the flowers that attract hummingbirds in Mexico's pine-oak forests.

with flowers of vivid, saturated colors and tubular shape, for this is prime hummingbird habitat. Because of their sheer abundance, reliable visits, and efficient pollination, hummingbirds have influenced the form of many unrelated kinds of flowers here. Among these floral jewels are the red-flowered mistletoes; the spikes of bromeliad blossoms that combine disparate blues and purples with pinks and reds; the scarlet-flowered honeysuckle and bouvardia vines draped overhead; the hanging red bells of fuchsias and orange bells of abutilons; the stiff spikes of salvia flowers in deepest purple, scarlet red, and royal blue; the dense spikes of flame-colored Indian paintbrush; and the curiously sculpted orange, red, velvety purple, and rose blossoms of the bushy cupheas.

Both the oaks and pines here break the rules for what they are supposed to look like. Some pines wear long, gracefully drooping needles (some nearly vertically hung), while oaks bear leathery, unlobed, paddle-shaped, broadly ovoid, or elliptical leaves with prominent rugose veins.

The Botanical Refuges of Oregon-California Siskiyou Mountains

The Siskiyou Mountains quietly straddle the western border between California and Oregon, tumbled between Oregon's Rogue and California's Klamath Rivers. Although these mountains seldom exceed 6,000 feet in elevation, their steep and varied topography, diverse soils, and near-inaccessibility make them an adventuresome and exciting place to visit. The Siskiyous are important because they represent an ancient refuge and meeting place of plants; they bring together elements from the mountainous forests of the Cascades and Sierra Nevada, the coastal rainforests of the Pacific Northwest, and the lowland forests of California's coastal range. Trees, shrubs, and wildflowers from all these regions grow together in strange, wonderful combinations in the Siskiyou Mountains.

Access to one of the Siskiyou's most botanically renowned areas is from the tiny town of Seiad Valley, located on the middle

Klamath River just east of Happy Camp, in California's far north. A little road runs north from Seiad Valley, climbing steeply up narrow twists and turns, skirting along cliff bases, crossing over streams and passing by waterfalls. The saddlelike summit is called Cook and Green Pass, and lies just in front of the Oregon border.

You start this journey in a typical northwestern mixed forest: immense Douglas firs (*Pseudotsuga menziesii*), old red-barked madrones (*Arbutus menziesii*), spreading multitrunked bay laurels (*Umbellularia californica*), old-growth tanbark oaks (*Lithocarpus densiflorus*), multitrunked California black oaks (*Quercus kelloggii*), and—along the river's edge—broad-canopied bigleaf maples (*Acer macrophyllum*) and soaring white alders (*Alnus rhombifolia*). This country bakes in summer heat and freezes in winter cold. As the road ascends, the higher mountains intercept the brunt of winter storms, remaining cooler in the intense summer sun. Here, you find pure stands of dense and scrawny knobcone pines (*Pinus attenuata*), fragrant coniferous forests of Douglas fir,

*The rolling mountains of the southwestern California-Oregon border are covered in lush coniferous forests. Here a line of endemic Brewer's spruce (*Picea breweriana*) graces the foreground.*

The tall spires of fragrant Washington lily (Lilium washing-tonianum) *blossoms are among the spectacular wildflowers of this remote region.*

ponderosa pine (*Pinus ponderosa*), white fir (*Abies concolor*), and incense cedar (*Calocedrus decurrens*). On the wettest, most sheltered slopes are comely stands of the endemic weeping Brewer's spruce (*Picea breweriana*). Tall oaks have nearly vanished from the forest mix, except during the second growth after a fire.

The understory of the forest is replete with acid-loving heather relatives, such as pipsissewa (*Chimaphila umbellata*), one-sided wintergreen (*Orthilia secunda*), rosebay rhododendron (*Rhododendron macrophyllum*), bilberry (*Vaccinium* spp.), black laurel (*Leucothoe davisiae*), and western azalea (*Rhododendron occidentale*) in company with beautiful lily relatives, such as bronze bells (*Stenanthium occidentale*), leopard lily (*Lilium pardalinum*), bear grass (*Xerophyllum tenax*), twisted stalk

(*Streptopus amplexifolius*), fairy bells (*Disporum hookeri*), trillium (*Trillium ovatum*), and Washington lily (*Lilium washingtonianum*).

The oaks that grow in the Siskiyou Mountains come in surprising packages. There are four different forms of shrubby, scrubby oaks: the shrub form of tanbark oak (*Lithocarpus densiflorus* var. *echinoides*), Brewer's oak (*Quercus garryana* var. *breweri*), huckleberry oak (*Q. vaccinifolia*), and Sadler's oak (*Q. sadleriana*). There are few other areas that so clearly divulge the disparate elements found here, for each oak has its own special ecological niche and its own floristic origin.

On sun-baked roadsides—places where the forest has retreated or has been cleared away—you'll find hedges of dense shrub tan oak, resembling its tree relative in flower and acorn, but with leaves devoid of sharp-toothed edges. The tough, leathery, dull green leaves are covered beneath with a thick growth of wooly hairs, reflecting tan oak's preadaptation to the rigors of full sun and quickly draining soils. Shrub tan oak is a local variety that persists in Northern California's driest mountains but is missing from the wetter, cooler forests closer to the coast, where its sister tree reigns.

Huckleberry oak likewise opts for exposed places. You see it growing out of rock shelves or between large boulders, where there is minimal space for roots to take hold and tap moisture. Huckleberry oak hunkers down in low two- or three-foot hedges covered with shiny, evergreen, huckleberry-shaped leaves that shimmer in the summer sun. The new leaves are a fetching bronzy red. Huckleberry oak typifies California's high Sierra but has wandered north into this wild, unpredictable country. Huckleberry oak belongs to the golden oak alliance.

Brewer's oak is another dwarf version of a much larger tree: the Garry or Oregon white oak (*Q. garryana*), which is a familiar sight from California's north coastal ranges all the way into Washington state. Its contorted and crooked twigs—bare in winter, pinkish in late spring when leaves unfurl, and decorated with deeply lobed leaves of a clear apple green in summer—seldom exceed five or six feet. The twisted scrubby branches may underlie larger shrubs or fringe the edge of piney forests. Brewer's oak follows the trail of its larger sister tree, but often climbs to higher places or drier sites, in company with other chaparral shrubs. Brewer's oak belongs to the white oaks.

Sadler's oak is the most remarkable of them all. An evergreen shrub with wide-reaching, horizontal branches, it scarcely grows to more than five or six feet. Sadler's oak shuns the bright sun, preferring to fringe the edges of dark forests or live as a low ground cover under coniferous trees. The leaves of this oak are reminiscent of a deep green, leathery version of an oversized chestnut, for they are uncommonly large—measuring up to six inches long—and are edged with coarse and conspicuously serrated teeth, like a sharp saw with widely spaced teeth. Sadler oak grows with rare wildflowers of the forest's shade: wintergreens (*Pyrola* spp.), woodland phlox (*Phlox adsurgens*), Siskiyou penstemon (*Penstemon anguineus*), and ghost orchid (*Cephalanthera austiniae*). Sadler's oak is not found beyond the confines of this mountainous realm; it's an indicator species for the region, with no like relatives closer than the mountains of Mexico. Although it too is a white oak, it belongs to a subsection that is rare in the United States.

California's Mediterranean: Santa Cruz Island

Lying just twenty miles south off the coast of Santa Barbara, the ruggedly mountainous ninety square miles of Santa Cruz Island are like a microcosm of a continent with a gentle Mediterranean climate, closely paralleling what you might encounter on islands in the Mediterranean Sea itself. Because the island is swathed by gentle summer fog and warmed in the winter by the surrounding ocean, it has served as a refuge for plants that have perished on the mainland, where the climate has become progressively hotter and drier during the last few million years. The island also operates as a place of evolutionary opportunism. It has remained isolated from the mainland its entire several-million-year life, with the channel separating it from the mainland as

a barrier to the migration of many species. The result is an evolutionary proving ground for those plants able to make the journey.

Here, plants live in combinations unheard of elsewhere, and
oaks play a variety of roles. Coast live oak (*Quercus agrifolia*), a
major mainland species, lines deep, well-watered canyon bottoms.
Its shade creates a home to plants that would otherwise find summer conditions overly dry: eight-foot-high, speckled, orange blossoms of Humboldt lily (*Lilium humboldtii*); festoons of scram-
bling purple fiesta flower (*Pholistoma auritum*); draperies of delicate maidenhair fern (*Adiantum jordanii*); brilliant scarlet blossoms of climbing penstemon (*Keckiella cordifolia*); and the tall
spires of golden canyon sunflower (*Venegasia carpesioides*). This
oaky refuge is also where the lovely, endemic, hummingbird-polli-
nated bush monkeyflower (*Mimulus flemingii*) resides.

By contrast, the steep, sun-washed, south-facing slopes of the
island support a quiltwork mosaic of evergreen chaparral shrubs,
including giant manzanitas (*Arctostaphylos insularis*); needle-leaved

*Graceful curves and
rugged mountains
epitomize Santa Cruz
Island's landscape.
The island is reminis-
cent of islands in the
Mediterranean Sea.*

213

Late afternoon light emphasizes the curious shapes of the endemic island scrub oak (Quercus pacifica).

chamise (*Adenostoma fasciculatum*); giant, yellow-flowered island poppy (*Dendromecon harfordii*); large-pod buckbrush (*Ceanothus megacarpus* var. *insularis*); and scrub oaks that differ from their mainland counterparts. Island scrub oak (*Quercus pacifica*) was only recently recognized as more than a variant of the mainland scrub oak (*Q. berberidifolia*). Island scrub oak has a distinctive appearance, and, instead of growing as a dense, low, multi-branched shrub, it creates miniature groves of multiple trunks with rounded crowns, resembling a liliputian forest.

Two more oak surprises await you on Santa Cruz Island. First you enter a dense, fragrant pine forest along the backbone of the wettest ridgetops, where summer fog lingers long and winter storms dump generous rains. This forest is an island version of the bishop pines that appear on California's central and northern coastal promontories. Amid these pines grows a delightful heather relative called summer holly (*Comarostaphylis diversifolia*), with vivid red berries at summer's end; a shrubby Indian paintbrush (*Castilleja lanata* spp. *hololeuca*) with wooly leaves and brilliant spikes of flame-colored flowers; and a low, sprawling ground cover oak (*Quercus parvula*) with glossy, evergreen leaves. This miniature oak does not fit the usual scrub oak profile. *Quercus parvula* looks like a semiprostrate version of interior live oak (*Q. wislizenii*) from California's hot, inland foothill country.

The second surprise hides deep in the island's narrowest coastal canyons, where summer sun penetrates for only a few hours a day and fog sweeps in off the ocean in the morning. These protected canyons harbor unique plants such as a giant version of the daintily bell-flowered island alumroot (*Heuchera maxima*); the island cherry (*Prunus ilicifolia* spp. *lyonii*), which is a large form of evergreen cherry resembling the Portuguese laurel; groves of the ferny-leaved island ironwood (*Lyonothamnus floribundus* ssp. *asplenifolius*), which is an ancient and unusual remnant of the rose alliance; and the tall spires of island oak (*Q. tomentella*). This beautiful evergreen oak looks for all the world like a close cousin of the tanbark oak, *Lithocarpus*, because its lance-ovate leaves are thick and leathery with deeply imprinted veins arranged in a herringbone pattern. But appearances are deceiving, and the hanging male catkins and acorns leave no doubt: this is a true *Quercus*, related to the Southwest's other golden oaks.

Yosemite Valley's Autumnal Wonderland: Grand Cliffs and Beautiful Trees

If you chance to visit this great national park in the fall, you'll notice the trees instead of the waterfalls. As autumn days rush into winter, ushering in the first blustery storms, a light dusting of snow hints at the changes to come. Hot Indian summer days grow short and cold at night, and signs of autumn are everywhere: California black oak (*Quercus kelloggii*) finishes coloring its yellow brown leaves, and they fall in great flurries amid the golden leaves of bigleaf maple (*Acer macrophyllum*), the crimson and orange leaves of flowering dogwood (*Cornus nuttallii*), the bronze leaves of western azalea (*Rhododendron occidentale*),

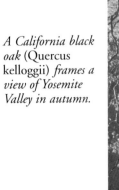

A California black oak (Quercus kelloggii) *frames a view of Yosemite Valley in autumn.*

and the fallow yellow leaves of cottonwoods and willows. Broad, open swaths of sedge- and grass-clad meadows are lined with the splendid, upswept canopies of aged black oaks. Now the deeply checkered black bark that gives them their name is evident, and the massive limbs and trunks of 200- and 300-year-old specimens are revealed in all their grandeur. The mosses and lichens they wear, revived and refreshed from gusty rains, contrast dramatically with the nearly barren bark of ponderosa pine (*Pinus ponderosa*) and incense cedar (*Calocedrus decurrens*).

Now is the time to search among the thick leaf litter for the black oak's large acorns, tucked into their shingle-scaled caps or lying separate from them. Black oak acorns were a favorite food for California's mountain Miwok Indians, who frequently burned areas such as this one to assure a healthy acorn crop.

Because of the myriad insects and fungi that infect and digest their acorns, competition for this rich food was intense. So Indians built ground fires beneath the great oaks to destroy breeding places for acorn predators and allow a full, healthy acorn crop. Fires also devoured competing saplings, keeping the forest open and parklike and giving the Native Americans easy access to the mature fruiting trees. The practice of burning not only produced a large crop of acorns for the Indians, but also assured better reproductive potential for the oaks themselves.

Today, a stroll through a pine-oak forest along the valley bottom reveals a diametrically different situation: the old stately trees are crowded with saplings of shade-tolerant incense cedar, white fir (*Abies concolor*), and myriad shrubs, offering up a scene of

Fiery colors temporarily paint flowering dogwood (Cornus nuttallii) *leaves in October before winter winds strip them from their branches.*

scraggly, unkempt undergrowth. This brush provides more fuel for wildfires and increases the likelihood that they will perish along with the big trees that grace the forest.

Which of these two situations is the natural one? Likely it is the one the Indians discovered, for they were emulating what nature was already doing. Natural brush fires were kindled by lightning every few years throughout the Sierra.

If you walk from the bottomland forests toward the valley's edge, where glaciers have dumped tons of unsorted boulders of all sizes, you come into a different vegetation, one that lacks the distinctly seasonal look at the meadow's edge. Here, at the foot of the valley's granite walls, evergreens rule. Yet these trees do not always remain the same; in spring, flushes of needles on ponderosa pine and incense cedar announce a new round of leaf production, and the stalwart, broad-leaved evergreens—bay laurel (*Umbellularia californica*) and goldcup oak (*Quercus chrysolepis*)—also put on a burst of new leaves. The goldcup oak, often the only tree on the steepest, rockiest slopes, makes leaves that flush bronze, then deepen to a luminous dark green. Their acorn crop lights up branches in fall, for the warty acorn cups wear a dense powdering of gold set off by the deep mahogany of the plump acorns.

High in the Heart of the Western Colorado Rockies

The lofty metamorphic peaks of the La Plata Mountains rise abruptly from the big sagebrush and pinyon-juniper country of the desert Southwest. These mountains wear a mosaic of upland pine, spruce, and fir forests, interlaced with beaver ponds, rushing streams, quiet lakes, aspen groves, and rocky shelves. Thick stands of ponderosa and limber pines (*Pinus ponderosa* and *P. flexilis*) seamlessly blend into Engelmann spruce (*Picea engelmannii*) and subalpine fir (*Abies lasiocarpa*) as you climb the mountain heights. Slopes that have been only recently forested still support their immense, cloned populations of quaking aspen (*Populus tremuloides*), whose shimmering, summer-green leaves turn to luminous shades of gold and amber in October.

Southwestern Colorado's Animas Valley and La Plata Mountains exemplify the rugged terrain of the western Rockies.

Lying in the arms of these forests, often on wetter ground, are vast meadows of colorful summer wildflowers: blue and white columbines (*Aquilegia caerulea*), yellow cinquefoils (*Potentilla* spp.), white and blue violets (*Viola canadensis* and *V. adunca*), green gentians (*Swertia radiatum*), vivid orange paintbrushes (*Castilleja* spp.), yellow daisylike arnicas (*Arnica* spp.), golden dandelions (*Taraxacum* sp.), and white bog orchids (*Platanthera dilatata*). Where the ground turns from deep and well-watered soil to craggy rock, the vegetation changes once again.

In the heart of these rocky outcrops are woody shrubs and low, cushiony matted plants, including a creeping manzanita known as kinnikinnick (*Arctostaphylos uva-ursi*) and the prickly-needled mat juniper (*Juniperus communis saxatilis*). When the

Thick stands of quaking aspen (Populus tremuloides) *turn luminous gold in the chill air of Colorado's October.*

rock has relented for a while and pockets of soil have formed, the first signs of tree life appear. Among the early tree pioneers is Gambel's oak (*Quercus gambelii*), which in time comes to dominate large swaths of steep, rocky slopes. Gambel's oak, as would be expected in a climate with sharply etched growing seasons, is deciduous, with the characteristic pattern of deeply lobed leaves so typical of such oaks. Gambel's oak creates an intricately interlaced network of horizontally trending branches and twigs, leafing out late in May or June, then briefly flaming russet and scarlet before shedding its leaves in October.

Despite the constancy of its foliage and acorns, Gambel's oak is a variable, changeable plant; it may assume forms that are dependent partly on genetic disposition and partly on ecological circumstances. The low, sprawling mats are common in the high mountains, but every now and then you'll unexpectedly meet a small tree and, on fertile bottomlands, a sizeable grove of trees.

The Oak Savannahs of California's Interior Foothills

A savannah is a broad expanse of open country, covered in grasslands and dotted with widely spaced trees, and the foothills that ring California's great Central Valley represent oak savannah at its best. The word *savannah* originally described the vast, open acacia thorn forests of dry tropical Africa. California's savannahs are not unlike their African counterparts in appearance and climate, for they also occur where it's brutally hot and dry one part of the year and cool and wet the other. But the kinds of plants that make up these two savannahs belong to different alliances: California's grasslands were once covered with tufted perennial bunchgrasses, and its picturesque trees remain oaks, while Africa's undergrowth consists of different kinds of perennial grasses, and acacia trees are still the mainstay.

There is also a fundamental difference in the fauna we see. Africa's savannahs are home to large mammals, including numerous kinds of predators, grazers, and browsers. California's savannahs, in the recent past, were preferred habitat for vast herds of elk and deer, both browsing mammals that were hunted by mountain lions and other predators, but they have always lacked the tall-necked browsers and the great crush of grazers that typify Africa's savannahs. Oaks have never been shaped into the flat-topped forms of Africa's acacias by the likes of giraffes, but deer certainly take their toll, greatly slowing the growth of oak saplings.

Spring is the time to take a leisurely tour through the remnants of California's oak savannahs. Following drenching winter rains, the landscape is magically transformed for a few brief weeks. Amidst verdant grasses, intertwined annual wildflowers grow and glow in varied hues of yellow, blue, and purple, which are all strong bee colors. Yellow buttercups (*Ranunculus* spp.) join blue-eyed grasses (*Sisyrinchium bellum*); magenta red maids (*Calandrinia ciliata*) mingle with golden poppies (*Eschscholzia* spp.); white popcorn flowers (*Plagiobothrys nothofulvus*) sprinkle their blossoms amid those of rose purple owl's clover (*Castilleja exserta*); and sky blue baby-blue-eyes (*Nemophila menziesii*) and royal purple larkspurs (*Delphinium* spp.) vie with goldfields (*Lasthenia californica*). Oaks quickly awaken, putting forth their golden male catkins before bursting into leaf. Oak leaves turn from palest green to blue green, deep green, or apple green, according to kind (be it blue oak, interior live oak, or valley oak, respectively). Birds sing, bees hum, and flowers waft potent perfumes across vast fields. This prosperity is brief, for soon wildflowers set seed and die or go dormant, young birds soon mature, and bees retreat underground into hidden burrows. The hot summer sun scorches the savannahs, grasses turn golden brown, and the land awaits the late fall rains. But oaks are quietly busy, with roots probing for the last bits of water, leaves slowly photosynthesizing, and acorns accumulating food stores for winter germination.

Spring carpets of golden buttercups (Ranunculus californicus) *in front of blue oaks in California's oak savannahs.*

The oaks that provide the framework for these savannahs vary according to slope and latitude. On steep hills, deciduous blue oaks (*Quercus douglasii*) dominate or share space with coast or interior live oaks (*Q. agrifolia* and *wislizenii*). On valley bottoms, majestic valley oaks (*Q. lobata*) throw out immense leafy canopies that create welcome shade below gracefully drooping branches.

Owl's clover (Castilleja exserta) *weaves rose-purple tapestries at the foot of majestic valley oaks in California's South Coast Ranges.*

Arizona's Chiricahuas: A Mountain Island in the Sonoran Desert

Tucked into Arizona's southeast corner, close by the Mexican border, the Chiricahua Mountains soar to over 9,000 feet. Encircled by a sea of desert, these mountains are an island oasis in the midst of a harsh, inhospitable environment. The abundance of all-year springs creates canyonlands that are unexpectedly lush with riparian vegetation. Giant Fremont cottonwoods (*Populus fremontii*) stand beside Arizona walnut (*Juglans major*), box elder

maple (*Acer negundo*), and Arizona sycamore (*Platanus wrightii*).
Tree limbs are softened by the ropy trusses of Arizona grape
(*Vitis arizonica*) and Virginia creeper (*Parthenocissus quinquefolia*),
and by thickets of poison ivy (*Toxicodendron radicans*). The
topography of these mountains also includes severe cliff faces and
sun-baked scree slopes; other plant communities include cool
upland pine forests and transitional woodlands adrift in an ocean
of tufted grasses.

Because the Chiricahuas provide so many habitats, they serve
as a refuge to plants, birds, reptiles, and trees that once were continuous from Mexico's Sierra Madre to Colorado's Rocky
Mountains. Here, too, oaks of several backgrounds mix in unusual associations, creating a fascinating mosaic that can't be found
anywhere else.

Ascending from the canyon bottoms, you first come to an
open woodland of multitrunked Emory oaks (*Quercus emoryi*)
and alligator juniper (*Juniperus deppeana*). The hot summer temperatures and shallow, rocky soils create an open parkland superficially reminiscent of California's oak savannahs, but with an
entirely different mix of plants. Emory oaks often grow in small
groves, surrounded by drought-adapted bunchgrasses, fishhook
cacti (*Mamillaria* spp.), prickly pear cacti (*Opuntia engelmannii*),
bear grass nolinas (*Nolina microcarpa*), sotol (*Dasylirion wheeleri*),
and agaves (*Agave* spp.). These stem and leaf succulents under-
score the environment's overall aridity.

Moving into the cooler uplands, the composition changes,
particularly on north-facing slopes, where you can find the first
remnants of Mexican-style pine-oak forests. A mix of three pines
of the yellow pine alliance—ponderosa pine (*Pinus ponderosa* var.
arizonica), Chihuahua pine (*P. chihuanana*), and long-leaf pine
(*P. leiophylla*)—create the framework of the forest, but Emory oak
is present too, joined by silver-leaf oak (*Quercus hypoleucoides*) in
a nearly continuous understory. The silver-leaf oak is predomi-
nantly a Mexican species with leathery, distinctively narrow,
lance-shaped leaves that are dark green above and silvery white
beneath. Throughout these forests, unexpected juxtapositions of

Branches of Gambel's oak (Quercus gambelii) frame the flame-colored cliffs of the Chiricahua's Cave Creek.

Daggerlike spears of maguey (Agave sp.) shoots on the rocky, sun-drenched slopes of the Chiricahua Mountains.

plants present themselves, such as moisture-loving meadowrues (*Thalictrum fendleri*) living close to droughty Schott's yucca (*Yucca schottii*), or ranks of fragrant lupines (*Lupinus* spp.) growing near agaves (*Agave* spp.) and claret-cup cacti (*Echinocereus triglochidiatus*) with their vivid red flowers. To complete the picture, flocks of raucous parrots—now being reintroduced—and Mexican jays forage for pine nuts and acorns. Acorn woodpeckers also live here.

Where volcanic tuffs cap the hilltops, the rapid runoff, exposed wind-whipped rocks, and shallow soils create a wonderland of stunted trees. Twisted, tortured, and tufted trees offer impeccable re-creations from the world of bonsai; in this habitat, Arizona cypress (*Cupressus glabra*), with its long shreds of peely bark, joins rank with miniaturized silver-leaf oak, Gambel's oak, and a truly dwarf form of goldcup oak (*Quercus chrysolepis*).

Crowning the highest mountains are parklike aisles of cool coniferous forest, dominated by ponderosa pine and a blue-needled form of the West's far-flung Douglas fir (*Pseudotsuga menziesii*). White fir (*Abies concolor*) and Engelmann spruce (*Picea engelmannii*), a Rocky Mountain species, also occur here. In these moist uplands, other trees from the Rocky Mountains, such as bigtooth maple (*Acer grandidentatum*) and Gambel's oak (*Quercus gambelii*) join company with Mexican netvein oak (*Q. rugosa*) in the understory along with colorful fields of blue lupines (*Lupinus* spp.), yellow false lupine (*Thermopsis pinetorum*), vivid scarlet paintbrushes (*Castilleja stricta*), and pale lavender blue mountain iris (*Iris missouriensis*).

Along Costa Rica's Dry Northern Pacific Coast

Our next excursion is to the Central American country of Costa Rica, where one can find habitats of tremendous diversity within a small area. Costa Rica's northern coastal plains, which lie west of a series of perfectly shaped volcanic cones, are winter-spring dry and summer-fall wet. Those two long seasons present startling contrasts. The lush-leaved trees of the wet season contrast dramatically with the barren, leafless trees of the dry season.

The encino, or Costa Rican live oak (*Quercus oleoides*), however, keeps its good-looking canopy of deep green leaves in thriving groves and open forests year-round. The encino is one of the few "tropical" American oaks that lives in the lowlands; most others keep to the cool, misty heights of cloud forests.

If you visit the province of Guanacaste at the beginning of the dry season—late January to early February—look for colorful companions to the encino's stately and timeless beauty. Then the deciduous hardwood trees announce their preparations to go dormant with a brief, showy flurry of colorful blossoms. Tabebuias (*Tabebuia* spp.) are covered with orchid pink or buttercup yellow chalice-shaped flowers brimming with nectar; mata-raton (*Gliricidia sepium*), a pea relative, is smothered in pale pink pealike blossoms; and silk-cotton tree (*Cochlospermum vitifolium*) sends out clusters of golden, saucer-shaped blooms rife with pollen. Other curious trees punctuate the forest with their own signature traits: kapoks (*Ceiba pentandra*), with their blocky thorns ascending grayish trunks, and gumbo-limbo (*Bursera*

The seasonally arid woodlands of northern Costa Rica's Pacific coast (Guanacaste province) is home to the subtropical encino (Quercus oleoides).

The four-inch golden flower saucers of the silk-cotton tree (Cochlospermum vitifolium) *provide dramatic color at the beginning of north-western Costa Rica's dry season.*

simarouba), whose boles are covered by curious, papery sheets of red and green bark.

Though it lacks exotic accoutrements, the encino carries on in the manner of its temperate counterparts, except that its flowering is brief and mercurial. Records indicate that encinos may bloom in seven months out of twelve, but different stands bloom at different times, according to subtle climatic cues that differ from locale to locale.

The encino's acorn crop ripens in just a few months (encino is a white oak) and is important food for many birds and mammals. Among the more exotic mammals it attracts are large rodents known as agoutis, piglike peccaries, and white-faced monkeys. These animals, like the acorn woodpeckers of temperate forests, take advantage of the oak's generous bounty without returning the favor by dispersing the tree's seeds. White-faced monkeys spend most of their time in tree canopies and never bury what they gather.

The encino resists fire and so survives where other trees and grasses are devastated. Conflagrations caused by humans and lightning are shaping Costa Rica's dry country more than ever, and the encino is one of this land's stalwart survivors.

In the Pine-oak Forests of Mountainous Greece

The Mediterranean Basin, which is the homeland to so many diverse human cultures, was also the cradle of many flower and tree species during the ice ages. Here, dry, hot summers and richly varied topography have accelerated the processes of adaptation and evolution. When ancient cultures began to make use of the Mediterranean's rich natural resources—especially the great cedar, fir, and oak forests that once covered so many mountainous slopes—their way of life was forever altered. The forests seemed to go on forever and offer an endless supply of wood for smelting ore, building ships, and constructing towns. From its sparkling isles to its mountain fastnesses, the Mediterranean Basin was one of the first places to suffer the effects of massive deforestation; the result was rapid, climate-changing desertification. Today, only remnants of those once-splendid forests stand as testament to what existed before.

For our visit here, we'll focus on a foothill band of still-intact forest facing the northern Adriatic Sea, in the rugged coastal mountains of Greece between sea level and 3,000 feet. Today's forest is mostly dominated by coniferous trees, especially the drought-adapted aleppo pine (*Pinus halepensis*), with its bunches of thin, wispy green needles and sturdy cones. Oaks also play a role here, appearing as trees that sometimes mix with the pines, but more often stand by themselves in localized groves. This secondary role is what remains from a time when oak woods dominated large areas.

Two oaks that are frequently found amongst the legions of pines are Kermes oak (*Quercus coccifera*), with shiny, leathery, spine-toothed leaves and acorn cups covered with conspicuously spiny, turned-down scales, and holly oak (*Q. ilex*), with similar leaves, felted with whitish hairs beneath, and acorn cups that have more ordinary scales. Both oaks may either grow into trees that resemble large hollies or be dwarfed into scrubby shrubs, depending on the environment.

Kermes and holly oaks provide us with an excellent example of parallel evolution within the multifarious genus *Quercus*. They belong to different sections of the immense white oak subgenus, yet they superficially resemble each other and oaks from similar habitats in California, such as the Palmer's oak (*Q. palmeri*) and goldcup oak (*Q. chrysolepis*), which belong to the small, distinctive New World subgenus *Protobalanus*. All four oaks make tough, shiny, spiny evergreen leaves designed to take the brunt of summer heat and drought, doing service for two or three years at a stretch.

In the understory of these pine-oak forests are fragrant-leaved shrubs that do double duty in many places, growing both in wooded and exposed habitats. Among them we see a kind of pistachio (*Pistacia lentiscus*); the renowned myrtle of the Bible (*Myrtus communis*); the madronelike strawberry tree (*Arbutus unedo*), with its peely reddish bark and colorful red strawberry-style fruits; shrubby heathers (*Erica* spp.), with their needle leaves and tiny pink bell blossoms; and the ancient and revered olive (*Olea europea*), which assumes a variety of forms, from full-fledged tree to stunted, twisted shrub.

This same array of shrubs, together with several others, compose the *maquis,* a plant community that appears on rocky hills, sometimes where soils have been eroded by deforestation. This kind of vegetation typifies all areas with a Mediterranean climate. In California and Arizona it is called *chaparral;* in South Africa's Cape Province it's known as *fynbos.* Joining the shrubs of this "elfin forest" in Greece are the same two oaks—Kermes and holly oaks—and colorful, aromatic shrublets such as rockroses (*Cistus* spp.), with their oversized, crepe-petalled white or pink flowers, and rosemary (*Rosmarinus officinalis*), with its sky-blue, mintlike blossoms.

When soils are even further degraded, plants shift from large shrubs to stunted, fragrant-leaved subshrubs, forming the

The rugged, arid slopes of Delphi, Greece. The spire-shaped trees are Italian cypress (Cupressus sempervirens).

The showy, pink, roselike blossoms of a rockrose (Cistus sp.) lend color to Greece's drab maquis vegetation.

phrygana or *garigue*. This is the natural home for colorful spring-blooming bulbs such as grape hyacinth (*Muscari* spp.), and culinary herbs, including thymes (*Thymus* spp.) and savories (*Satureja* spp.). And the Kermes oak persists here, too, as a stunted dwarf. Phrygana vegetation seldom reverts to forest, for the ecological balance of the soil has been altered in favor of these tolerant, undemanding shrublets. Here, the environment has been inextricably changed.

China's Mountains: The Mother of Gardens

The mountains of China form a nearly continuous backbone that runs from Southeast Asia to the country's northern border with Russia. Large areas receive abundant, evenly dispersed rainfall, promoting an unbroken chain of rainforests from the tropics of southern China up to the taiga at her northern extremities. The *taiga* is a boreal forest of somber hemlocks, spruces, and larches that covers vast tracts of land just south of the tundra, extending across the entire Northern Hemisphere.

No other place on earth now has this continuous connection of forest from tropical to subarctic. And these extensive forests occur where immense mountains add to the diversity, supplying myriad ecological niches. As a consequence, China is the home to a richness of woody plants—trees and shrubs alike—that is perhaps unequaled anywhere, save certain bastions of tropical diversity in the heart of Amazonia or in the jungles of New Guinea, Borneo, and Sumatra. Add to this unparalleled diversity the fact that a high proportion of these plants are eminently ornamental, and it's easy to see why China is revered as "the mother of gardens." From its mountain expanses come such familiar favorites as camellias, rhododendrons, azaleas, maples, viburnums, hydrangeas, dogwoods, and a large helping of coniferous trees.

Oaks and their relatives play prominent roles in these forests, except in the taiga or near timberline in the highest mountains. In some places, oaks grow intermingled with many other kinds of hardwood trees, both in deciduous and mixed evergreen

Mixed evergreen forest of Yunnan province shows Lithocarpus, Castanopsis, *and* Quercus.

associations; in others, they join with pines, firs, and spruces; in still others, they form nearly exclusive canopies under which other lesser woody plants live. For a glimpse into the richness and beauty of these great forests, let's look at the western foothills of the province of Hubei.

Located in rolling terrain in central China, Hubei is about equidistant from all four of China's borders—north, south, east, and west. Western Hubei is particularly noteworthy for the mixtures of trees in its forests, including some fascinating evolutionary "fossils" such as the recently discovered dawn redwood (*Metasequoia glyptostroboides*) and other little-known members of the redwood alliance, the genera *Cunninghamia* and *Cryptomeria*.

Climbing the hills above the mostly conifer-dominated flood plains, you enter a deciduous forest where two striking Chinese oaks—*Quercus variabilis* and *Q. acutissima*—live. The feeling in these forests is reminiscent of eastern North American hardwood

Bare in winter, the living fossil, dawn redwood (Metasequoia glyptostroboides), *is part of the diverse spectrum of central China's woody plants.*

forests, for many of the trees of Hubei have close relatives there. In China, you'll find hop-hornbeam (*Carpinus laxiflora*), a birch relative with inflated seed scales; sour gum (*Nyssa sinensis*), a tree with vividly colored autumn foliage; Chinese maple (*Acer davidii*), a maple whose leaves more resemble a fat willow than the archetypal maples of North America; a dogwood (*Cornus controversa*) without the showy petal-like bracts of the famed eastern dogwood; sweet gum (*Liquidambar glauca*), a tree with maplelike leaves that wear striking autumn colors; a snowbell tree (*Styrax japonicus*), with graceful, white, bell-shaped flowers; and a chestnut (*Castanea seguinii*), whose leaves and fruits recall the American chestnut (*Castanea dentata*).

Despite this seeming déjà vu, there are many trees that North Americans and Europeans would find unconventional. We see, for example, *Clerodendron mandarinorum,* a tree that belongs to the verbena alliance and has flowers resembling those exotic tropical vines; *Cercidiphyllum japonicum,* a small, graceful tree with delicately pleated leaves that belongs to a unique primitive alliance; *Ficus heteromorpha,* an unusual fig relative whose closest allies are in the tropics; and several unique, scattered evergreen conifers, including a Chinese plum yew (*Cephalotaxus fortunei*) and a Chinese version of a true yew (*Taxus chinensis*).

These forests harbor all sorts of oak relatives, including a beech (*Fagus longipetiolata*) with especially long leaf stalks, and an evergreen tan oak (*Lithocarpus viridis*).

The forests of western Hubei serve as a bridge between latitudes, combining elements from the tropic, temperate, and subarctic climes and reminding us of the unbroken band of forest that once joined the temperate hardwood forests of Asia, North America, and Europe.

aks dominate many landscapes—scrublands, woods, and forests alike—and they are inextricably linked to a staggering number of other organisms, from fungi to bacteria, birds to bears, and wasps to ants. Humans, too, have always had a strong connection to oaks. They have figured largely in our knowledge and myths. Throughout history, oaks have served as signs of permanance, eminences of hardihood, and figures of enduring beauty. They have provided food, dye, shelter, and wood for implements, furniture, and fuel. Whether you live in the uplands of Mexico, on the searing desert edge of North Africa, in the stunted juniper-pinyon forests of the southwestern United States, in the mountains of the Pacific Northwest, in the steamy rainforests of Borneo, in the denigrated hills of the Mediterranean, or in the lush temperate hardwood forests of

These Nature Conservancy volunteers are busy planting acorns to restore valley oaks' habitat at the Consumnes Nature Preserve in California's Central Valley.

eastern North America and China, you live among oaks. And oaks show no signs of stagnating; despite their ancient lineage, new hybrids are constantly cropping up in new places, as genetic combinations are tried and retried. Some of these natural, ongoing experiments will surely succeed in carrying oak evolution a step further.

But perhaps we should not blithely assume that oaks' permanence in the world's ecosystems is ensured. The onslaughts of logging, overgrazing by domesticated livestock, and overbrowsing by wild animals that have exceeded the environment's carrying capacity, along with rapidly increasing desertification and massive soil erosion, pose serious threats to oaks all over the world. We can read the story of what passed centuries ago in the Mediterranean basin, when oak forests were considered infinite

and so were felled without qualm. We can look at English litera-
ture to see how oaks have imbued that island with many myths,
including those of the famed Sherwood Forest, and see today
how few of the natural oak woods remain, because their trunks
provided sturdy ship masts. We can travel to California's foothills
and see how rapidly oaks are now disappearing to housing devel-
opments, malls, and the monocultures of orchards and vegetable
crops. Despite their cultural importance to humans, wherever we
go, oaks seem to be losing out.

There are still vast landscapes dominated by oaks: desert
mountains and expanses of chaparral carpeted with scrub oaks,
mountainous pine forests interspersed with an oak understory,
swaths of montane tropical forests where oaks were spared the
loggers' saws. But we desperately need to educate people about
the importance of preserving the trees that have shaped our world
for so long in myth, legend, and artifact. Even with the losses of
habitat and the overly aggressive appetites of browsers, oaks
remain a sturdy and vigorous offshoot from the evolutionary tree
of flowering plants. Remove the sources of destruction, and new
saplings appear once again, their acorns buried by opportunistic
squirrels and jays. Plant new oaks in places where they once
thrived, and watch them re-create woodlands of past splendor.
Encourage them in inhabited places, and gain a strong presence
of lasting beauty.

So here's to oaks and their continued successes. They will
undoubtedly outlast us all.

Fagaceae

The following is a summary of the various groups in the family Fagaceae:

Description of Fagaceae.

Monoecious trees or shrubs with buds of overlapping scales; stipules generally deciduous; leaves alternate, simple, petioled, with entire, dentate, or deeply pinnatifid margins; evergreen or deciduous; male flowers generally arranged in catkins or tassels, with a four- to eight-lobed calyx; stamens variable in number, with thin filaments, anthers opening lengthwise; female flowers in spikes, small heads, or short racemes that sometimes occur at the base of the catkins, with a four- to eight-lobed calyx that adheres to the inferior ovary; trilocular ovary (rarely six- or seven-loculed), styles equal to locules in number, ovules one or two in each locule, but all ovules abort except one; fruit a nut partly or completely enclosed by an involucre or cup of bracts; one seed per fruit, with thick, food-rich cotyledons and no endosperm.

Subfamily Fagoideae. Beech subfamily.

Genus *Fagus*. True beeches. Around fifteen species across the Northern Hemisphere except in western North America and Mexico. Deciduous trees with oval to ovate, usually serrated leaves. Male flowers borne in umbels on long slender peduncles, wind-pollinated; female flowers borne in small clusters inside four cuplike bracts with hooked appendages on the back. Fruits ripening into small, sweet (but not necessarily edible) nuts.

Genus *Nothofagus*. Southern beeches. Around forty species in the Southern Hemisphere, including South America, New Zealand, Tasmania, eastern Australia, New Caledonia, and New Guinea. Deciduous or evergreen trees and shrubs with alternate lance-shaped to ovate, usually serrated leaves. Male flowers borne singly on short stalks, wind-pollinated; female flowers borne in small clusters inside four cuplike bracts, sometimes with appendages on the back. Fruits ripening into small nuts.

Subfamily Castanoideae. Chestnut subfamily.

Genus *Castanea*. True chestnuts. Around twenty species across the Northern Hemisphere, except in western North America. Deciduous trees with alternate, usually large ovate, coarsely serrated leaves. Male flowers in stiff upright whitish catkins, insect-pollinated; female flowers usually borne near the base of the male flowers. Two large enveloping bracts, covered on the back by dense, sharp spines, surround a few female flowers. Fruits are large, angular, sweet, edible nuts.

Genus *Castanopsis*. Evergreen chestnuts. Over 100 species in Asia. Evergreen trees with alternate, simple, usually entire (untoothed) leaves. Male flowers borne in stiff upright whitish catkins, insect-pollinated; female flowers are usually produced near the base of the male flowers or mixed with them. Four large enveloping bracts, usually covered with dense spines on the back, surround a few female flowers. Fruits are angular, often edible nuts.

Genus *Chrysolepis*. Chinquapins. Two species in western North America. Evergreen shrubs or trees with alternate, simple, entire leaves, covered underneath with golden or tawny scales. Male flowers are borne in stiff upright whitish catkins, insect-pollinated; female flowers occur near the base of the male flowers. Four irregularly splitting bracts covered with dense spines on the back envelop a few female flowers. Fruits are small, angular, sweet, edible nuts.

Genus *Lithocarpus*. Tanbark oaks. Over 100 species found mainly in Southeast Asia, but one also occurs in northwestern North America. Large evergreen trees (occasionally shrubs) with tough, lance-shaped to ovate, simple leaves, sometimes coarsely serrated but often smooth-margined. Male flowers are borne in stiff upright whitish catkins, insect-pollinated; female flowers are borne near the base of the male flowers. A single acorn sits in a scaly cup. Details of cup scales vary from thin and shinglelike to bristly, or are fused together in ringlike collars. The fruit is a single, often bitter nut.

Subfamily Quercoideae. Oak subfamily.

Genus *Quercus*. True oaks. Estimates vary, but between 300 and 400 species widespread across the Northern Hemisphere, with great variety, particularly in the highlands of Mexico. Small shrubs to large evergreen or deciduous trees with variable leaves: leaves can be entire, toothed, or deeply lobed. Male flowers are borne in slender, hanging catkins, wind-pollinated; female flowers are borne along twigs singly or in small clusters, or are arrayed along slender peduncles. A single acorn sits in a cup covered with shinglelike, warty, bristly, or ringed bracts. The fruit is a single, usually bitter nut.

Genus *Trigonobalanus*. No common name. Three species restricted to Borneo, Southeast Asia, and a few adjacent islands, plus one anomalous species from Colombia. Despite overall similarities among the species, there have been recent proposals to separate each species into its own genus: *Trigonobalanus verticillata* from Malaysia and Borneo; *Formanodendron doichangensis* from Thailand; and *Colombobalanus* from Colombia. The whole group is characterized by evergreen trees with whorled or alternate leaves that are narrowly ovate with serrated margins. Male flowers are borne in catkins separate from female flowers; wind-pollinated. A three-angled acorn is borne inside a four-lobed cup of bracts covered with soft bristles. The fruit is a nut.

Glossary

Abscission layer. A layer of cells that forms where a leaf is severed from its stem.

Accessory pigment. Extra pigments found in leaves, such as carotenoids and xanthophylls, which absorb other wavelengths of sunlight and pass the energy on to chlorophyll.

Acorn. The special nut associated with oaks and tanbark oaks.

Active transport. The process of moving charged mineral ions and other substances across a living membrane. Active transport requires metabolic energy.

Adaptation. A modification of some plant part that allows the plant to function better in a certain kind of environment.

Aerobic respiration. The process of burning sugars and other foods to create energy through the use of oxygenation. Aerobic respiration tears glucose back down into the original starting components of photosynthesis: water and carbon dioxide.

Alga(e). Simple primitive plants with a rather unspecialized body plan. Most algae live in or near water. There are several major divisions of algae, according to pigmentation.

Alternation of generations. Plants have two separate generations in their life cycles: a spore-bearing generation and a gamete-producing (sperm and eggs) generation. In flowering plants, the spore-bearing generation dominates and lives a long time; the gamete-producing generation is tiny and ephemeral. (It consists of pollen grains for the male gamete-producing generation and the embryo sac for the female gamete-producing generation.) In the life cycle of cynipid wasps, a generation of female wasps that produce fertile eggs through parthenogensis alternates with a generation of male and female wasps that mate.

Anaerobic respiration. The process of burning sugars and other foods to create energy in the absence of oxygen. Anaerobic respiration doesn't completely break glucose back down into the original starting components of photosynthesis; rather, either carbon dioxide and ethyl alcohol or carbon dioxide and lactic acid are produced.

Annual ring. The juxtaposition of large vessels in spring wood next to small vessels in summer wood produces what, to the naked eye, looks like a ring. Counting annual rings gives a fairly accurate idea of a tree's age.

Anther. The hollow, pollen-producing sacs of the stamen.

Ascus (pl. asci). Elongated saclike, spore-bearing structures that line the reproductive fruiting bodies of a major group of fungi called Ascomycetes.

Bract. Any modified leaf associated with flowers. Bracts may be green and leaflike or colorful and petal-like, but they're basically below or outside the flower proper.

Bud, axillary. A bud borne in the angle between the base of the leaf and the stem.
Bud, mixed. A bud that contains both leaves and a stem as well as potential flowers.
Bud, simple. A bud that contains either potential leaves and a stem or future flowers.
Bud, terminal. A bud that is situated at the tip of a shoot.

Bundle sheath. A several-layered group of thick-walled supporting cells that surround major veins and the midrib of leaves.

By-products. Substances produced as a result of some important metabolic process but seemingly without obvious function themselves.

Calyx. The collective term for all the sepals of a flower.

Cambium. A layer or layers of dividing cells that add to the girth of a tree.
Cambium, cork. A series of arcs or a cylinder producing cork and cork parenchyma in the bark of trees.
Cambium, vascular. A thin cylinder of cells that produces wood (xylem) to the inside and phloem to the outside in trees. The vascular cambium lies between the bark and wood.

Carbon dating. The process of comparing the ratio of radioactive and ordinary carbon in a substance to determine its age.

Carotenoids. Yellow or orangish pigments that occur in leaves and sometimes in fruits. Carotenoids make carrots orange and bell peppers red.

Catkin. A chainlike arrangement of many tiny, petal-less greenish or brownish flowers.

Chaparral. A thick growth of evergreen, drought-tolerant shrubs typical of hot rocky slopes in California.

Chromosome. A more or less rod-shaped structure that carries an organism's hereditary material.

Chlorophyll. A green pigment in leaves and stems that traps the sun's energy and converts it into chemical energy in order to power photosynthesis.

Chloroplasts. The microscopic green bodies inside leaf cells that contain chlorophyll and carry on photosynthesis.

Class. A major group of plants under division. The flowering plants are differentiated into two major classes: the monocots (Monocotyledonae) and the dicots (Dicotyledonae).

Cohesion-tension. The tendency of water molecules to cling together to form a column that under tension, can be pulled high through the vessels of the tree's wood.

Compound. A leaf that is divided into two or more separate parts (leaflets). Oaks do not produce compound leaves, but peas, beans, and ash trees do.

Conch. Shelf fungus whose fruiting body is tough and woody and lasts for many years, forming conspicuous growths on dead or dying trees.

Conidium (pl. conidia). Tiny, sporelike body that some parasitic fungi bud off in chains. Conidia grow directly into more fungi just like the strands that produced them.

Coppicing. The practice of cutting shrubs and trees back severely to encourage straight stump sprouts to grow from the base.

Cork. Thick, waxy dead cells that form the bulk of bark in trees.

Cork parenchyma. Delicate living cells that occur between layers of cork in the bark of shrubs and trees.

Corolla. The collective term for petals of a flower.

Cortex. The soft tissue between the vascular tissue and epidermis of roots and stems.

Cotyledons. The first leaves of a seedling. Cotyledons usually look quite different from the other leaves. Sometimes, as in the case of oaks, cotyledons don't emerge from the seed at all.

Crustose. Lichens that grow as a dense, close crust on tree bark and rocks. Many crustose lichens are brightly colored.

Cuticle. The waxy layer secreted on the outside of epidermal cells to protect internal tissues from drying out.

Damping off. Fungi that flourish in damp situations and invade a seedling's vascular tissue, thereby bringing about its death.

Deciduous. Plants that lose their leaves all at once, usually at one particular time of the year.

Dehiscence. The opening of a structure, such as the dehiscence of anthers or seed pods.

Dendrochronology. The science of dating trees by studying annual rings.

Dentate. Teeth along the margins of leaves that point outward.

Division. The most inclusive groups of plants, comparable to the term phylum in zoology. The flowering plants are sometimes considered to be a division, although not all botanists agree on this.

Double fertilization. Special kind of fertilization found in flowering plants where one sperm fuses with the egg, the other with the two polar nuclei.

Drip tip. Narrowly tapered, pointed, turned down tips of leaves that channel water from the leaf surface away from the leaf.

Ectomycorrhizae. Relationships of roots and mycorrhizal fungi that are highly specialized. The fungal strands are mostly restricted to the outer layer of roots.

Egg. Special nucleus in the embryo sac with which a sperm from the pollen tube fuses in the process of fertilization.

Embryo. The young plant in miniature, enclosed inside the seed.

Embryo sac. A microscopic sac that produces the egg nucleus and a few other nuclei inside the ovule of flowering plants. Technically, the embryo sac is a highly reduced, female, gamete-bearing plantlet.

Endine. The inner layer of the wall around each pollen grain.

Endodermis. A cylindrical ring of cells surrounding the core of the root's vascular tissue. The endodermis regulates water pressure in the root.

Endosperm. The nutritive tissue that surrounds the embryo in the seeds of many flowering plants. Oak endosperm is digested by the cotyledons, which then store food for the developing embryo.

Entire. Leaves that have no lobes or teeth along their margins.

Epicotyl. The growing tip of the embryo. This growing tip ultimately produces the entire above-ground shoot system that eventually becomes the trunk, branches, and leaves of the mature oak tree.

Epidermis. The outer skinlike covering of leaves, stems, and roots.

Epiphytes. Plants that grow on tree branches to obtain light and avoid competition. Epiphytes do not harm their hosts the way parasites do.

Evergreen. Plants that retain at least some leaves at all times. Evergreen leaves do not last forever; however, they're gradually replaced over two to five years' time.

Exine. The outer waxy covering of pollen grains.

Family. A category containing one or more genera of plants that show several traits in common. A family is most often the highest "natural" category of classification and is often as intuitive as it is concrete.

Fertilization. The union of a sperm and egg, restoring the original chromosome number of a plant.

Fibers. Long, narrow, tapered cells with thick lignin-containing walls that give tissues strength and durability.

Filament. The stalklike portion of the stamen. It positions the anther in the right place for effective pollination.

Foliose. Lichens that look like flattened ribbons or thin blades. Foliose lichens usually have a differently colored bottom surface as compared to the upper surface, and are anchored by thin, hairlike rhizoids to the rocks or bark they grow on.

Fox fire. The glow produced by rhizomorphs containing the oak root fungus *Armillariella mellea*.

Fruit. The ripe ovary of flowering plants, regardless of edibility. Fruits can be papery seed pods, fleshy berries, or in the case of oaks, tough-shelled nuts.

Fruticose. Lichens that resemble twiggy shrubs or densely branched lacelike patterns.

Fynbos. The Afrikaans term for South Africa's chaparral.

Gall. A tumorlike growth that is made after an egg laid in plant tissues hatches. Something in the hatching larva reprograms the plant tissues around it to grow into the gall.

Garigue. The term used for the chaparral-like shrub communities common on hot, rocky slopes of the Mediterranean basin.

Genus (pl. genera). The next major category under family. Most families have more than a single genus. Each genus has a suite of features that separates it from related genera. Thus, oaks, chestnuts, chinquapins, and beeches are each in a separate genus although they all belong to the same family, Fagaceae.

Germination. The process of a seedling growing from a seed. A seed has germinated when the root of the embryo has pushed through the seed coat.

Glucose. A simple six-carbon sugar produced as the main end product of photosynthesis. Glucose can be converted into many other substances, stored for later use, or broken down again to yield energy.

Gradients. Changes in concentration of molecules from one area to another. The denser the molecules in a given area, the more likely they are to move to an area of sparser concentration.

Guard cells. Pairs of cells in the leaf's epidermis that swell or shrink to open or close a stomate.

Hardwood. Trees with relatively hard wood, typical of flowering plants, such as ashes, maples, sycamores, willows, cottonwoods, chestnuts, and oaks. Hardwoods usually have vessels to transport the water in their wood, and fibers to give structural rigidity. Softwoods, by contrast, have tracheids to transport water and lack specialized fibers.

Haustorium. The protuberance of a parasite, such as mistletoe, which enters into the host tissues to obtain water and food.

Heartwood. The inner layers of wood that fill with substances that block the movement of water. Heartwood is generally darker in color than the functional sapwood outside of it.

Herb. A plant that lacks bark and wood.

Hormones. Chemical substances that act on or affect some process away from the area in which they're produced. In other words, hormones have to be carried to the place where they function.

Hyphae. Tubular growths of the main fungus body. Hyphae are usually hidden inside whatever the fungus is growing on—bark, wood, or leaf.

Hypocotyl. The part of the embryo plant between the epicotyl and root (radicle) and responsible for the stem of the new seedling up to the cotyledons.

Inferior (ovary). The ovary of the flower is situated below all the other flower parts: sepals, petals, and stamens.

Involucre. A row of bracts enveloping a cluster of flowers or fruits. In the beech family, there is a spiny involucre surrounding the nuts of the chestnut, for example.

Ion. An atom or molecule that carries a negative or positive charge. Many mineral nutrients that plant roots absorb are ionic.

Isoprene. A hydrocarbon substance sometimes produced as a by-product from oak and other tree leaves and contributing to the problem of smog.

Keystone species. An all-important species in a given ecosystem, on which numerous other plants and animals depend and interact.

Leaf primordia. Tiny preformed leaves inside vegetative buds.

Leaflet. The individual segments of a compound leaf. For example, in roses, each leaf is divided in pinnate fashion into several serrated leaflets.

Lenticel. Porelike openings in the young bark of tree and shrub twigs through which the twigs breathe.

Lichen. A compound organism consisting of a fungal body inside which live green algae or blue-green bacteria. The two organisms function as a single entity: the fungus provides a safe home for the algal partner and absorbs water and mineral nutrients; the alga or blue-green bacterium photosynthesizes, producing food for both.

Lignin. A complex carbohydrate substance that gives woodiness to cell walls.

Lobed. Shallow to deep indentations in a leaf's margin.

Locule. The chamber inside a flower's ovary.

Malesia. A region encompassing the East Indies and adjacent mainland Southeastern Asia, including Malaysia, Indonesia, New Guinea, and southern Thailand.

Maquis. The name for the plant community of dense evergreen shrubs adapted to the Mediterranean region. Similar in overall appearance and adaptation to western North America's chaparral.

Mast. An oak's bountiful production of acorns.

Megaspore mother cell. The cell inside each ovule that divides by meiosis to produce four megaspores.

Meiosis. A kind of cell division that creates four daughter cells from an original single cell and, in the process, reduces the number of chromosomes from two complete sets (diploid) to one complete set (haploid).

Meristem, apical. Area of active cell division at the tip of each shoot or branch.

Meristem, root. Area of active cell division near the tip of each root or rootlet.

Micropyle. The minute canal at the end of the ovule that leads into the embryo sac.

Midrib. The main vein and accompanying tissues that run down the middle of each leaf.

Mistletoe. A group of parasitic flowering plants belonging to the family Loranthaceae (Viscaceae), many of which live in tree crowns and produce fleshy berries.

Mixed buds. Buds that contain new shoots and preformed flowers.

Monoecious. Where male and female flowers are both borne on the same plant. Oak trees are monoecious.

Mutation. A change in the genetic code of the cell's DNA. Most mutations are harmful.

Mycorrhizae. Mutualistic relationship between roots of plants and certain fungi. The fungus provides water and mineral nutrients to the plant roots; the roots give the fungus sugars.

Nectar. A sugary solution used to attract and reward pollinators that visit flowers.

Nectar guide. Patterns of lines or spots on petals that lead pollinators toward the source of nectar.

New World. The Americas: North, Central, and South.

Nitrogen fixers. Bacteria that convert nitrogen into a form that plant roots can use. Some bacteria make ammonia available, while others produce nitrates.

Nut. A large, single-seeded fruit with a hard shell and a seed filled with rich food stores. Oak acorns qualify as nuts, as do also filberts, chestnuts, and coconuts.

Old World. Europe, Africa, and Asia.

Order. A group of related plant families. For example, the order Liliales consists of the lily family (Liliaceae), the amaryllis family (Amaryllidaceae), and the iris family (Iridaceae).

Ovary. The saclike structure at the base of a flower's pistil. It contains the ovules, or future seeds. The ripe ovary becomes the fruit, with seeds inside.

Ovule. The tiny egglike structures inside the ovary that later become seeds.

Palisade parenchyma. Columnar, vertically arranged cells in the upper half of a leaf which contain numerous chloroplasts and are the main area where photosynthesis takes place.

Parasite. An organism which lives off another living plant or animal.

Parenchyma. Unspecialized cells that are living when mature. Parenchyma cells occur in a variety of tissues in roots, stems, and leaves, and carry out a variety of functions, including food storage, general metabolism, and production of pigments and nectar. Kinds of parenchyma include cork, spongy, and palisade parenchyma.

Parthenogenesis. Eggs which develop into new organisms without fertilization. Many insects produce parthenogenetic eggs in their life cycles, including certain parts of the cynipid wasp life cycle involved in forming oak galls.

Passive diffusion. Where water and other molecules pass across membranes without the expenditure of cellular energy.

Peduncles. The stalks to which flowers are attached.

Pericycle. A thin cylinder of cells just inside the root's endodermis which are responsible for initiating branch roots.

Petal. The (usually) colored parts of a flower, responsible for attracting pollinators to the flower.

Petiole. The stalk of a leaf. Some leaves may be sessile—that is, they may lack a petiole.

pH. The logarithmic scale that measures the acidity, neutrality, or alkalinity of soils. In chemical terms, pH measures the concentration of hydrogen ions (on the acid side) or hydroxyl ions (on the alkaline side). A soil with a perfectly neutral pH is rated at seven. Lower values are increasingly acidic; higher values are increasingly alkaline.

Phloem. The part of the vascular system that carries food throughout the plant. Phloem consists in large part of long, tubular cells called sieve tube members.

Photosynthesis. The process of combining carbon dioxide and water in the presence of sunlight and chlorophyll to produce glucose and oxygen.

Phrygana. The European name for scrub vegetation that consists of low, often fragrant-leaved bushes and shrublets in the Mediterranean region.

Phyllotaxy. The spatial arrangement of leaves on their twig.

Phytochromes. Special leaf pigments that are sensitive to red and far red light and are involved in initiating flowering according to day length.

Pinnate. The featherlike arrangement of veins, leaflets, or leaf lobes.

Pistil. The female part of a flower. Each pistil consists of an ovary with ovules inside, a style, and a stigma.

Polar nuclei. Two of the nuclei inside an embryo sac. Polar nuclei eventually fuse with a sperm to produce a nutritive tissue called endosperm, which will nourish a seed's embryo plant.

Pollen. The microscopic, sporelike male cells that carry the potential to grow pollen tubes and sperm after arriving at the pistil of the flower. Pollen is produced inside the stamen's anther sacs.

Pollen mother cells. Cells inside anthers that divide by meiosis to produce pollen grains.

Pollen tube. The tube which grows from a pollen grain, boring its way down the style into the ovary and to an ovule there. The pollen tube delivers two sperm to the embryo sac inside each ovule.

Pollination. The process of transferring pollen from the stamen to the stigma.

Preadaptation. Some trait which has appeared by chance, without special adaptive value. Such a trait may, however, become useful if environmental or climatic conditions should change.

Radicle. The future root end of the embryo inside a seed.

Rhizoid. Hairs that anchor mosses, liverworts, and lichens to bark or soil and absorb water and minerals.

Rhizome. A modified horizontal stem which grows near the surface of or beneath the soil.

Rhizomorph. The structure the fungus *Armillariella mellea* produces in oak roots.

Ring porous. A pattern in wood, where rings of large diameter vessels contrast strikingly with rows of small diameter vessels. The large vessels represent spring growth; the small vessels, summer growth. Oaks are noted for this pattern in their wood.

Root cap. A protective jacket over the delicate root meristem cells at the very tip of each root.

Root hairs. Fuzzy protuberances from the root's epidermis that absorb water and minerals from the soil.

Root pressure. A pressure produced by a difference in osmotic concentrations of salts, causing water to move into the root's xylem.

Saprophyte. Organisms that live off dead remains of animals and plants.

Sapwood. The outer layers of a tree's wood that carry the water and minerals upward.

Scales. Fishscale-shaped appendages that cover acorn cups and buds.

Sclereids. Tough, thick-walled cells reinforced with lignin that give body and strength to plant tissues.

Secondary compounds. Organic substances that are not the primary components of cells or parts of cells.

Section. A group of closely related species. In *Quercus*, subgenera are subdivided into series, which are, in turn, subdivided into sections.

Seed. The ovule after fertilization, consisting of a seed coat and embryo.

Semipermeable membranes. Living membranes that control the flow of various substances across them. Water usually can pass freely in either direction, but various mineral ions and larger molecules are selectively allowed to pass one way or the other.

Sepal. The outermost part of a flower, usually green and protective in function.

Series. The subgenera of oaks and other large genera are further subdivided into smaller units called series. For example, the white oaks consist of numerous series such as the *Prinus* oaks of eastern North America and the *Cerris* oaks of the Mediterranean region.

Serrate. Sawtooth-like edges on a leaf's margin.

Shelf fungi. Fungi whose fruiting bodies resemble flattened rounded shelves that extend out from logs or tree trunks. Many shelf fungi are destructive, feeding on tree wood or bark.

Sieve tube members. The long cylinder-shaped cells of the phloem that transport sugars and other foods throughout the plant.

Simple (leaf). A leaf which is not divided into more than one piece.

Species. The basic unit of classification, corresponding more or less to the mundane word "kind." For example, there are many different species of oaks within the genus *Quercus.*

Spongy parenchyma. Thin-walled, chlorophyll-containing cells in the lower half of leaves, with convoluted air chambers and passageways between them.

Spore. Microscopic cells which grow into new plants directly. Spores are not involved directly in the process of fertilization, as eggs and sperm are.

Stamen. The male part of a flower, consisting of a stalk and anther sac. The anther contains the male pollen grains.

Stellate. A starlike pattern of hairs, best seen under a hand lens or low-power microscope.

Stigma. The tip of the flower's pistil. Usually the stigma is fuzzy or sticky, in order to receive pollen grains from the stamens.

Stipules. Little leaflike appendages arranged in pairs at the base of a leaf. Some plant leaves have no stipules; others, like oaks, have inconspicuous stipules; still others, like geraniums, have obvious, permanent stipules.

Stomates. The openings in the leaf's epidermis through which carbon dioxide enters the leaf, and oxygen and water leave it.

Style. The slender stalk of the pistil that extends upward from the ovary. The style is capped by one or more stigmas.

Subfamily. The major divisions of a plant family. In the beech family Fagaceae, three subfamilies are recognized: Castanoideae (chestnut subfamily), Fagoideae (beech subfamily), and Quercoideae (oak subfamily).

Subgenera. The major subdivisions of a genus. In the oak genus *Quercus,* four subgenera are recognized: *Quercus* (white oaks), *Erythrobalanus* (black oaks), *Protobalanus* (golden oaks), and *Cyclobalanopsis* (ring-cupped oaks).

Subspecies. The major subdivisions under species. Some species don't have recognizable subspecies, while other species are so variable that they do.

Taiga. The hemlock-larch forests of the far north, generally forming a continuous band around the Northern Hemisphere just south of the tundra.

Tannin. Phenolic compounds with a bitter taste which inhibit fungi in large quantity and deter browsers and munchers in smaller quantity.

Taxonomy. The science of classifying and naming plants and animals.

Terrane. Sections of earth and rocks that somehow get glued to continental land masses from distant origins.

Testa. The seed coat or outer wrapping of a seed.

Tracheid. Water-conducting cells that are long, narrow, with tapered end walls. Tracheids are usually less efficient at moving water than are vessels.

Transpiration. The evaporation of water from leaf surfaces.

Tyloses. Penetrations of bulging wood parenchyma cells into vessels of an oak's wood.

Umbel. Arrangement of flowers where the flower-bearing stalks form a spokelike pattern.

Variety. Variations within a species. Variety has a number of different definitions and so is difficult to pin down. Horticulturists use the term in less precise ways than do botanists.

Vascular cambium. The thin cylinder of dividing cells in tree trunks and branches that add to their girth. Vascular cambium produces new wood to the inside and new phloem to the outside.

Vascular rays. Wedgelike groups of horizontal cells in the inner bark and wood. Vascular rays move water sideways.

Vascular tissue. Tissues involved with the transport of food and water in plants. There are two kinds of vascular tissue: phloem carries food in its sieve tubes, and xylem (wood) carries water and minerals in its vessels or tracheids.

Vegetative reproduction. Reproduction by roots, stems, or leaves. This kind of reproduction doesn't involve flowers or seeds and faithfully propagates the original plant's genetic material.

Vein. The vascular tissue in leaves.

Verrucate. A pimply surface or texture. Oak pollen grains have a slightly verrucate exine.

Vessel. Efficient, thick-walled, squatly tubular cells in the wood that carry water.

Wood. Also known as secondary xylem. Wood is what accumulates in large quantity in old trees and is where the water-carrying vessels are located. There are other kinds of cells in wood as well, such as vascular rays and fibers.

Xanthophylls. Brownish or reddish pigments in leaves.

Xylem. The part of the vascular system that carries water. See wood for a more complete definition.

Zone of elongation. Region of the root just above the root mersitem where cells are lengthening and developing into their mature form.

Zone of maturation. Region of the root where the cells have reached their maximum size and have assumed their mature form.

Index

A

Abies concolor 210, 217, 226
  lasiocarpa 218
abscission layer 77
abutilon 208
ac 11, 124
accessory pigments 75
Acer davidii 234
  grandidentatum 226
  macrophyllum 209, 215
  negundo 224
  species 204
acorn 127, 152, 173
  burial 105, 134 137, 140
  cups 125, 160, 162–63, 172, 177
  development 105, 124, 125
  dispersal 128, 134
  features 125, 126
  germination 105, 141–42, 143
  nutrition 129, 130
  predation 131, 133, 135, 138–40
  ripening time 125–26
  shell structure 126, 164
acorns and Native Americans 130, 217
Acraspis erinacei 90
active transport 25
Adenostoma fasciculatum 214
Adiantum jordanii 213
Adriatic Sea 229
agave 224, 225
Agave spp. 224, 225
agouti 82, 135, 228
alder, white 209
algae 50, 55–56
  green 56
Alnus rhombifolia 209
alternation of generations in galls 90
alumroot, island 215
ammonia 30
Anacardiaceae 170
Andricus californicus 93
annual rings 40–41, 42

anther 100, 101, 104, 108, 110, 111, 115
Anthophyta 149
ants 94, 132, 140
Aquilegia caerulea 219
Arbutus arizonica 48
  jalapensis 48
  menziesii 48, 209
  unedo 230
Arctostaphylos insularis 213
  species 48
  uva-ursi 219
Arisaema triphylla 204
Arizona 223–26
Armillariella mellea 32–33
arnica 219
Arnica species 219
ascus (asci) 55
aspen, quaking 218, 220
Asplenium nidus 53
ATP 61, 62
azalea 210, 215, 232

B

bacteria, blue-green 56
  nitrogen fixing 30
bark 39, 42, 46, 48
  color 46, 157
  diversity 158–59
  mature 47
  pattern 160
  structure 45, 46
  young 47
Basidiomycetes 26
bay laurel 209
bear grass 210
  nolina 224
bears 132
beech 151, 178, 179, 185, 235, 238
  family 150, 167, 190–91,
  southern 151, 167, 178, 179, 180, 185, 238–39
  subfamily 150, 167, 177–78, 238
bees 94, 100

Betula species 204
birch 204
blue-eyed grass 221
Blue Ridge Parkway 202–5
boars, wild 137
Bocconia species 205
bolete, king 27
Boletus edulis 26-28
bouvardia 208
bract 116,117, 125
bromeliad 53, 54, 206, 208
bronze bells 210
Bucculatrix albertellia 80
buckbrush, large-pod 214
bud scales 72, 73
buds 71–73, 104–5
  axillary 72, 79, 80, 107, 117, 119
  flower 119
  mixed 106, 107, 109
  terminal 79, 107, 109
  vegetative 72, 73
bundle sheath 63, 80
Bursera simarouba 48, 227
buttercup 221, 222
butterfly, purple hairstreak 81
by-products 42, 95

C

cactus, claret-cup 226
  fishhook 224
  prickly pear 224
Calandrinia ciliata 221
California 208–18
  oak savannah 221–23
Calocedrus decurrens 48, 210, 216
calyx 100, 101
Cameraria agrifoliella 80
carbon dating 184
carbon dioxide 60, 62, 64
carotenoids 76
Carpinus laxiflora 234
Castanea 150, 151, 167, 176, 239
  dentata 175, 235
  seguinii 235
Castanoideae 150, 151, 167, 174, 175, 239–40

Castanopsis 151, 174, 176, 189, 202, 233, 239
  species 167, 175, 176
Castilleja exserta 221, 223
  stricta 226
Casuarina species 170–71
Casuarinaceae 170
catkin
  male 104, 106, 107, 109, 110, 111, 173, 181
  structure 107
cattle 82, 135, 136
Ceanothus megacarpus var. *insularis* 214
cedar, incense 48, 210, 216, 217, 218
  red 48
Ceiba pentandra 227
cellulose 39–40
centipede 140
cêpe 26–28
Cephalanthera austiniae 212
Cephalotaxus fortunei 235
Cercidiphyllum japonicum 235
Cerris 164, 194
chamise 214
chaparral 213
chêne 11
cherry, island 215
chestnut 151, 175, 176, 235, 239
  American 235
  evergreen 151, 167, 174, 175, 176, 202, 239
  subfamily 150, 167, 174–77, 239
  tropical 176
chicken of the woods 44
Chimaphila umbellata 210
China 189, 232–35
chinquapin 151, 167, 174, 175, 176, 239
Chiricahua Mountains 223–26
chlorophyll 61, 70, 75
Chlorophyta 56
chloroplast 61, 64
chromosome 108, 124
Chrysolepis 151, 174, 176–77, 239
  species 167
cinquefoil 219
Cistus species 230, 231
class 150
Claytonia virginiana 204
Clerodendron mandarinorum 235
cocoons 80, 81
Cochlospermum vitifolium 227, 228

cohesion-tension 37
Colorado Rockies 218–220
columbines 219
Comarostaphylis diversifolia 214
conch 43–44
  artist's 44
conidia 81, 82
convection currents 114
Cook and Green Pass 209
coppicing 44–45
cork 39, 41
  cambium 41, 46
  parenchyma 39, 41, 46
Cornus controversa 234
  nuttallii 215, 217
corolla 100, 101
cortex 23, 24
Corvids 132
Costa Rica 58, 226–29
cottonwood, Fremont 223
cotyledon 124, 126, 127, 142
Cretaceous 187
Cryptomeria 233
Cunninghamia 233
cuphea 207, 208
Cupressus glabra 226
Curculio proboscideus 138, 139
currant 186
cuticl 62, 69
Cyanobacteria 56
Cyclobalanopsis 150, 166, 167, 169, 189, 202
cynipid wasps 84, 85–87
Cynipidae 84
cypress, Arizona 226
Cypripedium acaule 203, 204

D

Daedalia quercina 44
dandelion 219
Dasylirion wheeleri 224
deciduousness 67–68
deer 82–83, 135, 136, 221
Delphinium species 222
dendrochronology 40
Dendromecon harfordii 214
Disporum hookeri 211
division 149
dogwood 232, 234
  flowering 215, 217
drip line 22

E

Echinocereus triglochidiatus 226
ectomycorrhizae 25, 32
egg 103, 105, 118, 123
eiche 11
eik 11
embryo 103, 105, 123, 124, 126, 127
embryo sac 105, 118, 123
encino 11
endodermis 23, 24, 35
endosperm 123, 124
Eocene 187, 191
epicotyl 126, 127, 143
epidermis leaf 62, 63
  root 23, 24
Epigaea repens 204
epiphyte 47–60, 200
Erica species 230
Erythrobalanus 150, 165–67
Erythronium americanum 204
Eschscholzia species 221
evolution
  flowering plants 184, 185, 187
  oaks 182, 187, 188–94
evolution, parallel 186
exine 112

F

Fagaceae 150, 151, 167, 184, 190–91, 238
Fagoideae 150, 151, 167, 178, 238
Fagus 150, 167, 178–181, 185, 238
  longipetiolata 235
fairy bells 211
fairy ring 34
family 150, 188
fern, bird's nest 53
  maidenhair 213
  resurrection 52
ferns 50, 51, 52, 200
fertilization 105, 121, 123
  double 123
fibers 36, 39–40, 126
Ficus heteromorpha 235
fiesta flower 213
filament 100, 101, 108
fir, Douglas 209, 226
  subalpine 218
  white 210, 217, 226

flower design 100, 174
    female 102, 105, 116, 117, 119,
       152
    initiation 100, 106
    male 102, 104, 107, 108, 110,
       152, 179
    structure 100, 101, 102, 117
foam flower 204
fossils 182–84, 186, 187
foxfire 33
fructose 61
fruit 103, 128, 181
fuchsia 208
fungus 43, 50, 132, 133, 140, 144
    damping off 144
    fruiting body 26–27, 43
    hyphae 26, 27

G

gall 84–94
    apple 91, 92
    chamber 94, 95
    defenses 94, 95
    definition 84
    development 86, 87
    hedgehog 90, 91
    honeydew 94
    jumping 91, 92
    kinds 88–89
    life cycles 86, 87, 90, 92
    makers 84
    potato 93
    predators 93–94
    structure 86, 95
Gandoderma applanatum 44
garigue 232
gentian, green 219
genus 150, 151, 188
geologic time scale 182, 187
Gliricidia sepium 227
glucose 60, 61
gnat, fungus 140
goldfields 222
Gondwanaland 185
grape, Arizona 224
grape hyacinth 232
granary, acorn woodpecker 138
Great Smoky Mountains 69, 203
Greece 229–32
Grevillea robusta 170, 171

Guanacaste province 227
guard cells 63
gumbo-limbo 48, 227,

H

haustoria, mistletoe 57, 59
heather 230
Heuchera maxima 215
holly, summer 214
honey mushroom 32–33
honeysuckle, scarlet 208
hop-hornbeam 234
hormones 79, 121, 122, 142
Hubei province 233–35
hummingbirds 58, 208
hybridization 194–96
hypocotyl 126, 127

I

Indian paintbrush 208, 214
Ipomoea arborea 205
iris, mountain 226
Iris missouriensis 226
ironwood, island 215
isoprene 96
ivy, poison 224

J

jack-in-the-pulpit 204
jay 132
    behavior 134, 135
    distribution 132, 134, 136–37
    pinyon 135
    scrub 134, 135
Juglans major 223
juniper, alligator 224
    mat 219
Juniperus communis var.
       saxatilis 219
    deppeana 224

K

Kalmia latifolia 205
kapok 227

Keckiella cordifolia 213
keystone species 132
kinnikinnick 219

L

Laetiporus sulphureus 44
La Plata mountains 218–20
larkspur 222
Lasthenia californica 222
Laurasia 185
laurel, bay 218
    black 210
    mountain 205
leaf
    adaptations 67, 68–70
    arrangement 66
    attacks 78, 79
    blade 60, 65
    browsers 82–83
    color 69, 74–75, 153
    color change 73–76
    deciduous 66, 67
    decomposition 77
    defenses 74, 79, 80, 82, 83
    design 64–65, 67, 146
    development and growth 73
    diversity 153, 154–55
    drip tip 168
    evergreen 66
    fall 76, 77
    fungi 81–82
    hairs 69, 73, 74, 153, 156, 157
    lobes 69–70
    margin 65, 83, 153
    miners 80
    position 66, 70
    predators 78–82
    primordia 72
    shade 71
    shape 65, 205
    stages 71
    structure 62, 63, 64
    teeth 153
    water wasteful 69
lenticel 47
Lepidobalanus 150, 161
Leucobalanus 161
Leucothoe davisiae 210
lichens 50, 52, 55–56
    crustose 51, 55

foliose 49, 51, 55
 fruticose 51, 55
 lace 54
 nitrogen-fixing 56
 old man's beard 54
lignin 35, 39, 40
Lilium humboldtii 213
 pardalinum 210
 washingtonianum 210, 211
lily, Humboldt 213
 leopard 210
 Washington 210, 211
linden 204
Liquidambar glauca 234
Liriodendron tulipifera 204
Lithocarpus 151, 167, 171–77, 189,
 202, 233, 239–40
 densiflorus 171, 173, 209
 densiflorus var. *echinoides* 211
 viridis 235
live oak ribbed casemaker 80
liverworts, leafy 50, 51, 52
locust, black 204
Loranthaceae 57
Loranthus 58
lupine 226
Lupine spp. 226
lycopods 50
Lyonothamnus floribundus ssp.
 asplenifolius 215

M

Macrobalanus 164
madrone 48, 209
Malaysia 52, 199–202
Malesia 185–86, 189
Mammillaria species 224
manzanita 48, 213
maple 141, 204, 232
 bigleaf 209, 215
 bigtooth 226
 box elder 223–24
 Chinese 234
mast 129, 131
mata raton 227
maze gill 44
meadowrue 226
Mediterranean basin 229
megaspore, mother cell 118
meiosis 108, 118

importance of 108
membrane, semipermeable 24
meristem 24
 apical 72, 73
 root 24
Metasequoia glyptostroboides 233, 234
Mexico 52, 53, 205–8
micropyle 122
midrib 63, 64, 65
mildew 81–82
Mimulus flemingii 213
mineral nutrients 30
mistletoe 56–60, 200, 206, 208
 flowers 58, 59
 fruits 59, 60
mites 132
 beetle 140
Mitrastemon yamamotoi 33, 34
moccasin flower, pink 203, 204
monkeys 82, 135, 228
monkeyflower, bush 213
morning glory, tree 205
moss, Spanish 54–55
mosses 49, 50, 51, 52
moth, acorn 132, 133, 139, 140
mountain lions 136
Muscari species 232
mycorrhizae 25–26, 27
myrtle 200, 230
Myrtus communis 230

N

nectar guide 100
Nemophila menziesii 221
Nepenthes 200
Neuroterus saltitarius 92
nitrates 30
nitrogen, atmospheric 30
Nolina microcarpa 224
North Carolina 202–5
Nothofagus 151, 167, 178–81, 185,
 238–39
Nyssa sinensis 234

O

oak, acute-leaved 155
 ancient 38
 Arizona white 155

Asian cork 155, 161, 162
black 47, 110, 122, 130, 165–67,
 192–94
blackjack 154, 163, 165, 188,
 205
blue 12–13, 68, 74, 85, 195,
 222, 223
Brewer's 18, 161, 211, 212
California black 73, 76, 110,
 159, 196, 209, 215, 216
chestnut 154
coast live 68, 81, 145, 158, 163,
 194, 213, 223
cork 155, 159, 160, 161, 162,
 194
cup-flowered 162
desert scrub 163
Diamyo 155
eastern white 90, 121
Elmer's 155, 168
Emory 224
encino 155, 162, 227, 228
Engelmann's 74, 129, 154, 158
English 11, 121, 155, 161, 194
Gambel's 17, 146, 147, 154, 158,
 220, 225, 226
Garry 18, 57, 150, 161, 164, 211
goldcup 17, 84, 161, 163, 166,
 193, 218, 226, 230
golden 166, 167
golden-haired 155, 168
ground cover 215
holly 121, 155, 230
huckleberry 19, 20, 166, 211
Hungary 155
interior live 84, 161, 194, 196,
 215, 222, 223
island 154, 166, 215
island scrub 214
Keranga 162, 168
Kermes 229, 230, 232
King's 162
leather 19, 154
live 66, 161, 227
Mexico blue 75
Mexican netvein 155, 163, 226
Morehus 196
overcup 163
Palmer's 154, 163, 166, 230
poison 170, 171
post 154
red 47, 167, 205

ring-cupped 166, 167, 168, 189, 192, 202
Sadler's 211, 212
Sarawak 162, 168
scale-ringed 162
scarlet 76, 121, 154, 165, 188, 205
scrub 17, 20, 112, 164, 165, 214
sessile 194
she 170–71
shrub tan 211
silk 170, 171
silver-leaf 20, 165, 224, 226
tanbark 151, 171, 173, 174, 177, 209, 211, 239–40
thick-leaved 155
turkey 146
Turkish 162, 165, 194
valley 70, 71, 92, 120, 158, 163, 195, 222, 223
white 47, 85, 122, 130, 154, 161, 164–65, 167, 192–94, 205, 230
willow 154, 163
oak conservation 132, 236–37
oak design, advantages 14-15, 17, 128
weaknesses 15–16
oak distribution 136–37, 192–93
oak domination 16–17, 235
oak evolution 184
oak features 37–38, 41, 152–53
oak hormones 38
oak life cycle 103–6
oak moth 78, 79, 80
caterpillars 78, 79
oak subfamily 240
oak variation 14, 17, 19, 153
Olea europaea 230
olive 230
Opuntia engelmannii 224
orchid 52, 54, 127, 200
bog 219
epiphytic 206
ghost 212
order 150
Oregon 208–12
Orthilia secunda 210
ovary 100, 101, 105, 116, 117–18, 123, 127–28
ovule 100, 101, 103, 105, 116, 117–18, 123, 127–28

owl's clover 221, 223
oxygen 62

P

Pangaea 185
parasite 32, 33–34
flowering 56
parenchyma 127
palisade 63, 64
spongy 63, 64
Parthenocissus quinquefolia 224
parthenogenesis in galls 90
peccary 135, 228
peduncle 117
penstemon, climbing 213
Siskiyou 212
Penstemon anguineus 212
peperomia 54
pericycle 23, 24
petal 100, 101, 108
petiole 65
petunia 100, 101, 102
pH 30
phacelia, fringed 204
Phacelia fimbriata 204
phloem 23, 24, 35, 39, 41, 45, 46, 63, 64
phlox, woodland 212
Phlox adsurgens 212
Pholistoma auritum 213
Phoradendron species 58
photosynthesis 60–64
equation 61
importance 62
phrygana 232
phyllotaxy 65–66
Picea breweriana 209, 210
engelmannii 218, 226
pigs 29, 135, 137, 138
pine
aleppo 229
Chihuahua 224
knobcone 209
limber 218
long-leaf 224
ponderosa 210, 216, 218, 224, 226
white 204
Pinus attenuata 209
chihuanana 224

flexilis 218
halepensis 229
leiophylla 224
ponderosa 210, 216, 218
ponderosa var. arizonica 224
strobus 204
pipsissewa 210
pistachio 230
Pistacia lentiscus 230
pistil 100, 101, 102
pitcher plant, Malaysian 52, 200
Plagiobothrys nothofulvus 221
Platanthera dilatata 219
Platanus occidentalis 48
species 186
wrightii 48, 224
pocket gopher 29, 32
polar nuclei 118, 123
pollen 100, 104–5, 115, 120–21, 186
color 112
grain 108, 110, 112, 123, 181
mother cell 108
size 112
structure 112
tube 121–23
tube growth 121
pollination
animal 99, 113–14, 174
cross- 102, 117
self- 102
wind 99, 102, 103, 104, 107, 108, 110, 113, 114, 116, 120
Polypodium polypodioides 52
polypody 52
popcorn flower 221
poppy, golden 221
island 214
tree 205
Populus fremontii 223
tremuloides 218, 220
porcini 27
Potentilla species 219 ·
prairie dog 32
preadaptation 19
protea family 170
Proteaceae 170
Protobalanus 150, 166, 167, 193, 230
Prunus ilicifolia spp. lyoni 215
Pseudotsuga menziesii 209, 226
Pyrola species 212

Q

Quercoideae 150, 151, 167, 240
Quercus 150, 151, 167, 171, 174,
      190, 202, 233, 240
Quercus acuta 155
Q. x acutidens 195
Q. acutissima 233
Q. agrifolia 68, 81, 145, 158, 163,
      165, 194, 213, 223
Q. agrifolia var. oxyadenia 163
Q. alba 90, 91, 121, 154, 161, 205
Q. arizonica 155
Q. berberidifolia 88, 112, 164, 214
Q. cerris 162
Q. chrysolepis 17, 84, 88, 161, 218,
      226, 230
Q. chrysotricha 155, 163, 166, 168
Q. coccifera 229
Q. coccinea 76, 121, 154, 165, 188,
      205
Q. cornelius-mulleri 195
Q. crassifolia 155
Q. dentata 155
Q. douglasii 68, 74, 75, 85, 88, 89,
      195, 223
Q. durata 19, 154
Q. elmeri 155, 168
Q. emoryi 224
Q. engelmannii 75, 129, 154, 158,
      195
Q. faginea 155, 162
Q. frainetto 155
Q. gaharuensis 162, 168
Q. gambelii 17, 146, 147, 154, 158,
      220, 225, 226
Q. garryana 18, 57, 150, 161, 164,
      211
Q. garryana var. breweri 18, 150,
      161, 211
Q. gemelliflora 162
Q. humboldtii 165
Q. hypoleucoides 20, 165, 224
Q. ilex 121, 155, 229
Q. kelloggii 73, 74, 76, 110, 159,
      165, 195, 196, 209, 215,
      216
Q. kerangasensis 162, 168
Q. kingiana 162
Q. lamellosa 162
Q. lobata 70, 71, 88, 91, 92, 158,
      163, 195, 223

Q. lyrata 163
Q. macrocarpa 158
Q. marilandica 154, 163, 165, 188,
      205
Q. montana 154
Q. x morehus 195
Q. oblongifolia 75
Q. oleoides 155, 162, 227
Q. pacifica 214
Q. palmeri 89, 154, 159, 163, 166,
      230
Q. parvula 165, 215
Q. petraea 194
Q. phellos 154, 163
Q. pumila 146
Q. robur 11, 121, 155, 161, 194
Q. rubra 205
Q. rugosa 155, 163, 226
Q. sadleriana 211
Q. sinuata 158
Q. stellata 154
Q. suber 155, 159, 160, 161, 162,
      194
Q. tomentella 154, 166, 215
Q. turbinella 163
Q. vaccinifolia 19, 20, 166, 211
Q. variabilis 155, 159, 161, 162,
      233
Q. virginiana 88, 89, 161
Q. wislizenii 84, 88, 89, 161, 194,
      195, 196, 215, 223
Quercusia quercus 81

R

radicle 126, 127, 143
Rafflesiaceae 34
rainforest 199–202
Ramalina usneoide 54
Ranunculus species 221, 222
redwood 48
    dawn 233, 234
respiration
    aerobic 62
    anaerobic 62
rhizoid 48
rhizomorph 33
rhododendron 52, 200, 201, 232
    rosebay 210
Rhododendron macrophyllum 210
    occidentale 210, 215

Ribes species 186
ring porous 40
Robinia pseudoacacia 204
roble 11
rockrose 230, 231
rock sequences, geological 183
Rocky Mountains 224, 226
root cap 23, 24
    design 21, 23, 27
    hairs 24
    meristem 23
    pressure 35, 36
roots, branch 31
    feeder 22–23
    sinker 22
    tap 21, 31, 33, 143
rosemary 230
Rosmarinus officinalis 230
Rubus neomexicanus 186
    odoratus 186
    parviflorus 186

S

salvia 208
Santa Cruz Island 212–15
sapling 145–46
saprophyte 32
sassafras 204
Sassafras albidum 204
Satureja species 232
savory 232
sclereids 80
section 150, 161, 165
seed 103, 118, 124, 126–27
    coat 126
    structure 126
seedling
    establishment 144
    survival 142, 144
sepal 100, 101, 107, 116, 117
Sequoia sempervirens 48
Sequoiadendron giganteum 48
series 150, 161
serpentinite soils 19
Sierra Madre 194, 205–8
Sierra Nevada 194
sieve tube member 39, 45–46
Silene virginiana 205
silk-cotton tree 227, 228
Siskiyou Mountains 208–12

Sisyrinchium bellum 221
snails 140
snowbell tree 234
soil
   importance 29
   microorganisms 31
   organisms 31–32
   structure 30–31
Sonoran desert 223–26
sotol 224
sour gum 234
species 150, 188
sperm 105, 122, 123
spiderwort 204
spring beauty 204
spruce, Brewer's 209, 210
   Englemann 218, 226
squirrels 29, 32, 130, 132
stamen 100, 101, 108
steinpilz 27
Stenanthium occidentale 210
stigma 101, 102, 116, 127
   design 118, 119, 120
   shape 117
stipules 65
stomate 47, 62–63
Streptopus amplexifolius 211
style 100, 101
Styrax japonicus 234
subfamily 150
subgenera 150, 161, 196
subspecies 150
sucrose 60-61
sugars 95
sun spectrum 70
sunflower, canyon 213
sweet gum 234
Swertia radiatum 219
sycamore 48, 186
   Arizona 224

T

Tabebuia species 227
taiga 232
tannins 42, 48, 78, 83, 94, 95, 129,
      130, 144–45
Taraxacum species 219
taxonomy 149, 151, 169
Taxus chinensis 235
terpenes 95

terrane 188
testa 126, 127
Thalictrum fendleri 226
Thermopsis pinetorum 226
thimbleberry 186
Thuja plicata 48
thyme 232
Thymus species 232
Tiarella cordifolia 204
Tilia heterophylla 204
Tillandsia usneoides 54–55
Toxicodendron diversilobum 170, 171
   radicans 224
Tradescantia virginiana 205
trailing arbutus 204
Trametes versicolor 44
transpiration 37, 63
Trigonobalanus 151, 167, 181–82,
     185, 186, 188, 189, 240
   verticillata 181
trillium, painted 204
Trillium undulatum 204
trout lily 204
truffle 26, 28–29
Tuber species 26, 28–29
tulip poplar 204
turkey, wild 132, 135
turkey tail 44
twisted stalk 210
tyloses 42, 45

U

Umbellularia californica 209, 218
Usnea species 54

V

Valentina glandulella 139, 140
variety 150
vascular cambium 38, 41
vascular rays 40, 41, 42
vascular tissue 35
vegetative reproduction 146
vein pattern 153
veins 35, 63, 64, 65
Venegasia carpesioides 213
verrucate 113
vessels 35–37, 40
Viola adunca 219

   canadensis 219
   papilionacea 204
violet 204, 219
Virginia creeper 224
Viscum album 58
Vitis arizonica 224

W

walnut, Arizona 223
water column 14–15, 37
   molecule 36
   movement 24–25, 35–37
   splitting 61
weevil, acorn 132, 133, 138, 139
wintergreen, one-sided 210, 212
wood 38–39
   design 42
   heart 41, 42
   parenchyma 39
   quality 44, 45
   rot 43
   sap 41, 42
   structure 39–41, 42
woodpecker, acorn 132, 135, 138
worms, earth 31, 141

X

xanthophylls 76
Xerophyllum tenax 210
xylem 23, 24, 35, 36, 39, 41, 63

Y

yew, Chinese plum 235
   true 235
Yosemite 215–18
yucca, Schott's 226
Yucca schottii 226

Z

zone of elongation 23, 24
zone of maturation 23, 24